THE SOLDIERS
OF THE FRENCH REVOLUTION

A BOOK IN THE SERIES

BICENTENNIAL REFLECTIONS ON THE FRENCH REVOLUTION

General Editors: Keith Michael Baker, Stanford University
Steven Laurence Kaplan, Cornell University

THE SOLDIERS
OF THE FRENCH REVOLUTION

Alan Forrest

DUKE UNIVERSITY PRESS

Durham and London

1990

For Rosemary

CONTENTS

ACKNOWLEDGMENTS

EVEN A SHORT WORK OF SYNTHESIS CAN INCUR HEFTY debts for its author, and these should not pass unrecognized. Research grants from the University of Manchester helped me complete archival work on supply and on military clubs, and it was during study leave from Manchester in the winter of 1987–88 that the major part of this book was written. In the course of its preparation the librarians at the Bibliothèque Nationale and the archivists at Vincennes showed courtesy and tolerance, as did the staff of those departmental archives where I made the brief one- and two-day appearances that must be the bane of any archivist's life. One section of the book, on the recruitment of the armies, emerged from much more detailed research that I had undertaken for a previous work, *Déserteurs et insoumis sous la Révolution et l'Empire,* published in spring 1988 in Paris. To its publishers, Perrin, and especially to Sybille Billot, go my warmest thanks for their encouragement and forebearance.

I would also like to thank Richard Cobb, Colin Jones, Peter Jones, and Isser Woloch for advice and inspiration on different aspects of the military history of the period. I have benefitted greatly from presenting parts of the present work as seminars at the Centre Pierre Léon in Lyon and at the Ecole des Hautes Etudes in Paris, and from the constructive criticisms of François Furet, Yves Lequin, and Mona Ozouf. The final draft of the book owes much to the careful and thought-provoking comments of the series editors, Keith Baker and Steven Kaplan; I wish to express my appreciation to them and to the editor, Lawrence Malley.

Finally, a word of thanks to those fellow historians and friends who helped ensure that my stay in France would be pleasant and productive. In particular, I should like to thank John and Carol Merriman, on the terrace of whose home in Balazuc the plan of this book took shape; Jon Skinner, with whom I spent several companionable days in the archives of the Southeast; Godfrey Rogers and Jane Dougherty, who provided such stimulating friendship during the greater part of a year in Paris; and Jean-Paul Bertaud, who, as France's leading expert on the Revolutionary armies, might have been excused for rebuffing me as a poacher, but who extended his customary generous help. To them all, *salut et fraternité*.

My greatest debt, of course, is to my wife, Rosemary Morris. It is to her that this book is dedicated.

EDITORS' INTRODUCTION

"IN PARIS, IN THIS SYMBOLIC NIGHT OF 14 JULY, NIGHT of fervor and of joy, at the foot of the timeless obelisk, in this Place de la Concorde that has never been more worthy of the name, [a] great and immense voice . . . will cast to the four winds of history the song expressing the ideal of the five hundred Marseillais of 1792." The words, so redolent in language and tone of the instructions for the great public festivals of the French Revolution, are those of Jack Lang, French Minister of Culture, Communications, Great Public Works, and the Bicentennial. The text is that of the program for the grandiose opera-parade presenting "a Marseillaise for the World," the internationally televised spectacle from Paris crowning the official celebration of the bicentennial of the French Revolution.

The minister's language was aptly fashioned to the occasion. It was well chosen to celebrate Paris as world-historical city—joyous birthplace of the modern principles of democracy and human rights—and the Revolution of 1789 as the momentous assertion of those universal human aspirations to freedom and dignity that have transformed, and are still transforming, an entire world. It was no less well chosen to leap over the events of the Revolution from its beginning to its end, affirming that the political passions engendered by its momentous struggles had finally ceased to divide the French one from another.

The spectacle on the Place de la Concorde exemplified the unavowed motto of the official bicentennial celebration: "The Revolution is over." Opting for a celebration consonant with the predominantly centrist, consensualist mood of the French in the late 1980s, the presidential mission charged with the organization of the bicentennial celebrations focused on the values which the vast majority of French citizens of all political persuasions underwrite—the ideals exalted in the Declaration of the Rights of Man. It offered the nation—and the world—the image of a France finally at peace with itself: a people secure in the tranquil enjoyment of the human rights that constitute France's true revolutionary patrimony, confident in the maturity of French institutions and their readiness to meet the challenges and opportunities of a new European order, firm in the country's dedication to securing universal respect for the democratic creed it claims as its most fundamental contribution to the world of nations. No hint of subsequent radicalization, no echo of social conflict, no shadow of the Terror could mar this season of commemoration. It followed that the traditional protagonists and proxies in the great debate over the Revolution's character and purposes, Danton and Robespierre, were to be set aside. The hero for 1989 was Condorcet: savant, philosopher, reformer, "moderate" revolutionary, victim of the Revolution he failed to perfect and control.

But the Revolution—ambiguous, complex, subversive as it remains, even after two hundred years—still proved refractory to domestication. Not even the solemn bicentennial spectacle on the night of 14 July was sheltered from certain treacherous counterpoints. Spectators watching the stirring parade unfold down the Champs-Élysées toward the Place de la Concorde already knew that this same route would shortly be followed by participants in a counterrevolutionary commemoration returning a simulacrum of the guillotine to its most notorious revolutionary site. These spectators were moved by the poignant march of Chinese youths pushing their bicycles in evocation of the recent massacre in Tienanmen Square, even as this brutal silencing of demands for human rights was being justified in Beijing as reluctant defense of the Revolution against dangerous counterrevolutionary elements. The spectators were stirred by Jessye Norman's heroic rendition of the *Marseillaise,* even as it reminded all who cared to attend to its words that this now universal chant of liberation was also a ferocious war song calling for the letting of the "impure blood" of the enemy. On the very day of the parade a politely exasperated Margaret Thatcher, publicly contesting the French claim to the paternity of the Rights of Man and insisting on the identity of Revolution with Terror, reminded the world of the jolting equation, $1789 = 1793$. For their part, the performers sent by the USSR to march in the parade, garbed in dress more Russian than Soviet, raised questions about the socialist axiom that the Russian Revolution was the necessary conclusion to the French. As men and women throughout the communist world rallied for human rights, was it any longer possible to see 1917 as the authentic future of 1789?

The tensions and contradictions of commemoration have their own political and cultural dynamic, but they are nourished by the tensions and contradictions of historical interpretation. If the Revolution has been declared over in France, its history is far from terminated—either there or elsewhere. Indeed, the bicentennial of the French Revolution has reopened passionate historiographical debates over its meaning that began with the Revolution itself. As early as September 1789, readers of the *Révolutions de Paris*— one of the earliest and most widely read of the newspapers that were to play so powerful a role in shaping the revolutionary consciousness—were demanding "a historical and political picture of everything that has happened in France since the first Assembly of Notables," to be offered as a means of explaining the nature of "the astonishing revolution that has just taken place." Observers and participants alike sought from the outset to grasp the causes, nature, and effects of these remarkable events. And if they concurred on the momentous character of the Revolution, they differed vehemently on its necessity, its means, its fundamental mission. Burke and Paine, Barnave and de Maistre, Condorcet and Hegel were only among the first in a dazzling succession of thinkers who have responded to the need to plumb the historical identity and significance of a phenomenon that has seemed from its very beginning to demand, yet defy, historical comprehension.

This rich tradition of political-philosophical history of the Revolution, which resounded throughout the nineteenth century, was muted and profoundly modified in the wake of the centennial celebrations. In France, 1889 inaugurated a new age in revolutionary historiography dedicated to that marriage between republicanism and positivism that underlay the very creation of the Third Republic. This marriage gave birth, within the university, to the new Chair in the History of the French Revolution at the Sorbonne to which Alphonse Aulard was elected in 1891. From this position, occupied for more than thirty years, Aulard directed the first scholarly journal devoted to the study of the Revolution, presided over the preparation and publication of the great official collections of revolutionary documents, and formed students to spread the republican-positivist gospel. He established and institutionalized within the university system an official, putatively scientific history: a history dedicated to discovering and justifying, in the history of the Revolution, the creation of those republican, parliamentary institutions whose promise was now finally being secured in more felicitous circumstances. Danton, the patriot, determined in 1793 to institute the emergency government of the Terror to save the Republic in danger, but opposed in 1794 to continuing it once that danger had eased, became the hero of Aulard's French Revolution.

Given his institutional authority, his posture as scientific historian, and his engaged republicanism, Aulard was able to marginalize conservative interpretations of the Revolution, ridiculing the amateurism of Hippolyte Taine's frightened account of its origins in the philosophic spirit and culmination in the horrors of mass violence, and dismissing, as little more than reactionary ideology, Augustin Cochin's analysis of the genesis and implications of Jacobin sociability. Within the university, the revolutionary heritage became a patrimony to be managed, rather than merely a creed to be inculcated. But this did not preclude bitter divisions over the manner in which that patrimony was to be managed, or its now sacred resources deployed. Aulard's most talented student, Albert Mathiez, became his most virulent critic. The rift was more than an oedipal conflict over the republican mother, Marianne. Mathiez questioned Aulard's scientific methods; but above all, he detested his mentor's Dantonist moderation. As an alternative to an opportunistic, demagogic, and traitorous Danton, he offered an Incorruptible, Robespierre, around whom he crafted a popular, socialist, and Leninist reading of the Revolution. The Bolshevik experience reinforced his Robespierrism, investing it with a millennial hue, and stimulated him to undertake his most original work on the "social movement" of the Terror. Thereafter the relationship between the Russian Revolution and the French Revolution, between 1917 and 1793, haunted the Marxianized republican interpretation to which Mathiez devoted his career.

Although Mathiez was denied Aulard's coveted chair, he taught in the same university until his early death. His exact contemporary, Georges Lefebvre, shared much of his political sensibility and his interest in history from below, and succeeded him as president of the Society for Robespierrist Studies. Lefebvre's election to the Sorbonne chair in 1937 proved decisive for the consolidation, and indeed the triumph, of a social interpretation of the French Revolution based on the principles of historical materialism. More sociological than Mathiez in his approach, and more nuanced in his judgments, he broke fresh ground with his monumental work on the peasants (whose autonomy and individuality he restituted) and his subsequent studies of social structure; and he rescued important issues from vain polemics. His rigor, his pedagogical talent, and the muted quality of his Marxism—most effectively embodied in the celebrated study of 1789 he published for the sesquicentennial of the French Revolution in 1939—earned him, his chair, and the interpretation he promoted worldwide prestige. After 1945, and until his death in 1959, he presided over international research in the field as director of his Institute for the History of the French Revolution at the Sorbonne. Under Lefebvre's aegis, the Marxianized republican interpretation of the French Revolution became the dominant paradigm of revolutionary historiography in France following the Second World War; and it was largely adopted, from the French leaders in the field, by the growing number of historians specializing in the subject who became so striking a feature of postwar academic expansion, particularly in English-speaking countries.

Lefebvre conveyed his mantle of leadership to his student, Albert Soboul, who succeeded to the Sorbonne chair in 1967. Soboul owed his scholarly fame above all to his pioneering thesis on the Parisian sansculottes, a work recently subjected to severe criticism of its sociological and ideological analyses, its understanding of the world of work, and its often teleological and tautological methods. But his influence far transcended this acclaimed monograph. A highly placed member of the French Communist party as well as director of the Institute for the History of the French Revolution, Soboul saw himself as both a "scientific" and a "communist-revolutionary" historian. Tireless, ubiquitous, and prolific, he tenaciously rehearsed the Marxist account of the French Revolution as a bourgeois revolution inscribed in the logic of the necessary transition from feudalism to capitalism. But his relish for confrontation, and his assertive defense of an increasingly rigid orthodoxy, eventually invited— and made him the chief target of—the revisionist assault on the dominant interpretation of the Revolution as mechanistic, reductive, and erroneous.

Challenges to the hegemony of the Sorbonne version of the history of the French Revolution were offered in the late 1950s and early 1960s by Robert Palmer's attempt to shift attention toward the democratic politics of an Atlantic Revolution and, more fundamentally, by Alfred Cobban's frontal assault on the method-ological and political assumptions of the Marxist interpretation. But such was the power of the scholarly consensus that, con-demned more or less blithely in Paris, these works drew relatively little immediate support. Not until the late 1960s and early 1970s did the revisionist current acquire an indigenous French base, both intellectual and institutional. The charge was led by François Furet, who left the Communist party in 1956 and has subsequently gravitated toward the liberal political center. One of the first French historians to become intimately familiar with Anglo-American scholarship (and with American life more gener-ally), Furet served as the third president of the École des Hautes Études en Sciences Sociales, accelerating its development into one of Europe's leading centers for research in the social sciences and humanities—and a formidable institutional rival to the Sor-bonne. Disenchanted with Marxism, he also turned away from the *Annales* tradition of quantitative social and cultural history vig-orously espoused in his earlier work. For the past fifteen years he has sustained a devastating critique of the Jacobin-Leninist "cate-chism," redirecting scholarly attention to the dynamics of the Revolution as an essentially political and cultural phenomenon; to the logic, contradictions, and pathos of its invention of demo-cratic sociability; to its fecundity as a problem for the political and philosophical inquiries of the nineteenth century upon whose inspiration he insists historians must draw.

It is one of the great ironies of revolutionary historiography, then, that whereas the centennial of the Revolution inaugurated the consolidation of the official republican exegesis, so the bicen-tennial has marked the distintegration of its Marxist descendant. The field of inquiry is now more open, more fluid, more exciting than it has been for many decades. By the same token, it is also shaped by concerns and sensibilities deriving from recent changes and experiences. These latter are many and varied. Any com-prehensive list would have to include the eclipse of Marxism as an intellectual and political force; the dramatic decline in the fortunes of communism, especially in France; the resurgence of liberalism in the West, with its rehabilitation of the market as model and morality, asserting the intrinsic connection between political liberty and laissez-faire; the dramatic shifts in the East from Gulag to glasnost and perestroika, from Maoism to Westernization, with their oblique and overt avowals of communist failure and ignominy extending from Warsaw to Moscow to Beijing. But such a list could not omit the memory of the Holocaust and the traumas of decolonization among colonized and colonizers alike, from the Algerian War to the sanguinary horrors of Polpotism. It would have to include the stunning triumph and the subsequent exhaustion of the *Annales* paradigm, with its metaphor of levels of determination privileging a long-run perspective and quantitative techniques; the emergence of a new cultural history, pluralistic and aggressive, fueled by diverse disciplinary and counterdisciplinary energies; the striking development of the École des Hautes Études en Sciences Sociales as counterweight to the traditional French university; and the efflorescence of a tradition of French historical studies outside France whose challenge to Parisian hegemony in the field can no longer be ignored. Neither could it neglect the dramatic eruption of the revolutionary imagination in the events of 1968, and the new radical politics of race, sex, and gender that have become so profound a preoccupation in subsequent decades.

The implications of this new situation for the study of the French Revolution are profound. Many fundamental assumptions, not only about the Revolution itself but about how to study it, have been called into question. Though the Revolution is better known today than ever before, the collapse of the hegemonic structure of learning and interpretation has revealed egregious blindspots in what has hitherto counted for knowledge and understanding. While the republican-Marxist view innovated in certain areas, it sterilized research in many others. Today it is no longer possible to evoke complaisantly the bourgeois character of the Revolution, either in terms of causes or effects; the roles, indeed the very definition, of other social actors need to be reexamined. A rehabilitated political approach is avidly reoccupying the ground of a social interpretation in serious need of reformulation. Questions of ideology, discourse, gender, and cultural practices have surged to the forefront in fresh ways. Fewer and fewer historians are willing to accept or reject the Revolution "en bloc," while more and more are concerned with the need to fathom and connect its multiple and contradictory components. The Terror has lost the benefit of its relative immunity and isolation. And despite extravagant and often pathetic hyperbole, the Right has won its point that the Vendée in particular—and the counterrevolutionary experience in general—require more probing and balanced treatment, as do the post-Thermidorian terrors. Finally, there is a widespread sense that the narrow periodization of Revolutionary studies must be substantially broadened.

When the bicentennial dust settles, there will therefore be much for historians of the French Revolution to do. Many questions will require genuinely critical research and discussion, searching reassessment, vigorous and original synthesis. Our ambition in editing these Bicentennial Reflections on the French Revolution is to contribute to this endeavor. In organizing the series, which will comprise twelve volumes, we have sought to identify fundamental issues and problems—problems that have hitherto been treated in fragmentary fashion; issues around which conventional wisdom has disintegrated in the course of current debates—which will be crucial to any new account of the French Revolution. And we have turned to some of the finest historians in what has become an increasingly international field of study, asking them to reassess their own understanding of these matters in the light of their personal research and that of others, and to present the results of their reflections to a wider audience in relatively short, synthetic works that will also offer a critical point of departure for further work in the field. The authors share with us the belief that the time is ripe for a fundamental rethinking. They will of course proceed with this rethinking in their own particular fashion.

The events that began to unfold in France in 1789 have, for two hundred years, occupied a privileged historical site. The bicentennial has served as a dramatic reminder that not only our modern notions of revolution and human rights, but the entire range of our political discourse derives from them. The French Revolution has been to the modern world what Greece and Rome were to the Renaissance and its heirs: a condensed world of acts and events, passions and struggles, meanings and symbols, constantly reconsidered and reimagined in the attempt to frame—and implement—an understanding of the nature, conditions, and possibilities of human action in their relation to politics, culture, and social process. To those who would change the world, the Revolution still offers a script continuously elaborated and extended—in parliaments and prisons; in newspapers and manifestoes; in revolutions and repressions; in families, armies, and encounter groups. . . . To those who would interpret the world, it still presents the inexhaustible challenge of comprehending the nature of the extraordinary mutation that gave birth to the modern world.

"Great year! You will be the *regenerating year,* and you will be known by that name. History will extol your great deeds," wrote Louis-Sébastien Mercier, literary anatomist of eighteenth-century Paris, in a rhapsodic *Farewell to the Year 1789.* "You have changed *my Paris,* it is true. It is completely different today. . . . For thirty years I have had a secret presentiment that I would not die without witnessing a great political event. I nourished my spirit on it: there is *something new* for my pen. If *my Tableau* must be *redone,* at least it will be said one day: In this year Parisians . . . stirred, and this impulse has been communicated to France and the rest of Europe." Historians of the French Revolution may not bid farewell to the bicentennial year in Mercier's rapturous tones. But they will echo at least one of his sentiments. Our tableau must be redone; there is something new for our pens.

Keith Michael Baker and Steven Laurence Kaplan
26 August 1989

1

THE REVOLUTION AND ITS SOLDIERS

ON APRIL 20 1792, THE FRENCH GOVERNMENT DE-
clared war on Austria and brought to an end a long
period of uneasy coexistence between revolutionary
France and the monarchies of Europe. It was to prove a momentous decision, affecting the domestic history of the French Revolution almost as crucially as it affected international relations
throughout Europe. However confident contemporaries might be
in predicting a speedy and successful outcome, this would not
turn out to be a short war, to be won in a single glorious campaigning season. Hostilities were to last, virtually continuously,
throughout the remainder of the decade, consuming an increasing
part of the effort and resources of revolutionary governments and,
in the process, changing the character of the Revolution itself.
With the war came economic controls and special taxes, forced
loans on the rich, requisitions of food and livestock, extensive
recruitment, and finally annual conscription. Winning the war
became, unavoidably, the major political priority of the day, with
the result that other measures were dropped or distorted in order
to provide for the armies. New levels of constraint and compulsion
entered everyday life, often justified by military necessity or
introduced as emergency expedients that must be endured for the
duration of the war. Even political terror could be explained and
popularized as an exceptional measure needed to ensure the success
of French arms. In the process, the army itself gained new author-

ity and status until, under the Directory, it came to represent an alternative focus of power to the constitutional government of the day and allowed Napoleon Bonaparte to launch his successful challenge on 18 *brumaire.*

This book is not the place to consider in detail the military history of these years; others have done so, often at very great length.[1] A general picture of the progress of the war is perhaps necessary, however, if only to provide a context for the social and political discussion that follows. The declaration of war in April 1792 was made in an atmosphere of some confusion, after months of saber rattling by both sides and amid bitter political disunity in France. Nor did the early news from the battle zones do anything to dispel that confusion. The first encounters were ominously unsuccessful for the French, deepening the political divisions within the country and increasing the levels of fear and panic that already existed among the population. Military defeats and indecisive campaigning during these early months convinced many that the Revolution was being deliberately undermined, that ministers and generals were betraying the trust placed in them, and that France was being projected on a path that would lead to humiliation and political chaos. A war that had been declared against Austria was extended to include the Prussians by early July; on July 11, the *patrie* was declared *en danger;* and during August French territory was invaded from both the North and the East. The revolutionaries who had launched the war with such confidence and bravado just a few months before were fighting for their very survival.

Toward the end of 1792, it is true, the French armies staged a spectacular recovery, chased their enemies out of France, and were everywhere on the offensive—in the South they entered Nice and Savoy, in the East they attacked Mainz and Frankfurt, and in the North they had Brussels and Antwerp at their mercy. Two famous battles marked what many at the time saw as a great turning point in the war. At Valmy on September 19, the forces of Dumouriez and Kellermann used massed artillery to turn back the Prussians;

and at Jemmapes on November 6, Dumouriez's army inflicted a further defeat, this time on the Austrians, which showed the quality of French infantry and cavalry in hand-to-hand combat.[2] But these successes were soon eclipsed, and by the spring of 1793 the Revolution was again threatened.

Tormented by serious outbreaks of rural counterrevolution in Brittany and the West, the French were faced with the combined strength of the First Coalition, which included not only the military power of the major land armies of Europe, but also the naval strength of Britain and Spain. In time, this crisis, too, passed. Under the Jacobins the French armies recovered from their early setbacks, turning back Austrian and Prussian advances in the East and pushing the Spaniards across the Pyrenees into Spanish Catalonia. Morale inevitably improved. Whereas early victories like Valmy and Jemmapes could justifiably be regarded as the outcome of a certain good fortune, the armies of 1794 were able to hold their own against the best professional armies of Europe. By June of that year, following victory over the Austrians at Fleurus, the north of France was liberated and the French found themselves once again in a position to attack Belgium. And with both the Prussians and the Austrians seeking peace, the First Coalition was effectively over. The key settlement was the Treaty of Basel, signed with Prussia on April 5, 1795. By its terms Prussia abandoned her allies, recognizing French claims to the left bank of the Rhine if France would agree to the neutralization of North Germany. This in turn allowed the French to impose the Treaty of the Hague on the Dutch on May 16 and to prepare for the permanent annexation of Belgium. Spain made peace two months later.[3] The Republic had been saved, national pride had been restored, and the reputation of the citizen army—the myth of "les soldats de l'an II"—was born.

The treaty proved, however, to be little more than a short respite from fighting, and again it was the French who opened hostilities, taking advantage of the apparent weakness of their enemies. Austria and Prussia remained disunited, their mutual antagonism fueled by the question of Polish partition. And Britain's ill-fated landing at Carnac in June 1795 to help the royalist rebels in Brittany—the three thousand British and émigré troops were quickly cornered on the Quiberon Peninsula by a French army under Hoche—served only to confirm French suspicions of English perfidy and to harden their own political resolve. But the principal change in the conduct of the war, as Georges Lefebvre noted, was that until Basel France was largely on the defensive, seeking to defend herself against enemies who believed her cause lost. In this second phase of the war, the French government launched itself into conflict in an offensive mood, intent on holding onto gains in Holland and the Rhineland and on taking advantage of divisions and weaknesses among her opponents.[4] Ranged against the French was a renewed coalition, which included many of the north German states but in which only England and Austria could be counted as serious belligerents. This was not a war to protect "la patrie en danger," to defend the French people against invasion and the gains of the Revolution against destruction.

It would be difficult, indeed, to claim that the wars of the Thermidorians and the Directory were in any real sense ideological in inspiration. Rather, they resembled the traditional wars of conquest fought by the kings and princes of the eighteenth century, conducted with the single-minded aim of acquiring territorial advantage. To secure its conquests, but also to feed its armies, the Directory ordered the invasion of the German states and of Italy. Its military ambition, indeed, seemed limitless. By 1797, France had set up a series of buffer states to protect her military acquisitions—dependencies like the Batavian Republic in Holland, the Helvetic Republic in Switzerland, or the Cisalpine and Ligurian republics in Italy, while a victorious French army had ignored papal sensibilities and had entered Rome. The Treaty of Campio-Formio, imposed on the Austrians by Bonaparte on October 18 with only the most cursory reference back to his political masters in Paris, demonstrated both the extent of France's imperial aspirations and the degree of independent authority which the military had obtained. In these circumstances any thought of a permanent peace could be little more than self-deception; Campio-Formio was rightly interpreted, both in Paris and in Vienna, as little more than a lull in the fighting.[5] By the end of the year Napoleon would be preparing the Egyptian campaign, and the Second Coalition would be born. Far from being a temporary expedient, war had become an integral part of the politics of the revolutionary state. The power of the army was already a political reality, as was volubly demonstrated by the *journée* of 18 *fructidor,* when the military overthrew the Constitution and brought Bonaparte to power. The army was no longer a passive onlooker, no longer a mere instrument of the government of the day. It had a professional interest in the pursuit of victory and in the continuation of hostilities.

There is no clear consensus about the essential character of the revolutionary wars. The traditional interpretation, at least in France, has placed great emphasis on ideology, seeing the wars as the clash of two opposed and mutually intolerant political systems.[6] The French, according to this rather apocalyptic vision of foreign policy, were motivated by much more than the simple desire for conquest. They were not simply imitating the ambitions of their predecessors, seeking to take advantage of the weakness of others to grab a slice of the Rhineland or to seize the trading cities of the Netherlands. Nor was war to be explained by a desire to establish natural frontiers—perhaps the most traditional of all French foreign policy aims under the monarchy. Nationalism and a sense of dedication to the cause of the *patrie* made this a war of principle in which the rational assessment of gains and losses gave way to a much more emotive gut reaction, that of protecting the territory and culture of the French people against the depredations of others. During the revolutionary decade, when so much was politicized and expressed in ideological terms, that "culture" was, of course, predominantly a political culture. Geographical and political expressions—France, *patrie,* Revolution, and ultimately

Republic—came to be used interchangeably and almost without distinction. The country and its political institutions, the people and their collective morality, all were easily assimilated into a common good. The war, like the Revolution itself, was presented as a cause that involved the interests of all the people. It was an ideological war between two irreconcilable forces, a war which, many believed, could end only in complete victory or in total defeat. And the prospect of defeat could not be contemplated because defeat would involve the reimposition of the Bourbons and the destruction of all that had been achieved since 1789.

This vision of war as the inevitable clash of two mutually antagonistic political systems finds ample illustration in the speeches and tracts of the period. The French Revolution combined nationalism with a sense of missionary zeal which many other European governments regarded as a threat to their own values and institutions. From the very earliest months the revolutionary leaders preached to the French people that their cause was the cause of all humanity, that of Reason and Enlightenment against the forces of social reaction and monarchical absolutism. For many among them the logic of war was inescapable. They saw their enemies on all sides—not just in foreign courts and foreign capitals, but in such French citizens as might be in foreign pay, like aristocrats and émigrés, army officers and refractory priests. Military mutinies and the defections of generals, financial panics and the collapse of markets, noble and clerical emigration, the vacillation and bad faith of Louis XVI, the treasonable correspondence of Marie Antoinette and her Austrian coterie, royalist insurgencies like that which drew some twenty thousand Catholic peasants to the Camp de Jalès in the Ardèche in 1790—it was little wonder that the Revolution developed a paranoia about national security, or that a war party came into being long before the formal declaration of hostilities. Indeed, it could be argued that from the very outset the French Revolution, almost necessarily, was placed on a war footing.

Popular opinion, especially in Paris, remained highly sensitive to the threat posed by the monarchies of Europe, by the much-feared machinations of "Pitt-Cobourg," the mythical two-headed monster which, in revolutionary propaganda, represented the unbridled fury of counterrevolution. But such fears were not restricted to the capital. In the countryside, too, the Grande Peur—the waves of rural rioting which had swept uncontrollably across wide tracts of agrarian France during 1789, linked to popular belief in an aristocratic conspiracy[7]—left a legacy of insecurity that would prove difficult to eradicate. The move to form National Guard units in provincial towns and cities during the months that followed reflected the degree of unease which lingered on. By 1792, the level of fear and suspicion was considerably heightened as a result of the international situation. The flight of the king to Varennes the previous summer had confirmed the worst suspicions of those who believed that constitutional monarchy could never be made to work with a Bourbon on the throne. The Declaration of Pilnitz and the Brunswick Manifesto, both issued in August 1791, had demonstrated the undying hatred of the Austrian court for the Revolution and its liberal reforms. At Pilnitz, the emperor and King Frederick-William of Prussia promised to use force to reestablish a monarchical system of government in France; in his manifesto, the Duke of Brunswick threatened that those Frenchmen captured in battle would be treated as rebels and held the people of Paris collectively responsible for the continued safety of Louis XVI.[8] Both documents were intended to spread fear and panic among the civilian population in France, and they provided clear evidence, if such evidence was needed, of the degree of influence enjoyed by French émigrés with Leopold and his advisers and showed how openly committed the Austrian Empire still was to the return of the Bourbon monarchy. As a result, many Frenchmen became convinced that war was no longer a simple policy option, but was necessary if the Revolution was to be saved from destruction at the hands of its enemies.

In 1792, this view was most closely identified with the Girondins, the group in the Assembly which most consistently advocated war against Austria if the Revolution were to be saved. While Robespierre and his supporters among the Paris Jacobins warned that war would only distract the French people from their real enemies within, Roland, Brissot, and other leading Girondin politicians insisted that there was no necessary contradiction between internal surveillance and external conflict. Brissot even went so far as to claim that he did not see a war policy as being in any sense dangerous because French troops would be welcomed in countries they invaded as liberators and missionaries of liberty.[9] But it was Vergniaud who put the Girondin case most succinctly in a major speech to the Legislative Assembly on January 18, 1792.

France, Vergniaud argued, could not afford to ignore the effects of its revolution on other countries or the fear it had caused among the crowned heads of Europe. Nor could it overlook the political consequences of that fear. The Revolution had provided a glorious example not only of a government based on liberty, but also of the destruction of that very despotism which supported and maintained monarchies. It was therefore unavoidable that despots should detest the French constitution and work to undermine it because "it makes men free, whereas they want to rule over populations of slaves." Vergniaud went on to demonstrate that the Austrian emperor, far from remaining aloof from French internal politics, was already engaged in a three-pronged campaign against the Revolution, a campaign against which France was ill-equipped to react as long as she remained at peace. The emperor had at his disposal three "armies of reptiles," each dedicated to the destruction of the Revolution and its achievement—an army of intriguers and slanderers who undermined the regime from within; an army of seditious priests who spread discord in the name of a God of peace; and an army of greedy financiers who speculated shamefully in human suffering. Vergniaud warned that only by taking up arms could the French people defend their liberty and give hope to the rest of the human race.[10]

Even within the Assembly Vergniaud's analysis was hotly contested. Robespierre spoke for many deputies when he queried the wisdom of spreading France's commitments too widely, or of risking the uncertainties of foreign war when there were enemies to be rooted out at home. He saw the war option as foolhardy and dangerous, plunging France into a European conflict which could only play into the hands of the court faction.[11] But it was one thing to criticize the war policy when it came up for discussion in the Assembly or at the Jacobin Club; it was quite another to continue an antiwar crusade once hostilities had been declared. By this time, French soldiers were engaged in fighting on the frontiers, patriotic propaganda had stressed the level of shared danger France faced, and the mobilization of men and resources had brought the war into every village in the land. To counsel prudence might seem dangerously like defeatism; to advocate peace might be mistaken for cowardice or treason. Besides, popular panic and the fear of an Austrian invasion were everywhere in evidence. Radical pamphleteers and sectional leaders rivaled one another in their patriotism and their commitment to destroy the last vestiges of despotism. Radical journalists whipped up emotive anger and sought scapegoats for failure. And theirs were no longer lone voices. They were guaranteed a ready audience in the teeming streets around the Paris markets and in those popular faubourgs in the capital—like Saint-Antoine and Saint-Marcel— where a radical tradition was developing. Here news of French setbacks gave rise to fear and consternation, as Parisians prepared themselves for invasion and for the bloody repression they expected at the hands of the Austrians; the extent of their fear became chillingly apparent only in September when alleged aristocrats and counterrevolutionaries were hunted down and massacred in Paris jails. By then all French politicians were agreed that the war had to be pursued vigorously, and if the Jacobins continued to attack the Gironde's war policy, it was not the principle of war but the inefficiency of their management which provoked criticism. By 1794, Billaud-Varenne could claim that the success of the war and the pursuit of the Revolution were in no sense conflicting policies. Rather, he argued, the war which at one time had appeared to threaten France with ruin had inspired the people with patriotism and with a sense of their common achievement. The war had increased the political consciousness of the French and had made them aware of the common dangers they faced. And he called for a stabilization of the political system in France to prepare a sound basis for military victory.[12]

The prevalence of this view does not, of course, prove that the revolutionary wars were ideological in kind or in origin. Nor is it incompatible with the interpretation, expressed most uncompromisingly by T. C. W. Blanning, that they should be seen less as a new kind of warfare than as the latest of a series of European wars which had pitted ruler against ruler, state against state. Even if ideological motives impelled French politicians to maintain the dynamic of their Revolution, there is no reason to think that Austrian, Prussian, or Russian governments accepted their logic. These governments would continue to think of war and diplomacy in terms of dynastic alliances and imperial advantage. They would not, in Blanning's view, have any interest in restoring Louis XVI to the full powers of Bourbon absolutism, nor yet in salvaging France from the debilitating chaos and self-destruction they perceived in revolutionary politics. Why should they? Their interest, after all, was in the maintenance of a weak France, in the continued loss of influence by one of the major units in the eighteenth-century European system. And the revolutionary wars were no more than the continuation, under a new and more passionate rubric, of the old rivalries which had surfaced in the War of the Austrian Succession and the Seven Years' War, and which had induced the French, arguably against their better judgment, to become embroiled in the issue of American independence in 1778. Seen in this light, Austria and Prussia were attracted by the prospect of war with France in 1792 not because France was revolutionary, but because France was weak. Russia, the most vigorous of the European powers when it came to antirevolutionary diatribe, nonetheless stayed out of the fighting until 1798—not because of politics, but because Catherine the Great had more pressing interests in Poland. And when France again began to inflict defeats on her rivals, to show every sign of a revival from the slump of mid-century, then the other great powers of Europe felt their interests sufficiently threatened to form an alliance against her. But it was not, insists Blanning, an alliance specifically directed against the Revolution, whatever the devices to which the apologists of war might resort. It was an alliance forged in the most traditional of causes, that of political self-interest. [13]

This view of the revolutionary wars, by underlining the importance of long-standing rivalries and traditional foreign policy objectives, provides a healthy antidote to the image of a European political order saturated in ideological absolutes. Governments have seldom hesitated to use almost any opportunity to increase their influence or to settle old scores. And by the time of the Directory, such considerations figured as prominently among the war aims of French governments as among those of their principal adversaries. It would be rash, however, to extend that judgment to the revolutionary governments of the earlier part of the decade. Girondin politicians may have used inflammatory language and appealed to heady ideals as they pressed their case for foreign war, but there was more to that case than traditional policy considerations such as territorial gain and political leverage. Jacobin orators may have whipped up popular patriotism and used the war to enforce measures of political terror, but there is no reason to doubt the reality of their underlying fears or the genuineness of their commitment to what they saw as a better society. It is easy to underestimate the intensity of political involvement in Paris and in some of the larger provincial cities from 1792 to 1794. Political morality demanded engagement and involvement in clubs, in sections, at the Commune, and in the wings of the Convention; among revolutionary militants, no issue caused greater interest or greater anguish than that of public safety, the defense of the Revolution against its enemies. Of course, political involvement at this level was restricted to a tiny minority of the population, and politics of such intensity could not last for more than a short time. But in this period, and especially during the Jacobin months of revolutionary government, the pressure for war did not come from politicians alone. Calls for emergency measures to save the Republic, demands that the war be pursued more ruthlessly, appeals for volunteers to fight on the frontiers, denunciations of the rich and *égoïstes* who made no sacrifices in the cause of victory, such issues dominated the agenda of popular politics. Enthusiasm for an ideological war against France's enemies could be found in the streets as well as in the committees of the Convention.

The perception of war, shared by both Republican politicians and radical militants, had important implications for the character of the military. The traditional eighteenth-century army might be well equipped to fight a war of conquest, but what the Revolution promised was a war of liberation, a war fought in the name of liberty and equality. This immediately raised fundamental and very troubling questions. Were small professional forces of the kind that had served Louis XV in his recurrent struggles with the other continental powers compatible with the new social and political order in France? Could an army of liberation decently continue to be raised by methods reminiscent of the press gang? In a country which had recently abolished feudalism and had declared that all its citizens were equal before the law, was it tolerable that the nobility should maintain its monopoly over the higher echelons of the command structure? In a society which had gloried in the Declaration of the Rights of Man, did soldiers have any rights, civil or political, or could they continue to be used and abused by their officers in the name of efficient discipline? What, indeed, was to be the relationship between civil and military society in a revolutionary state? And how was the role of the soldier to be defined—was it to be a policing role, bringing him into close contact with the population, or a more conventional military one, restricted to the defense of the state from external attack? Such questions could not be set aside in a country which was reforming its social and political infrastructure as was revolutionary France. The degree to which they excited contemporaries can be judged by the large number of tracts and treatises devoted to military reform. Already in the 1780s there had been lengthy discussions of the sorts of reform an efficient modern army required—changes that would have opened careers to talent and ended the stifling constraints of aristocratic domination.[14] A decade later the tone had become more peremptory, the discourse more idealistic. Dubois-Crancé, for instance, the career soldier who would be minister of war during the Jacobin period of government, was insisting that the organization of the military must follow the same principles as that applicable to civilian society. He therefore proposed that all citizens must be equally available to the army as soldiers, and that all soldiers must be equally able to accede to officer rank.[15] The era was past when all that was required was a plan of reform sufficient to improve the army's fighting capacity. In a political revolution it was unavoidable that the army should itself become a focus for political scrutiny and for political solutions.

The forces for change were not, however, entirely ideological. By 1789, highly practical reasons for reforming and restructuring the army were apparent to everyone at the time. Public opinion had made itself felt when the *cahiers de doléances* were drawn up for the consideration of the Estates-General. Complaints about the existing structure and regulation of the army came from both the nobility and the Third Estate, although, as Albert Soboul points out, the grievances of the nobility could as easily reflect an antiministerial stance, a *frondeur* mentality, as a strand of intellectual liberalism.[16] But the grievances of the Third could not so easily be dismissed, as many of them denounced the entire military regime as well as the specific obligations which fell upon their own members. Recruitment practices were attacked on the grounds of inequity and not just because they were so damaging to the peasant economy. Recruitment for the militia was considered especially repressive, cahier after cahier denouncing a process whereby a man would be dragged away from his friends and his community for six years simply because he had the bad luck to draw a low number in a ballot. Some cahiers went further, demanding that peasants be excused military service altogether and that the rich, the clergy, and the servants of the nobility be required to serve in their stead. From Rouen came the demand that the extent of service should be directly proportionate to land-holding, not, as was the case at the time, in inverse proportion to one's stake in society. The Third Estate of Troyes complained that the current conventions led to the devaluation of agriculture, to early peasant marriages by men who were desperate to escape the recruiting officer, and, in consequence, to a generation of young men bereft of the means to care for their families, who were left "weak and naked and impoverished."[17] And the Third of the bailliage of Nemours noted acidly that the imbalance in obligation was the exact antithesis of what had previously pertained. Although the nobility was now effectively excused service, it was precisely because they had had a military role in feudal society that they had been granted the enormous privileges they enjoyed over others.[18]

Other complaints concerned the way in which the army conducted its affairs and abused the young men in its ranks. Having deprived the community of the labor it so desperately required, the military was condemned for wasting the time and the talent of the young, at least during peacetime. Could not soldiers perform a useful civil function, undertaking road-building and public works that would benefit the community? Some cahiers went so far as to suggest that, except in times of war, the military had no use for the large numbers of recruits they demanded, with the result that the battalions encouraged idleness and squandered the resources of the local communities on which they were imposed. Billeting was particularly resented—the very common practice of insisting that local towns and villages accept responsibility for the lodging of troops while they were deployed in the area, a practice which did much to destroy such harmony as might have existed between the army and the civilian populations. In document after document the abuses of billeting are listed. Could not the army build sufficient barracks to house its own men? If billeting of individuals had to continue, should not the privileged orders, the nobility and the clergy, share in the obligations of the people? These were heartfelt grievances, for, like requisitions of food and fodder for the military, billeting seemed like a heavy and unequal additional tax arbitrarily imposed on local people. Some cahiers did not restrict themselves to those aspects of army life which affected them as civilians, but took up the cause of their sons and brothers in the regiments and complained indignantly about the humiliations to which young soldiers were subjected in the name of military discipline. Corporal punishments were especially loathed, not just by the young, on whom they were inflicted, but by whole communities which saw them as needlessly degrading and reminiscent of the treatment normally reserved for slaves. It is significant that such denunciations appear in the cahiers of the nobility as well as of the Third, that many officers in the ancien régime army were hostile to traditions which seemed more Prussian than French and which, they felt, undermined any concept of military discipline based on principles of honor.[19] Dissatisfaction was widespread, a dissatisfaction which would become politicized in the atmosphere of expectancy unleashed with the meeting of the Estates-General in May 1789.

The pressure for change was not restricted to the *cahiers de doléances,* nor, indeed, did it come exclusively from civilian sources. It would be foolish to dismiss the role played by the military themselves in bringing to the notice of the government the strength of opinion within their own ranks. Soldiers, too, were human beings, albeit human beings subject to military law and military discipline, and many of them looked to the Revolution to grant them the same Rights of Man that were being proclaimed for the population at large. The decrees of the National Assembly were of as much interest to the military as to the rest of French society, and their status as soldiers—answerable to the king at the very moment when relations between king and Assembly were most strained—gave them, obligatorily, a political role to play. Besides, the royal army had always played a policing role as well as a purely military one, maintaining public order, repressing riots and insurrections, and ensuring that the king's wishes were obeyed. It was almost unavoidable that if this role were to be continued, it would force the army to adopt a more overtly political stance, supporting the king against the Assembly and the expressed will of the people. Even before the calling of the Estates-General, indeed, the king had relied on his troops to ensure the maintenance of order in the countryside; the Grande Peur and the numerous disorders that marked 1788 and 1789 had necessitated the deployment of force, and it was to his line army—often to soldiers from the same province as the rioters—that Louis XVI had turned.[20] Likewise, when faced with the revolts of his *parlements* in Rennes and Grenoble, the king had called on the regiments to maintain his authority. But on both occasions their policing function had left the troops in a complex political dilemma. Was their first duty to the king in circumstances where they felt that popular opinion was ranged on the side of the *parlements?* And in the revolutionary circumstances of 1789, was it incumbent on them to open fire in French cities when crowds were clamoring for their civil rights and for the end of royal absolutism? The Revolution introduced a new and unprecedented ambivalence into the relations between the monarchy and the military.

Ordered to intervene in defense of royal authority, the various regiments of the line army responded very differently, but already there were clear signs of disaffection, from sudden increases in desertion rates to cases of open fraternization with the people. Such fraternization was most noticeable in Paris, where, by early July, more than twenty thousand troops had been assembled to defend the capital against radical insurgency. Although the full extent of popular sympathies among the troops cannot be estimated with any accuracy, it is surely significant that soldiers were observed aiding townspeople against the royal army and that they played a prominent part in organizing the attack on the Bastille.

It is significant, too, that Louis was deterred from turning to his army to put down popular insurrection in Paris or to close the sessions of the National Assembly. His ministers and closest advisers all counseled caution: the royal army could no longer be relied upon to obey orders. Given the extent of the Bourbons' dependence on the army to maintain their position of power, this was a critical change. As Marcel Reinhard points out, the refusal of obedience was itself a positive political action in the context of 1789, because if the army could throw its weight behind a political faction, it could also provoke a decisive change in the political balance by the withdrawal of its unquestioning support of the monarchy. This refusal of obedience was the army's most important role in the early months of the Revolution, a role which played a major part in ensuring the permanency of the Assembly. But Reinhard is right to be prudent in the interpretation he places on the meaning of the army's reaction. Did it indicate the spread of a new political consciousness among the troops, an immediate identification with the cause of the people, as some historians have suggested? Or was it, more prosaically, a reflection of their simmering discontent with pay and conditions in the regiments?[21] Politicians, perhaps predictably, were more forthright. Mirabeau, for example, saw the army's reaction as proof that it was already speaking with the same voice as the people, sharing its collective interests and fighting for its legitimate rights. He believed that the king might even provoke the army into armed insurrection in the popular cause, for, Mirabeau claimed, despite the brutalizing effects of blind obedience to their officers, "the troops will not forget what we are, they will see in us their parents, their friends, their families, busy looking after their most precious interests." Soldiers, argued Mirabeau, could never be persuaded to abandon their intellectual faculties because soldiers were an integral part of the nation itself.[22]

Given the draconian penalties reserved for men who disobeyed their superiors—acts of insubordination were commonly punished by life imprisonment or even death—even the relatively passive refusal of obedience which characterized these early months demanded courage and conviction. But as the political climate changed and the language of constitutionalism became more widely accepted, soldiers were induced to play a more active role in political affairs.[23] Some left their regiments to serve in the newly formed units of the National Guard, an act of desertion which had demonstrable political connotations even at a time when pay in the guard units was higher than in the line regiments. The guard was, after all, under local municipal control, and in the case of Paris, under the control of the sixty districts. Its principal novelty lay in the fact of the guard's local accountability, often to authorities who were pressing for a more radical policy than the one favored by central government. The guard also enjoyed a social and political prestige as yet denied to the regular troops: they were seen as young men of principle who had made a voluntary sacrifice for the defense of the Revolution when they could easily have continued to look after their own affairs. Others openly disobeyed the orders of their officers, especially where they believed that their officers harbored counterrevolutionary sympathies. In the aftermath of July 14, numerous individual acts of defiance occurred as soldiers refused to fire on the people, even when the king's authority was directly threatened. At Nancy, for example, men of the 105th regiment of infantry, the Infanterie du Roi, joined demonstrations in favor of the deputies to the National Assembly; at Bordeaux, troops called out to control a rioting crowd responded by joining the insurgents. Most memorably, the troops ordered to police the march of six thousand Parisians to Versailles on October 5 did nothing to impede the crowd's freedom of movement, some of the soldiers going so far as to hand over their cartridges to the Versailles National Guard. The authority of the officers was increasingly undermined as more and more soldiers placed their loyalty to the new political authorities above their established loyalty to the king and to their military superiors.

The problem of authority was made more intractable by the large number of officers who rejected the Revolution and remained loyal to the Bourbon monarchy. Such officers—men of noble birth who had never enjoyed close rapport with the men under their command—were rightly suspected by the troops they commanded of harboring counterrevolutionary prejudices and of working to secure the return of the old order. This in turn led to new questions being asked, questions which put traditional military discipline at risk. Was a man to be obeyed without question simply because of the rank that had been conferred upon him? Could those who had been given commands under the ancien régime be trusted to defend the Revolution? Should not those in command be obeyed as much for their political wisdom as for their seniority or their tactical skill? With the growth of prorevolutionary sentiment among sections of the soldiery, often particularly marked in garrison towns where soldiers mixed with townsmen and rubbed shoulders with the local battalions of the National Guard, such questions were increasingly asked, and the relations between officers and men in the regiments of the line army became tense and strained. Orders were given and refused. Officers known to be unsympathetic to the Revolution were abused and insulted by their troops, the soldiers confident that they would find support for their defiance from their new political masters. As a result the very foundations of the line army came to be questioned, and the army itself was threatened by the spring and summer of 1790 with a complete breakdown in its structures of authority.

Mutinies broke out in regiments throughout France—in Perpignan, Brest, Epinal, Longwy, Metz, Sarrelouis, Compiègne, and Hesdin, to list only some of the more serious. Often they originated in complaints about pay or the misappropriation of regimental funds, but other sources of grievance included the alleged ill-treatment of soldiers by officers, especially where these officers were disliked because of their politics. Often, too, the mutineers enjoyed considerable support from local people. Soldiers, especially those on garrison duty in cities along the French frontier, had plenty of opportunity to forge links with the local population. Clubs and popular societies, mayors and municipal councils all tended to listen favorably to the tales of outrage and abuse the mutineers related. Wrongful imprisonment, savage punishments, careless phrases, or insulting rebukes were all deemed sufficient cause for the denunciation of an officer and the rejection of his authority. Denunciations, indeed, began to be encouraged by the political authorities as they became ever more suspicious of the loyalties of the officer class, while infantrymen with a grievance did not hesitate to turn their denunciation into a political catechism.[24] Among more radical sections of the public, interest did not stop there, and there was an increasing clamour for the reform of perceived abuse. By the spring of 1791, the Jacobin clubs, both in Paris and in the provinces, devoted long and acrimonious sessions to the question of military reform, sessions at which extreme anti-officer feeling was expressed. Officers were frequently assumed to be suspect by the very fact of their rank in the line. In Cherbourg, for example, the club demanded the dismissal of the entire general staff and the replacement of all nobles who still held military commands.[25]

Matters came to a head in August 1790 with the most serious single mutiny of that mutinous summer, affecting three regiments stationed at Nancy. Only one of the three was a French infantry regiment (again, the Infanterie du Roi), the others being a regiment of Swiss mercenaries and one of cavalry. Yet this unlikely combination of units was responsible for the Nancy mutiny and for bringing the army close to civil war. Details of the mutiny are well-known.[26] Relations between officers and troops within the Infanterie du Roi had become badly soured, especially after the National Assembly voted to abolish political associations in the army—a desperate and somewhat forlorn measure to enforce discipline in the face of the new spirit of democracy which had spread among the troops. They had established a soldiers' committee in the regiment, maintaining close links with the local Jacobin Club, the Nancy National Guard, and other soldiers' committees in other regiments. It was this committee which demanded to audit the regimental accounts and which subsequently arrested the regimental quartermaster and confined all their officers to barracks. The other regiments, impressed by their example, also made demands about pay, discipline, and the administration of funds in their own units. The fact that the officers of the Swiss regiment, that of Châteauvieux, chose to reject their men's demands and to have the soldiers' representatives publicly whipped as an example to their fellows drove all three regiments to mutiny and won for the mutineers a large measure of public sympathy from local people. It was a stunning instance of insensitivity and political miscalculation by noble officers who had lost touch with the mood of their men. Yet Nancy might have remained just another name in the long list of soldiers' mutinies in 1790, but for the change in the government's response. The Assembly was frightened by the extent of insurrection in the ranks and afraid that the spirit of defiance would spread like a cancer throughout France's fighting units. It therefore attempted to restore army discipline by entrusting the command of the entire eastern frontier to the Marquis de Bouillé, and it backed Bouillé's attempts to reimpose strict obedience among the troops. In the case of Nancy, Bouillé was determined to make an example of the mutineers, and he answered their demands by marching on the town with a force of four and a half thousand men, many of them trusted troops from foreign regiments who could less easily be contaminated by egalitarian propaganda. He took Nancy and forced an unconditional surrender, but only after three hours of fighting and a hundred casualties. French troops had fired on one another in the name of the Revolution. The standing of the line army had sunk to its nadir.

If the mutiny shocked French opinion, the repression which followed was even more damaging to the army. Bouillé was intent on impressing on the soldiers the need for a strict and traditional military discipline, and those who had been responsible for mutiny and bloodshed could expect no quarter. He had demanded as part of the terms of the surrender that each of the three regiments hand over their four most mutinous soldiers. And the men of the

Châteauvieux regiment, who had been largely responsible for the fighting, were punished mercilessly: official attitudes to mercenaries had changed little since the ancien régime. One member of the soldiers' committee of the regiment, identified as the principal source of the disruption, was broken on the wheel, and twenty-two other members of the regiment were sentenced to be hanged. Forty-one soldiers were condemned to thirty-year terms in the galleys, and many others to lengthy periods of imprisonment. It was draconian justice, the application of military codes which dated from the ancien régime to defend the authority of noble officers against their own men. The cruel irony of the situation was not lost on the French public, especially when the National Assembly went out of its way to congratulate Bouillé on his effective action to restore order. In Paris especially, radical opinion turned violently against Lafayette, whose decree repressing acts of insubordination in the army was blamed for the judicial bloodletting at Nancy, and against Bouillé, reviled as the *massacreur des patriotes*.[27] In political terms, the government's response to the mutiny caused widespread anger and revulsion, but the implications were just as serious for the military. Nancy emphasized the need for a durable and truly revolutionary change in the character of the army. It underlined the contradictions between the aims of the Revolution and the military means at its disposal. And it exposed in a particularly lurid light the true character of the line army that had been inherited from the ancien régime.

The experience of Nancy also contributed to the widespread disaffection which undermined the loyalty of the officer class during the early years of the Revolution. The extent of insubordination and anti-noble sentiment in the ranks persuaded many high-ranking officers that there was no place in the armies of the French Revolution for them and the ideas they represented. It fueled the already widespread suspicion that noble birth was incompatible with the new political order, and provoked a fear that not even the most liberal of noble officers would be acceptable to the politicians in the Assembly. The officers' responses were predictably varied. Some, like Lafayette, had served in the American war and had drunk in its libertarian philosophy, although this did not necessarily endear them to the idea of revolution at home.[28] Others were natural conservatives who quickly became disabused about the nature of revolutionary politics in France. All had taken an oath of loyalty to their monarch, and thus many felt torn between their patriotic duty as Frenchmen and their responsibility as soldiers of the king. As time passed and the Revolution became more radical—both in its relations with Louis XVI and in its treatment of the army—increasing numbers of officers saw no future for themselves in revolutionary France. For many—and especially for the younger, ambitious men whose promotion had been rapid during the 1780s—emigration seemed an increasingly attractive option. As early as 1789, a small proportion of them had joined the first émigrés in Turin and Coblentz, ready to serve the king's brothers Artois and Provence in their crusade to restore the Bourbon monarchy to its former glory. Others, generally the younger brothers of landed families, would leave when their brothers and parents shuttered their châteaux and headed for the eastern frontier. Whether through fear or family pressure, the desire for vengeance or political commitment, these officers were prepared to choose temporary exile rather than come to terms with the demands of the new political order.

Their numbers remained relatively small until the spate of insurrections in 1790, and especially until the flight of Louis XVI to Varennes in 1791. Faced with a straight choice between a revolution from which they felt increasingly alienated and a monarchy which they could no longer serve on French soil, increasing numbers of nobles abandoned their military commands to join the émigré army in exile, encouraged as much by the unrealistic hopes of their families as by the bloodcurdling promises of the Duke of Brunswick. The trickle quickly became a hemorrhage that put the viability of the armies at risk. Between mid-September and the beginning of December 1791, some 2,160 officers emigrated; in some units it was almost impossible to find men with the skills and experience necessary for command.[29] The royalist press, papers like the *Ami du Roi*, gave the faltering every encouragement to join the emigration and carried optimistic reports about the military strength of the armies assembling across the Rhine. The Comte d'Artois had already established his headquarters at Coblentz, where he was talking of an imminent invasion of France by an émigré army, and that army was openly recruiting on French territory. The *Gazette de Paris* even carried a notice offering a signing-on bounty of fifty livres to all who would join them on the Rhine, together with details of the rates of pay and instructions for reaching the assembly points.[30] After the declaration of war, such emigration posed a direct threat to the ability of the country to defend itself, as individual generals not only abandoned their trust, but also often subverted a proportion of the men under their command. It was only too easy for politicians to place the blame for military defeat on the treason of the general staff.

Emigration placed intolerable strains on bonds of mutual trust within the army, encouraged surveillance and denunciation of suspect officers, and left the government uncertain of the loyalty of its own troops. It also left whole armies at the mercy of their Austrian and Prussian enemies and contributed to the miserable performance of the French during the first months of fighting in 1792. It was an abuse that could not be allowed to continue unchecked, and the succession of laws passed against émigrés was an accurate reflection of the increasing concern they caused. The first great law against emigration dates from April 1792; by September all émigré property was ordered to be confiscated, and in October all those who had left France were banished for ever from the soil of the *patrie,* with a death sentence hanging over them should they return.[31] The defection of Dumouriez in 1793 became one of the political causes célèbres of the revolutionary decade because he not only surrendered a number of border forts to the Austrians, but also tried to turn his army against Paris; he had also been a minister in Roland's government and had close ties with the Girondins in the Convention. But Dumouriez's was only the most sensational of a number of defections by sensitively placed army officers. Long before Dumouriez crossed the line to join the enemy, the combined forces of insubordination and emigration were threatening to sap the morale of the armies. As a result, an increasing number of politicians reached the conclusion that what was required was root-and-branch reform of France's military institutions. For pragmatic as well as for ideological reasons, the whole basis of the military was reexamined. Far-reaching reforms were discussed and implemented. These reforms affected every aspect of army life, from organization to command structure, from provisioning to political answerability. The line army of the ancien régime would not be disbanded, but it would be completely changed. Just how it would be changed, and how these changes would affect the lives of the soldiers who fought in it, will be the subject of the remaining chapters of this book.

2

RESTRUCTURING THE ARMIES

THE INFIDELITY OF LARGE NUMBERS OF ARMY OF-
ficers, the political awakening of the men under their
command, and the long-standing complaints of a large
section of the civilian population were all forces for change in the
structure and composition of the army the Revolution inherited in
1789. The reforms which followed would reflect the diversity of
these forces and would demonstrate the uneasy mixture of idealism and pragmatism which so often characterized the revolutionary achievement. They would be introduced piecemeal, replacing
the existing military structures and modes of recruitment, the
system of command and of military justice. The result was a
revolutionary change in the character of the royal army—the
regular troops of the line who had made a career of soldiering and
who formed the bulk of the king's regiments throughout the
ancien régime—yet at no stage was it disbanded or the existing
troops cashiered. For the first two years of the Revolution, before
the call to arms of the first volunteer battalions, it was the line
army and the line army alone which provided for the defense of
France. If citizen militias and National Guard units were created
locally, their powers remained limited to the defense of property
and local policing. Although politicians might view the line with
distrust, they had no choice but to rely on it, at least until major
changes could be implemented. Besides, in the early months of
the Revolution, politicians had no legal right to interfere with the

status quo because the army remained the personal responsibility of the king until a new constitution determined otherwise. It is therefore with the royal army of the ancien régime that any study of the military must logically begin.

The royal army was composed of three distinct elements: the household regiments, the line regiments, and the militia.[1] The first two constituted the standing army of the ancien régime, a permanent army that would be sustained in peacetime as well as in times of war. The militia, in principle at least, was recruited to supplement the line troops in moments of national emergency, although in practice it had come increasingly to be regarded as part of the standing army. During the eighteenth century, indeed, the only times the *milice* had been disbanded totally were from 1715 to 1719 and again from 1721 to 1726.[2] Of the two permanent forces, the Maison du Roi can scarcely be regarded as a fighting unit. These were the troops of the royal household to whom Louis XVI could turn in a personal capacity, the troops used to guard the royal palaces or take part in ceremonials. Their loyalty was to the king and to him alone. The Maison du Roi included some 7,200 men: the royal bodyguard and the Gardes Françaises, as well as the regiment of Swiss Guards which would earn such notoriety on August 10, 1792 when it fired on the Paris crowd at the Tuileries. In contrast, the line regiments constituted the principal fighting strength of the eighteenth-century army, totaling in 1789 some 113,000 infantry, 32,000 cavalry, and 10,000 artillery. The infantry regiments would form the backbone of the revolutionary army until the recruitment of the first volunteer battalions in 1791. At the end of the ancien régime they numbered 102 in all, of which 79 were French and the others drawn from among the mercenaries of Europe, from the Swiss cantons and the various German states, aud from Ireland and Liège. They tended to be recruited regionally, in the areas where their captains and higher-ranking officers could exercise social influence over the population. And they bore proudly traditional names which conjured up regional loyalties or the military glories of the past. French regiments fought in the names of La Couronne and La Reine, of Turenne and Condé; they had the arms of the old French provinces emblazoned on their regimental colors, Aquitaine and Anjou, the Vivarais and the Vexin. Foreign regiments were usually given names appropriate to their country of origin—for the Germans, names like La Marck and Royal Hesse-Darmstadt; for the Swiss, Châteauvieux or Diesbach; for the Irish, Walsh or Dillon.[3] In each case their particularism was emphasized, as was the strength of local tradition in their recruitment and in their choice of officers. The men of the old line regiments fought not for the nation, not even in any direct sense for the king, but for their local seigneur and their local provincial tradition.

From a purely practical viewpoint, this localness of perception did not reduce the troops' value as soldiers or damage their esprit de corps. But for the revolutionaries, the sense of identity which individual regiments could command was a source of intense irritation; it undermined the universality of the Revolution's appeal and stressed what was most parochial and most archaic about ancien régime society. Besides, the regionalism of regiments' names and titles was largely fraudulent. Titles did not necessarily represent the province of origin of the men; rather they depicted the areas of land-holding and seigneurial influence of the commanders or reflected the personal predilections of the officer class. For much of the eighteenth century, for example, as Jean-Paul Bertaud has shown, the Régiment d'Auvergne recruited heavily in the Cévennes for the simple reason that the regimental captains came from that region and showed an understandable preference for troops from back home.[4] It would be difficult to offer any immediate military explanation for the insistence of the revolutionaries that regiments should be relabeled, the picturesque and particularist names of the eighteenth century giving way to rather drab and unevocative numbers. The true reason had much to do with the symbolic significance of the old traditional names—the respect for tradition in a force where tradition was closely bound to monarchy and aristocracy, the loyalty to regions when the new order was laying so much stress on the nation and when regional power was indentified with the feudal fiefdoms of the ancien régime. A truly national army, bound to the state and committed to the defense of France and her Revolution, was the goal to which the men of 1789 subscribed. Like Mirabeau, they saw the need for army and people to be as one, and any trace of local loyalty or local attribution was taken as a symptom of lingering privilege.[5]

Such reforms were important to politicians, even if their military significance was largely cosmetic. The Royal Roussillon would not perform any more brilliantly simply because it was now designated the 54th Regiment of the line. And yet to make such a clear distinction between military and political inspiration, between practical and ideological change, is to misunderstand the mission the revolutionaries had set themselves and to forget the purpose of the Revolution's plan of reform for the army. That purpose was only partly to create a more efficient military machine. It was also to mold a fighting force that would reflect the character of a revolutionary society and which could be entrusted with the task of defending a revolutionary state. This double goal—efficiency and political virtue—was to remain intact, to a greater or lesser extent, throughout the revolutionary period, and especially during the period of Girondin and Jacobin control. Of course the two aims were often conflicting, even contradictory. In the short term at least, military advantage and ideological constraints did not always coincide. But when seen in a longer perspective, the arguments about military policy were often microcosms of wider political debates reflecting the different priorities and outlooks of revolutionary politicians. The army was a part of the polity.

From both a military and a political point of view, however, certain questions must be asked. How efficient was the army the Revolution inherited? Was it well respected by the public opinion of the day? Was there an evident need for reform? If the opinion of contemporary writers is to be believed, there was clearly considerable cause for alarm. The ancien régime army elicited little praise or support, and those who served in its regiments evoked condescension, distrust, and even open revulsion. Literary sources seemed virtually unanimous in their judgment that war was corrupt and that the army was necessarily corrupted by the values of war. This idea was not unique to the eighteenth century. The three great moralists of the seventeenth century, Pascal, Fénélon, and La Bruyère, had all condemned what they saw as the false ethics of war. To Fénélon, war could have no morality; it was, he declaimed, "an evil which dishonours the human race." For La Bruyère, the notion of human beings devoting themselves to "plundering, burning, killing and slaughtering one another" seemed utterly obscene; to carry out these atrocities more ingeniously, he added, "they have invented splendid rules which they call the art of war" and have over the centuries developed evermore efficient ways of slaughtering one another. Even in comedy the soldier did not escape censure. Molière created comic situations in which valets and footmen, dressed up as soldiers and officers, solemnly discussed before the audience the wounds they had received in the service of France.[6]

Worse still was the image of soldiering presented by the writers of the Enlightenment, who treated the individual infantryman with cavalier contempt. In the pages of the *Encyclopaedia*, he is presented as the dross of French society, to be judged only by the standards of the lowest rabble, "because he sells himself more cheaply." In *Candide*, Voltaire presents an unsavory image of the armies of Europe, "a million assassins organized into regiments, rushing from one end of Europe to the other inflicting murder and pillage because they have to earn their living and they do not know an honest trade." Voltaire, indeed, lambasted the military with unparalleled venom, seeing the armies of his day as composed of unprincipled mercenaries masquerading under the banner of patriotism and military honor. "The wonder of this infernal enterprise," he wrote in his *Dictionnaire philosophique* when discussing warfare, "is that the leader of each band of murderers has his flags blessed and invokes the support of God before exterminating his fellow-being."[7]

This sense of repugnance toward the army and the art of war was not confined to the writers of the Enlightenment or to a small coterie in the salon society of Paris and the larger cities. What posed a far greater threat to military recruitment was the gulf between the military and civilian society at large. Among the peasantry and among artisans and laborers in the towns, this alienation showed itself most damagingly in increasing numbers of deserters and refractories and in a widely expressed dislike of any form of personal service.[8] They had too much firsthand experience of the soldiery to be seduced by the propaganda of the recruiting sergeant, preferring to see in the armies a major source of civil disorder for their own communities. But in educated circles, too, the image the army enjoyed had never been less flattering. Soldiers were depicted as gratuitously violent and permanently drunk, a source of danger to such decent people as they might meet and of nuisance to the local communities on which they were imposed. The armies were commonly associated with a rise in violent crime and with a loose moral code. Soldiers, it was widely believed, raped and looted freely when they were on campaign or when the armies were on foreign soil, and it was feared that the habits acquired and even encouraged during periods of occupation must necessarily affect their conduct toward their fellow Frenchmen. Soldiers, like beggars and vagabonds, were a section of society that needed to be closely supervised and strictly policed.

If the frequent recourse to war in the eighteenth century meant that civilian society had more firsthand experience of a military presence, it should not be assumed that that experience led to better relations between soldiers and civilians. A serious shortage of barracks resulted in troops being billeted regularly in the towns and villages through which they passed, a practice that also raised the level of resentment against the army. Local communities did not relish the camp followers and prostitutes who attached themselves to the regiments, and French families feared for their daughters and sisters when the army was in town. By the end of the ancien régime, it is clear that troops were feared more than they were respected by wide swathes of French society. They were seen as rather marginal figures, men without any skills or sense of vocation who had drifted into a military life-style through boredom or misfortune. And when they left the army, often wounded or injured, without a trade or a home to live in, frequently without either wife or dependents, they again risked giving the impression of being among society's misfits, condemned to spend the rest of their lives in rootless poverty or in the local poorhouse. Too often, observation seemed to confirm what the writers had suggested, that the armies were for the very poor, for those without hope of earning an honest living, and for drifters and scoundrels who relished a culture founded on violence.

Of course this picture can be exaggerated: not all soldiers were cut off from their social roots, not all were tempted to crime or given over to debauchery. But this image of soldiering was so widespread that it was part of the popular culture of the eighteenth century, and it did great damage to the army. It not only soured relations between civilians and those who were responsible for their defense, but it also resulted in violent incidents when the army was used for internal policing within the community and helped to reduce respect for authority in all French society. It also led to a widespread contempt for the military life-style, a lack of esteem which undermined recruitment and reduced the willingness of the individual Frenchman to serve in the regiments. In times of war or national emergency, the call to defend one's home or one's community would still elicit an enthusiastic response, at least in those parts of the country most exposed to attack. But in peacetime, when there was no such obvious necessity, the response was generally sluggish, with peasant boys showing a marked resistance to any form of recruitment which would remove them from their farms and their villages. Why should young men, particularly in the areas of subsistence farming where their labor was so badly needed in building up their family smallholding, abandon their fields or their pastures for years on end to take up a career that brought so little glory or social respect? The result was an army drawn disproportionately from the ranks of the poor. In Paris after 1763, many of the recruits lied about their area of origin and gave false information about their occupation; they were often eager to conceal their true identity or to blot out some misdemeanor from their past. The majority of those incorporated in these years were unskilled and had only recently arrived in the capital from their native province; only 14 percent of them were Paris-born.[9] Military service would seem to have had little appeal to those who were already well-integrated into the life of the city.

It is clear that ministers and commanders in the eighteenth century would have preferred a volunteer army dedicated to a military career. The increasing complexity of weaponry and of military tactics convinced many contemporaries that an effective army must also be one that could muster a degree of conviction and commitment.[10] What they got was something very different—men devoid of any military vocation, a line army composed primarily of those who had neither the means nor the willpower to escape. The most normal method of recruitment for the line was that known as *racolage*—the soliciting of inscriptions on public highways and in village squares, at fairs and markets and in local taverns. The *racoleurs* would advertise the supposed benefits of army life to the local population by every means at their disposal, impressing village boys with the smartness of their uniforms, the martial music of their drummers, or the incisiveness of their slogans, the exhibition culminating in the offer of a generous bounty. These could be very tempting: in the Franche-Comté, for example, some of the bounties were in excess of a hundred livres, or as much as an agricultural laborer could hope to earn in a year.[11] Professional recruiting sergeants who would stoop to most forms of deceit lied brazenly to the more impressionable among the young, promising early promotions and claiming to be recruiting for prestige cavalry regiments. When their efforts elicited no response, their methods of persuasion often degenerated into violence and bullying of a kind which recalled the abuses of the press gang. There were frequent allegations of intimidation and strong-arm tactics, of peasant boys being recruited at the local fête when they were too drunk to offer resistance, of youngsters waking up to find that they had signed their lives away. When voluntary inscriptions were lacking, the military could so easily become mere *marchands d'hommes*.

From these abuses, others followed. Soldiers recruited by such means had little reason to show loyalty in return; they had, after all, signed on for cash rewards not to the French army but to the service of a particular officer. And the personal nature of much of this recruitment, as André Corvisier has remarked, was sufficiently feudal in character that it was not always clear whether the recruited soldier was a trooper of the king or a servant, a *domestique*, to his captain. The ties of personal fealty were certainly considerably more real, the element of personal obligation more consistently maintained, than any nebulous loyalty to a national army.[12] Only in time of war did officers find themselves sent into the towns to recruit on a large and impersonal scale, and contemporary opinion tended to regard that as rather repugnant, as a byproduct of war that would not be tolerated in peacetime. In the eyes of the recruit, his obligation was strictly limited. Once in the army, he would discover that there was little contact between officers and men, little camaraderie to strengthen the bonds between them. The officer was a distant figure, often feared and even loathed, who showed little respect for the person or the sensibilities of those in the ranks and who inflicted a harsh and unremitting discipline on his men. On the orders of his officers, a soldier could be hanged or shot in full view of his regiment; in extreme cases he might be broken on the wheel. Yet crime and lack of discipline were rife in all eighteenth-century armies. In particular, theft, pilfering, and pillage were everyday temptations when pay was so miserably low that men regularly went hungry and were forced to look around for part-time employment to make ends meet. In 1789, for example, an infantryman earned only seven sous and four deniers per day, or the equivalent of around four or five pounds of bread. And out of this he was to pay for his own food and drink, his clothing, and even his army boots.[13]

For the young peasant lured into service by the promise of wealth and the prospect of booty, daily life in the regiments could be a rapid source of disillusionment which only confirmed the whispered warnings of his boyhood friends. Instead of adventure, he faced tedium and neglect to the point where military discipline became hard to maintain. Soldiers acquired a very casual attitude about their service and could easily be tempted to leave their regiment for another if a second bounty were promised: the practice of changing units in this way, of betraying one officer for another, was known as *billardage* and was a major source of discord among eighteenth-century commanders.[14] And—especially at the end of a campaign or on the approach of the harvesting season—desertion could seem an obvious solution to men for whom army life had lost its charms. During the 1780s, there were some three thousand desertions in an average year—around 2 percent of the total strength of the regiments—but this figure rose considerably whenever the threat of war loomed.[15] Searching for deserters was one of the main tasks assigned to the police force in the countryside, the *maréchaussée;* they had been constituted "for the capture of deserters, the safety of travellers, and the transport of tax receipts."[16] Periodic amnesties were offered, but, with no guarantee that he would be released from service after a fixed period, the deserter had little incentive to return. There was always some farmer who would offer him work, some frontier over which he could escape, some lingering hope that he would be able to get back to his village. Faced with a choice between recapture and life on the run, the deserter saw little benefit in throwing himself on the mercy of his regimental officers.

Any sense of cohesion within the regiments was further vitiated by the structure and social origin of the officer corps. Not only were the day-to-day relations between officers and men made distant by regimental tradition, but they were rendered even more tenuous by the fact that all but a handful of officers in the line armies were of noble birth, and as such were the kind of men who in ordinary village life would have had little truck with the sons of sharecroppers and artisans. There was therefore no possibility of promotion from the ranks, of talent finding its reward. The promotion structures for officers and men were kept quite clinically distinct. In Louis XVI's reign, the number of soldiers who were not noble, but who aspired to officer rank was very small: of 211 lieutenant generals, for example, only 16 can be singled out as being of likely *roturier* origins. [17] Of the officer corps bequeathed to the Revolution in 1790, more than 90 percent were nobles. They were for the most part relatively modest provincial nobles, far removed from Versailles and the politics of the court; they were proud of regimental tradition as they were proud of their family tradition, and that tradition was one of service to the crown. They were opposed to any dilution of noble control over the army not only because it was the life-style they knew and loved, but also because they believed that such dilution would lead to a decline in the notion of honor on which the French army was built. The Ségur Ordinance of 1781, which demanded that recruits to officer rank must be able to demonstrate four generations of nobility, clearly did nothing to encourage the opening of careers to talent or the emergence of a dynamic new officer class from commoner stock. But, as David Bien has shown, that was never a great likelihood. What was perceived as a threat by the military was the entry into the army of large numbers of sons of *magistrats,* of ambitious bourgeois families which, through careers in the law or in business, had made a great deal of money and had bought titles of nobility. The aristocratic reaction which historians have detected in the Ségur Ordinance must therefore be seen for what it was, not as part of a generalized social reaction by the aristocracy—for it had no counterpart in other areas—but as a specific measure by the officer corps to defend their traditional values and to prevent an invasion of their ranks by rich officeholders. It was a way of excluding those who were regarded as being insufficiently serious in their commitment to the army. [18]

If the structure and recruitment of the line army aroused anger in the community at large, it was the third element in the military provision of the ancien régime—the militia—which provoked the loudest protest. Unlike the line regiments, the militia was a service in which all unmarried men between eighteen and forty were liable to serve—or one in six of the male population. As originally conceived, it had been intended as a reserve force that could be raised at short notice to defend the local community against enemy attack; it had first been introduced for this purpose by Louvois in 1688 to fill gaps in regular recruitment. [19] Its peacetime duties were scarcely onerous—a fortnight's training at irregular intervals—but in periods of war the militia assumed such ancillary duties as guarding regimental baggage, garrisoning frontier towns, and defending the rear of fighting columns. [20] Initially, when it still retained something of the character of a civic militia, the *milice,* in France as in much of Western Europe, had encapsulated an element of regional pride and had enjoyed a certain popularity in the local community. By the eighteenth century, however, the nature of the militia had significantly changed, its ceremonial role having given way to that of an army auxiliary, its voluntary character having been replaced by ballot. Service with the militia, which in the Middle Ages had been counted among the privileges of free men, was now quite devoid of status. [21] By the second half of the eighteenth century it had become a permanent reserve of some 75,000 men, regarded by the state as a necessary fund of auxiliary soldiers but treated with fear and loathing by the bulk of the rural community.

The roots of this fear lay in the method of recruitment employed for the militia, which involved a high element of chance and left the individual terribly vulnerable and exposed. Each district of the country had to find a set number of men to fill its quota, although provinces were at one time or another favored with exemptions, and the extent of the sacrifice demanded could appear desperately unequal to those involved. This sense that people were being treated unequally, without any element of social justice, lay at the root of the unpopularity of the *milice*. Those with means could buy themselves out by finding a replacement from among the less fortunate members of their community; thus in practice militia service was a burden which weighed heavily on the peasantry and the poor. Landowners, notaries, chemists, doctors, officeholders, merchants, and the richer peasants, those with land of their own or with large herds, would find themselves exempted from serving in person. So, to the dismay of the poorer peasantry, did the servants and footmen employed by the rich and aristocratic.[22] As Lazare Carnot, himself an army officer during the ancien régime, perceptively remarked, replacement on a large scale and on the basis of income was degrading as well as unfair because replacements were openly bought and sold in the streets and markets of provincial towns in a wholesale "commerce d'hommes."[23] Besides, so much hinged upon the outcome of a simple ballot on the village green. For those who had the misfortune to draw low numbers—the much-feared *mauvais numéro*—the sacrifice seemed frighteningly open-ended. By the second half of the eighteenth century the period of service had been extended from three years to six, and with so many wars and such great international uncertainty recruitment to the militia had come to involve real soldiering. It is little wonder that it was on the *milice* rather than on the line regiments that popular anger was focussed when communities were asked to list their grievances in 1789.

These grievances were in the main the grievances of civilians, but the army did not remain unaffected by opinion in the country. Army officers, just like their civilian counterparts, attended literary societies and masonic lodges. They, too, drank in the ideas of the Enlightenment, and they were particularly given to question the wisdom of current military practice. Within the army, indeed, reform plans and critical pamphlets became commonplace. Some of the ideas proposed smacked of control and repression. There were pamphlets proposing that all beggars and vagabonds should be rounded up and incorporated in the regiments, pamphlets that wished to recruit all domestic servants as a means of rooting out idleness in society, others that wanted orphaned boys to be forced to serve as a means of repaying their debt to the public purse.[24] But many of the *mémoires* emanating from the army reflected the same concerns as the general public. They wanted to reform the *milice*, to get rid of the blatant unfairness in its codes of recruitment, to move toward an army of volunteers who would make more motivated soldiers. Or they questioned the wisdom of maintaining strict social divisions at the very heart of the system of command. Other pamphlets concentrated on more practical questions like strategy and military tactics and sought to break with tradition and reform the army's military thinking from within. Some made a notable contribution to enlightened thought in their own right.

Perhaps the most remarkable of the military writers of the last twenty years before the Revolution was Hippolyte de Guibert, who combined the experience of high military rank with the critical thinking of the Enlightenment. Guibert had studied military reform in other European countries and felt that France had a great deal to learn, particularly from the armies of Frederick the Great. But he also felt that permanent reform would only come when patriotism, the love of the soldier for his country, became part of the military code. Contemporary tactics, he conceded, saved unnecessary loss of life, but they made no use of the patriotic spirit that lay dormant in the troops, preferring to pay the men miserable wages and to underestimate them as human beings. Guibert would become a close collaborator of the minister of war, Saint-Germain, and would be elected to the Académie Française in 1786. But his most lasting contribution was to the debate which raged in military circles about the role and the nature of a modern army: his anonymous pamphlet of 1772, *Essai général du tactique,* helped to forge a reformist climate among his peers in the high command.[25]

What Guibert was preaching—some twenty years before the Revolution—was the need to create an army that would be more closely identified with the nation and restructured to capture the patriotic spirit of the nation. He advocated a mass army which would use new tactics based on enthusiasm and sheer numbers. Others were less adventurous, or less rash. Among the most influential was Joseph Servan, like Guibert an army officer and a nobleman, whose revolutionary career would take him to the Ministry of War under the Girondins in 1792. Servan, too, insisted that the principles on which the royal army was conceived needed to be completely rethought. In a long and thoughtful tract published in 1780 and entitled, somewhat prophetically, *Le Soldat citoyen,* he dismissed the possibility of a mass army and argued that any resemblance to the militia must at all costs be avoided. In such circumstances, he contended, military strategists should be asking a new set of questions, questions his fellow officers seemed happy to ignore. What should be the ideal number of men to form the royal army? How many were required to defend the security of the state? What moral and physical qualities should be demanded of these soldiers? And, in the event of there being insufficient volunteers, how should their number be supplemented? Comprehensive change was needed, Servan argued, in an army where officers were often blind to wider issues and obsessively concerned with trivial questions of precedence, where subalterns were "brave but ignorant, careless and presumptuous" and were paid too little to inculcate any pride in their rank, and where, most serious of all, soldiers were so poorly paid, clothed, armed, and trained that they were wholly unsuited to defend the public good. In a modern and enlightened army of citizens, said Servan, it was indispensable that the soldier be fully integrated into civil society, that he enjoy a decent level of pay, a humane code of discipline, and a function that would command respect from others. He urged that soldiers should be men of peace, carrying out useful agricultural tasks in the community when they were not required to undergo military training or to defend the frontiers. For Servan, the eighteenth-century army was based on a faulty premise. He saw the soldier as a citizen first and foremost, and only in this way, by performing the normal tasks and duties of a citizen, could the soldier command the respect due him.[26]

Although Guibert and Servan spoke a new political language that was as yet unfamiliar to many of their peers, it should not be imagined that theirs were lone voices, or that the eighteenth-century army was impervious to change. In the last decades of the ancien régime, several reforming ministers, among them Choiseul, Saint-Germain, and Castries, looked for ways of improving the efficacy of the military. Their achievement, it may be felt, was limited. The virtual monopoly exercised by the country nobles over the officer ranks in the army was strengthened rather than weakened. The pay of a French sailor in 1789 remained what it had been in 1689, despite the massive increases in the cost of living over the intervening century. And the reforms in the disciplinary code which Saint-Germain introduced in 1776 were received scornfully by the soldiers. The minister had sought to reinculcate discipline in the army without resorting to brutality, replacing a range of punishments which he deemed to be cruel and demeaning with a single penalty, that of *coups de plat de sabre,* the administration of beatings with the flat of the sword across the victim's back. To the troops, on the other hand, it seemed a dishonorable form of punishment, and one that was imitated from foreigners, especially from the Prussian army.[27] But the failure to make major advances in the social field does not mean that there were no significant reforms in the prerevolutionary years. The poor performance of the French armies in the Seven Years' War had awakened politicians and generals to the urgent need for change, and military reformers enjoyed a ready audience. New weapons were developed, and tactics and strategy were subjected to a searching review. The result was very substantial technological development and greater maneuverability in the field. Gribeauval's artillery guns, for example, were the most modern and had the farthest range of any in Europe at the end of the eighteenth century. And the tactics Dumouriez deployed at Valmy were directly inspired by the tactical thinkers of the 1770s and the 1780s.[28]

There was, indeed, a large measure of continuity between the reforms being discussed in the last years of the ancien régime and those implemented in the early stages of the Revolution. The idea of a national army of the kind proposed by Servan and Guibert found wide support among members of the National and Constituent assemblies. And many believed that to be truly national an army must involve the service of all, or at the very least the availability of all for service. The principle was clearly mooted that "Tout citoyen doit être soldat, tout soldat citoyen" (every citizen must be a soldier and every soldier a citizen).[29] Among the deputies there was also a widespread distrust of the existing military leadership and a fear that too great a degree of professionalism in the army would necessarily distance it from the people and leave it as a privileged *corporation*.

Much of the early thrust of the Revolution was directed toward the abolition of such privilege, whether in the estates or in the towns and the *corps de métiers*. It would have been illogical to leave the army unscathed, especially because the army was potentially the most dangerous corporation of them all. Yet in practice the Assembly proved cautious in the reforms it proposed, limiting its activity to the removal of the most glaring abuses denounced in the cahiers. This might at first sight seem curious. The mood of the country was receptive to change, in this sphere as in others. Opinion in the Assembly was bent on transforming the country's political and social institutions, and most of the permanent gains of the Revolution were, quite demonstrably, made through the reforming legislation of this early period. Yet the army, arguably the institution in ancien régime France which was most tied to royal power and noble privilege, did not undergo any searching program of reform until the soldiers' mutinies and the king's flight had made the maintenance of the status quo unthinkable. Why?

One reason clearly lay in fears that by radicalizing the army the deputies would radicalize the Revolution itself. Although the experience of the Bastille might endear some among them to the concept of a popular army acting in close cooperation with the people, memories of the Grande Peur were too recent for risks to be taken with the one institution that could guarantee the maintenance of order. Although they might have serious reservations about the aristocratic profile of the officer corps, few in the Assembly saw any alternative to a gradual transfer of authority. Army officers did, above all, need to possess expertise, and the possibility of an army without a clear structure of authority was attractive to no one. The revolutionaries, like their predecessors, found themselves obliged to choose men who had graduated from the military academies of the ancien régime or who—in the case of the highly specialized artillery regiments—had passed through the elite artillery school at Mézières. Only gradually did the demand for new officers, combined with a glaring failure to found new training schools, lead to a preference for experience in the field over such specialist training.[30] The problem was compounded by the fact that there was no clear consensus about what sort of army the Assembly aimed to create. Was the principal aim to build up a strong military force capable of defending France and winning any war in which she became involved? Was it to create an army that would be politically pliant, a tool in the hands of the executive power that would carry out the instructions of the executive? Or was it rather to be a force for the politicization of the nation, a force which would represent in itself certain political values and political ideals? In this early period the main debate was between those who sought proficiency and professionalism and those who were eager to politicize the army in order to make it a tool of the nation. The third purpose—using the army to help forge the new revolutionary man—would not fully emerge until the period of the Convention.[31]

Fear that the army would become radicalized and independent of the state led the deputies to exercise caution in their reform plan. Yet between 1789 and 1792, considerable progress in mili-

tary restructuring was achieved.[32] Methods of military recruitment were carefully weighed; the Assembly rejected any form of
conscription, but accepted that citizenship implied duties and
obligations, among them that of giving military service when it
might be required. It also went a considerable way toward liberat-
ing the army from its ancien régime ties to the monarch and to the
nobility. Initially, it is true, the military remained subject to the
authority of the executive, and executive power was invested in
Louis XVI, but such unambivalent power was short-lived. By
1790, the Assembly voted itself the right of involvement in
executive decisions, and after August 10, authority over the
military passed directly to the Convention. Other changes sought
to tie the individual soldier more closely to the nation and in this
way remove the risk that the regiments would one day be turned
against the Revolution itself. In 1789, officers were required to
take an oath of loyalty to "the nation, the king, and the law"; they
further undertook that they would never use their troops against
civilians without express orders from the civil authorities.[33] In
1791, the nature of the engagement made by each serving soldier
was amended so that his contract was with the state rather than
with an individual. Also in 1791, the special statute accorded to
foreign regiments was abolished, and all infantry regiments were
considered equally responsible before the French state. Reform
after reform stressed that the soldier's duty lay in serving the
nation, the *patrie*—France itself.

The abolition of the provincial names and the traditional insig-
nia of individual regiments also dates from this period, with the
same aim of standardizing army procedures and abolishing distinctions that could easily be regarded as emblems of an outdated
feudal order. The degree of direct influence exercised by the
Assembly over the military increased dramatically. In part this
was done by sending to the various armies deputies who had
instructions to report on the political loyalty of their generals as
well as on more routine questions of supply, morale, and general
readiness for war. In part, too, it was achieved by the administra-

tive device of establishing at a very early date a special military committee of the Assembly that could provide the deputies with expert advice and thus strengthen the standing of the political leadership with the troops. This *comité militaire,* like so many of the specialist committees of the Constituent, soon evolved into a powerhouse of new ideas where reforms were born and legislation planned. Established by decree on October 1, 1789, it included among its members both Mirabeau and Dubois-Crancé, and it boasted a wide expertise on all matters affecting the military. In consequence, the Assembly was never allowed to lose touch with the armies or to see the officers as a specialist corps on whose judgment they had to depend. Long before the abolition of the monarchy, elected deputies exercised effective controls over the military, and the structure of authority binding the army to the state underwent a fundamental transformation.

Within the regiments, too, there were notable areas of reform.[34] The soldiers' mutinies had the salutory effect of reminding politicians that the long tradition of low pay and unquestioning obedience was not acceptable to free men. As early as 1790 it was accepted that soldiers who qualified as active citizens should enjoy the same rights as civilians, rights they were to exercise in their hometowns and villages. This was a very timid concession, although it was important as a point of principle; with the passage of time, soldiers would acquire a greater and greater measure of civil rights. From May 1791, they were permitted and even actively encouraged to take part in political clubs and societies in those towns where they were stationed, provided, of course, that their political activity did not impede their military exercises and garrison duties. From July of the same year soldiers were allowed to exercise their rights as active citizens in the communities where they served, and from August 1792, these rights were extended to all soldiers, regardless of their wealth or property, provided that they had reached the required age of twenty-five and that they remained loyally at their posts. All these reforms were intended to reduce the distinction which had existed in law between serving soldiers and the community at large. The trend continued under the Convention: in March of the following year, soldiers obtained a further right, much prized as a symbol of freedom, when they were allowed to marry without the express permission of their commanding officer. Such changes were not of merely marginal interest. They demonstrated a clear intention on the part of the political authorities to treat those who fought to defend the nation with all the dignity and respect that was their due.

The principle that soldiers enjoyed all the rights pertaining to citizenship had other implications for the running of the revolutionary armies. Officers could not continue to be a caste apart. The circumstances of 1790—and they were as much practical circumstances as the product of revolutionary ideology—demanded that the gulf between officers and men be closed. But such a transformation of attitudes in a traditional bastion of privilege like the army could not be easily achieved. In large measure, indeed, it was the high losses incurred among the ancien régime officers—losses caused as much by emigration and political dissension as death and injury in battle—which helped hasten the creation of a new and more egalitarian spirit within the line regiments. But the Assembly had still to find new men to replace the officers, men drawn from social groups that had not been immersed in the military traditions of the provincial nobility. Again there was a certain conflict between the professional and the political interest. Should promotions be decided on the basis of experience or of talent, of years of service or popularity in the ranks? Now that the criterion of birth had been rejected, how could a choice be made that would both satisfy the troops and guarantee effective military discipline?

The decisions that were taken suggest a certain blurring of these priorities, a willingness to compromise between the different interests that were represented in the army. A percentage of promotions to officer rank—in practice of promotions to the post of second lieutenant (sous-lieutenant)—was reserved to noncommissioned officers, appointed by their superiors, who had served the army well but who would have been ineligible to rise any further in the regiments of the ancien régime. However, others were to be selected by their peers, voted their promotions by the men with whom they served, the men who—it was supposed— were best able to recognize their human qualities. It was a most novel way of choosing young officers, one which allowed for a degree of answerability and reflected the democratic instincts of the new political order. In practice, the most significant outcome was the rapid promotion of men of ability who had served as NCOs in the last years of the monarchy, but who had seen their careers blocked by the structures of the eighteenth-century army, men who often combined military talent, personal dynamism, and an impatience to participate in political change. They were at once excellent soldiers, well-skilled in the art of war, and confirmed patriots, eager to implement the reforms of the new order. They formed an identifiable phalanx of military talent, since the quality of the *bas-officiers* had been massively improved in the years since the end of the Seven Years' War. From their ranks came such as Soult, Bernadotte, and Hoche, men who would make their mark on French military command during both the revolutionary wars and those of the First Empire.[35]

Changes in the disciplinary code were also implemented quickly. If soldiers had rights in law, they could not be suddenly deprived of these rights at the whim of their commanding officer. And because officers remained suspect politically, it was deemed particularly important that the soldier's independence of the political authority of the officer class should be maintained at all costs. Public opinion united with opinion within the regiments to ensure that the arbitrary powers of officers were curbed and that a disciplinary code was adopted which conflicted less blatantly with the ideals of the regime. The status quo was untenable in any case. The judicial system that pertained in the armies was steeped in custom and privilege: a soldier could be made to appear before any of four different sorts of tribunal, their authority overlapped, and some of them had no expertise in military law. And the penalties laid down by a succession of royal ordinances were of a savagery that was intended to deter. Capital punishment was invoked for any act of violence toward a superior officer, for failing to report sedition or seditious utterances, and for blasphemy or sacrilege. A soldier convicted of stealing sacred objects or of pillage on Church property was to be hanged and his body burned if he had in any sense profaned sacred objects. A soldier who threatened his superior with a weapon, or who struck him in anger, even if he had in his turn been ill-treated by the officer in question, was to have the offending hand cut off before being put to death by hanging and strangulation. In an army of free men a new code of law was a matter of urgency, a code that distinguished crimes against common law from those offenses against military discipline which had always been punished with an exaggerated ferocity during the ancien régime.[36] Discipline would have to be maintained, and there were among the professional soldiers those who expressed their fears that too liberal a reform would result in the collapse of the French armies as a cohesive fighting force. But under the Revolution that discipline was to be one that was freely consented to; it would no longer be a discipline imposed from above. Men were to be judged according to strict juridical norms. A clear distinction would be drawn between criminal offenses—which would be judged by civilian tribunals—and breaches of military discipline. And the army would be subject to a legal code based on the same legal principles that applied to their civilian counterparts. From the soldier's point of view, these were considerable gains, made for the most part during the months of the Constituent, during the high period of reformist legislation before the outbreak of war made government less sensitive to issues of liberal principle.

A new kind of army was coming into being, even though it was built around the rump of the old line army of the ancien régime. Gone were the mercenary regiments of Germans or Swiss; gone, too, were the regiments of militiamen forced reluctantly into uniform in periods of crisis. From 1791, political opinion, and especially that expressed by the Assembly's *comité militaire,* moved steadily away from the idea of a professional force and opted instead for an army composed of volunteers committed to the cause of France and the Revolution. By 1791, there were already those who feared the political ambitions of professional soldiers, and who foresaw the danger of Caesarism, the threat that high-ranking officers would develop their own power base in the armies and use it to challenge the authority of the state. Alternatives to the line were being actively created. In towns throughout France, National Guard units had formed to protect lives and property; in 1791, many of these guards would become the first true volunteers, forming themselves into new regiments to supplement the line armies on the frontiers. The ideal of a volunteer army was subsequently embraced with enthusiasm, and the recruitment of large numbers of volunteers in both 1791 and 1792 left France with two very different types of soldiers: the old line troopers, well-drilled in the eighteenth-century art of war, and the new volunteers, youthful and patriotic but often woefully lacking in even the most basic training. Or such was the theory: in practice these contrasting attitudes can easily be exaggerated because at least some of the old line troops were counted among the most fervent supporters of the revolutionary cause. What is certain, however, is that until 1793 they were organized, regimented, and disciplined differently; they even received different rates of pay. France still had two distinct armies rather than a single, integrated military force.

With such different traditions it was perhaps unavoidable that these two types of soldiers did not necessarily understand each other or appreciate each others' qualities. Frequent squabbles and confrontations occurred between regiments of volunteers and regiments of the line, confrontations which often ended in violence and bloodshed. Insults were thrown, and insults were easily followed with saber cuts. At Versailles in August 1793, soldiers of two French regiments—one composed of regulars, the other of volunteers—drew their swords on one another in the course of an angry altercation; and at Perpignan, when violence and disorder broke out between volunteers and men of the line, it was explained as the result of a long-standing "schism" between the two units.[37] One particular incident is graphically described by a young volunteer, Gabriel Noel, who was on garrison duty in the town of Sierck in January 1792. The garrison was manned by both a unit of volunteers and a unit of the Picardy regiment, grenadiers of the line. When on New Year's Day some of the grenadiers came across to wish the volunteers season's greetings, mutual antagonisms were fueled, perhaps by alcohol, and fierce fighting broke out which left sixteen grenadiers injured and four dead. What particularly frightened the young Noel was the fact that such violence and hatred could be sparked off by a single ill-considered remark; if the incident ended in reconciliation, that reconciliation was completely lacking in warmth as the two regiments continued to regard each other with ill-concealed loathing.[38] Disputes and rivalries of this kind were legion and were only increased by the differences of pay and conditions and by the contrasting uniforms of the different regiments. The line still dressed in white; the volunteer regiments wore blue. And if the men of the line reviled the volunteers for their higher daily pay—they scathingly referred to them as *soldats à quinze sols*—the volunteers were equally dismissive of what they saw as the servile mentality of the *culs-blancs*.

If the French army was to be molded into an effective fighting force, drastic structural reform was a matter of the highest priority. Volunteers and regular troops were organized differently, administered differently, even paid differently. The armies, subdivided into regiments and battalions, were widely dispersed and poorly integrated. The volunteer battalions, in particular, lacked the experienced quartermasters who alone could ensure some degree of administrative efficiency. The result was a level of administrative chaos which was itself an important contributing element in explaining French defeats. When the Convention wished to enforce reforms, it discovered that in many battalions there were no registers, no lists of enrollments, no account books, only disorganized piles of unpaid bills and crippling deficits.[39] Officers could not accurately assess losses through death and desertion; recruits were being sent to units that were already overstaffed; and the ministry did not really know what resources were at its disposal.

Underlying the entire debate was the political question: What form of army structure would be most acceptable to public opinion, and particularly to the volunteers themselves? What they clearly would not find acceptable was any form of incorporation whereby their battalions would be dissolved and the men added to existing line regiments. That would be seen as a political defeat and in military terms as the victory of the line, of discipline and experience over youth and republicanism. Yet the volunteer battalions were the greatest cause of military concern. Of the alternatives, any genuine amalgamation which involved the total restructuring of the army into new regiments would seriously prejudice the immediate fighting capacity of the armies in time of war. And incorporation had to be ruled out for political reasons. The third possibility was some form of *embrigadement,* the regrouping of the existing battalions to erode the differences that separated them while building on the skills and qualities each could offer. It was this third solution which Dubois-Crancé proposed and which the Convention voted in February 1793—the so-called law of the *amalgame,* the most critical measure of military restructuring to be undertaken during the revolutionary decade. As well as resolving the damaging differences between the volunteers and the men of the line, it was presented as a way of attaining new levels of military efficiency by getting rid of a multiplicity of small units, saving precious administrative manpower, and allowing for more effective instruction and training.[40]

Dubois-Crancé's proposal seemed beguilingly simple: to create a single national army, all differences between the line and the volunteers must be abandoned. They would henceforth wear the same uniform, receive the same pay, and march behind the same flags and regimental banners. They would be subject to the same discipline and would serve under the same officers. The separate battalions would disappear, and the men would be *embrigadés* through the simple device of placing one battalion of the line alongside two battalions of volunteers in a new military unit, the *demi-brigade*. The result—at least on paper—would be an army of 196 *demi-brigades* of infantry, each with a company of artillery attached, plus units of light artillery, engineers, and cavalry. The deputies accepted this form of amalgamation as a means of excising the very real problems of the existing army without, it was thought, so disrupting the military that the defense of the frontiers would become impossible. It was, by its very nature, something of a compromise between the politically ideal and the immediately practicable, a solution that was inevitably subjected to fierce criticism from both the right and the left of the Convention. Many felt that the politicians were putting the security of the state needlessly at risk by passing such a measure so close to the start of a new campaign season. The generals themselves showed no great enthusiasm for the change, some, no doubt, through a lack of revolutionary conviction, but many because they feared the practical consequences of such massive restructuring on battalions of men who had just recently learned the basic principles of soldiering. From the Armée des Pyrénées-orientales at Perpignan, the commanding officer, General Dugommier, complained to Paris that he had received instructions to proceed with the *amalgame* just as his troops were preparing to move on to the attack. The result, in his view, could only be catastrophic for an army which had just become accustomed to the maneuvers it would have to use, an army in which the officers and men had only recently got to know one another and where a measure of mutual trust had been established. Nor did the general want to delay the campaign: his troops had been inactive in their winter quarters for far too long, and boredom was setting in. Dugommier therefore overruled the deputy on mission to the army, Châteauneuf-Randon, and delayed the implementation of the law until the end of the 1793 campaigning season.[41] He was not alone. Of all Dubois-Crancé's proposals, the formation of the *demi-brigades* was the last to be put into effect.

Restructuring was not limited to reshaping the battalions. Much of Dubois-Crancé's effort was devoted to what he saw as a necessary corollary of that restructuring, the reform of the system of promotion.[42] Without such a change, the Republic could not be sure of the devotion of its commanders, while the individual soldier could have been forgiven for thinking that his lot had changed very little from the ancien régime. Besides, with the *amalgame,* some device had to be found to create a fair system of promotion for an army composed of very different sorts of troops. Were it to be geared too closely to battle experience, then the volunteers would surely suffer; yet a system that ignored the fruits of experience would be resented by the line. Dubois-Crancé's solution was both subtle and sensitive, although it was greeted with derision in the more conservative military circles. Generals and *chefs de brigade* would be appointed directly by Paris, so that account could be taken of their political qualities and their loyalty to the regime. For promotion to most other ranks, one-third would henceforth be taken on the basis of seniority, of years of service in the regiments; the other two-thirds would be elected by their peers. More precisely, the men of the rank below would elect three candidates for a post which became vacant; three from among their own number and the soldiers already in the higher grade would choose one of the three for promotion. In this way, it was believed, talent could be recognized—because the soldiers themselves would choose men in whose capacities they had faith— while the long service of those who had suffered as commoners during the ancien régime could at last be rewarded. At the same time officers would be more answerable to the men they led, less prone to form a caste apart. For Jacobin leaders like Robespierre, this was a highly significant change of direction, and one of which he approved even as he criticized Dubois-Crancé's proposal for its overall timidity and moderation. In Robespierre's eyes the real danger to the Revolution emanating from the armies was political—the danger of an overpowerful officer class, armed and privileged, which could at any moment take up those arms against the state. The law on the *amalgame* was quickly followed by a purge of the officers, especially of those generals whose aristocratic origins rendered them automatically suspect. The *sans-culottes* in Paris demanded vengeance; and the Jacobin coup d'état of May 31–June 2, 1793 gave renewed impetus to the purge of the high command, with generals like Custine wrenched from his command in the Nord and sacrificed to the guillotine. The purge had a powerful symbolic significance for the Paris popular movement: it represented in the clearest terms the victory of patriotism in the armies. On the other hand, it had a more complex objective for the Jacobins. The new citizen army at last had its own organizational structure, independent of the inheritance from the ancien régime, and it had at its head a new generation of officers on whom the political power could rely.[43]

The solutions the Jacobins applied to the problem of military authority were much the most radical of the revolutionary period, yet they were in their turn fraught with ambiguity. The attitude of the political power toward its officers was never wholly clear. Were officers intended to exert authority and impose discipline when circumstances demanded it, or was such action to be construed as potential tyranny? Were officers expected to show individual initiative, or was their role to be restricted to the channeling and implementing of political instructions? Was the officer chosen for his expertise or for his political worth? Was he, indeed, first and foremost a technician or a political appointee? These are important questions, for there is no doubt that the general staff of 1793 and 1794 was placed in an ambivalent and often unenviable position in relation to the executive. It is significant that, in practice, officers were judged much more harshly for political crimes than for abusing their authority over their men. Allegations of arbitrary arrest or ill-treatment of soldiers are relatively rare, whereas there were regular denunciations of those suspected of disloyalty or hostility to the regime. Some of the officers who won rapid promotion in Year II were unquestionably political figures before they were career soldiers—men who left political missions to lead armies or who had served their apprenticeship in the Paris sections. The minister of war, Bouchotte, himself defined the qualities of the good general in largely political terms. He should, said Bouchotte, be sober and upright, devoted to his duty and exuding fraternity in his relations with others; he should also provide the men with an example that they might follow of "courage, devotion, patriotism, and a hatred for kings, tyrants and those who depended on them." For a brief period, at least, the qualities of political virtue took precedence over those of military expertise.[44]

Yet even at the height of the Terror, appearances can deceive. Virtue could be interpreted as an essential ingredient in the efficacy of a revolutionary army. If generals were put on trial for political disloyalty, they were also tried and executed for losing battles. Virtue and technical excellence were qualities the commander of 1794 was expected to possess in equal measure. What had disappeared from speeches and from the preambles to legislation was the insistence on the civil rights of the individual soldier which had been such a dominant theme with the Girondins. With the Jacobins in power the army's purpose was more incontrovertibly to carry out the wishes of the executive. And for that purpose, discipline, whether or not it was a discipline of consent, was once again important: the virtuous soldier of the Year II was not expected to question the orders he received. The rights he was accorded—the full rights of citizenship, the right to receive newspapers and join political societies, the right to a fair trial, the right to appear as a witness in court like any other Frenchman[45]— were rights which in no way clashed with his efficacy as a soldier. They could even be seen as raising his political consciousness and strengthening his resolve. In February 1793, critics of Dubois-Crancé saw in his scheme for promotions a significant move away from the principle of free election in the direction of technical expertise. Why else, they asked, did he leave the final choice of candidate to those already promoted to the higher grade? Their suspicions were probably well founded. Dubois-Crancé was, after all, a career soldier, a former general who understood as well as anyone the needs of an army and the constraints of war. However tempting it is to view the *amalgame* in primarily political terms, his main purpose was to create an army that would be effective on the battlefield and a military structure that could turn defeat into victory.

There had always been an element of conflict between ideas of liberty and participation and those of discipline and obedience. The Jacobins added to this ambiguity by their almost pathological suspicion of the officer class and by their insistence on political surveillance to avert the ever-present threat of conspiracy. This in turn could only encourage discussion and questioning of orders by the soldiers, and risked producing an army that was itself part of the political process. Yet the Jacobins never took the side of participation at the expense of effective military discipline. It was, after all, during their period in office that the conflict was largely resolved in favor of discipline and efficiency, with officers increasingly chosen on merit for their strategic intelligence and technical knowledge. After 9 Thermidor, any vestige of a dilemma rapidly disappeared as the army command became largely depoliticized and technocratic. A new spirit of military professionalism crept in, among both the officers and the men, as the years passed and they became increasingly inured to a military life-style. By the end of the 1790s, indeed, political commitment played little part in the armies; obedience rather than militancy was what was expected of the soldiers of the Republic. There was little mention either of the camaraderie and fraternity which had distinguished the volunteers of 1793, ideals which gave way to a more single-minded concern for grade and promotion. Men who had been recruited as volunteers in the heady days of 1791 and 1792 increasingly saw themselves as professional soldiers, as men who had no real alternative to a career in the military. In spirit, at least, they came to resemble career soldiers. Gradually the gains made by the soldiers in 1793 and the Year II were also dissipated, as the armies reverted to a more traditional and more authoritarian structure, especially in matters of discipline. In Year III a much stricter system of military police was established, with a new military code which prescribed the death penalty for a wide range of crimes and offenses. Soldiers were again judged by their superior officers rather than by civilian tribunals. It was a change indicative not of a return to the ancien régime, but of the evolution of a military machine that was increasingly devoid of political idealism and independent of political control.[46]

3

RECRUITING THE SOLDIERS

THE SUCCESSION OF REFORMS AIMED AT RESTRUC-
turing the armies left unanswered the most pressing question of all, that of recruitment. If France was to have a
volunteer army, there would have to be a sufficient number of
young men willing and eager to defend the Revolutionary cause.
Peasant boys who had declined to serve in the armies of the ancien
régime, and who had gone into hiding rather than submit themselves to the ballot for the militia, would now have to respond
with unprecedented enthusiasm to the call of the nation. It was
always a rather risky assumption. The ideal of the "nation in arms"
might be prominently enshrined in the Revolution's legal codes,
but it was a difficult ideal to translate into practice. Dubois-
Crancé's slogan that every citizen must be a soldier and every
soldier a citizen had little immediate appeal in a country where the
idea of soldiering enjoyed such a poor popular image. It would
take time and careful propaganda before popular fears of the army
could be allayed, especially in those areas of France which had
proved refractory in the past.

The reactions to soldiering had varied sharply from one region
of the country to another; desertion and draft-dodging were regional problems before they were national ones. In the eighteenth
century, for example, some areas of France, most notably in the
plains of the North and East, had always provided their quota of
soldiers without serious complaint, whereas others, especially in

the Midi and the Southwest, had failed to find more than a few recruits. In Alsace, noted the Chevalier des Pommelles in 1789, there was one soldier for every sixty-one inhabitants, whereas the *généralité* of Auch had difficulty in raising one for every 628.[1] André Corvisier has reconstructed from regimental records the map of regional recruitment patterns in 1716, and it generally confirms des Pommelles' claims. Enthusiasm in the East was matched by the sullen hostility of regions like Pau and Perpignan, although Corvisier stresses that such hostility was not a southern monopoly. Brittany was the province with the worst recruitment record of all in 1716.[2]

In areas like Brittany, Guienne, Gascony, and the Auvergne, the task the revolutionaries set themselves was a daunting one. They had, in practice, to transform local mentalities and reverse age-old prejudices if they were to generate the sort of enthusiasm which the notion of a volunteer army presupposed. They had, in particular, to disabuse local people of the associations which they stubbornly maintained between any sort of military obligation and the hated militia service, and to persuade them that there was no necessary conflict of interest between their duty to the nation and their duties as peasants, sons, and fathers in the agricultural community. In 1789 and 1790, when recruitment was conducted in the familiar context of the old line regiments and when there was no direct military threat from abroad, such a transformation proved impossible. Enthusiasm was reserved for the newly formed National Guard companies, largely because they were perceived as having the predominantly civil role of defending the Revolution inside France. The population at large made a clear distinction between Guard service and soldiering.[3] And although in rural France the Guard was drawn from a wide cross-section of the community, it could never claim to have had a truly popular catchment in the towns. There, with its heavy concentration on the defense of property, it became a respectable and rather bourgeois institution whose ranks were closed to those who were not active citizens. It is true that with the passage of time Guard units did get embroiled in fighting and that individual guardsmen volunteered for active service. But there were also instances where the very rumor that the Guard might have a serious military function led to allegations of deception and to mutinous rumblings among local people, as happened in the Périgord in 1790.[4] Guard service, in short, was not recruitment; rather, it was seen to be safe, respectable, and rather enjoyable. Urban merchants' and country lawyers' sons who flocked to join were participating in a public demonstration of their patriotic principles, generally in the company of their friends and social peers. For the great majority of them, their sense of obligation ended there. They did not for a moment imagine that they were signing up for service in a real army, or that their service might involve a sustained period of absence from their local community.

The realization that rather more would have to be demanded of the citizenry became clear from the early months of 1791, when fears of an imminent war against Austria persuaded a number of municipal councils that they must prepare themselves for hostilities. In Clermont-Ferrand, for instance, an enrollment book was opened and the young of the town were invited to volunteer for active service when their country needed them. By July, war fever gripped the Assembly as rumors spread of the existence of a counterrevolutionary army, commanded by the Prince de Condé, assembling on the frontiers and preparing for an invasion of French soil. The result was the first decree calling for volunteers to present themselves to their town halls, prepared to march to protect France in its current emergency. Like the reforming generals of the ancien régime, the political leaders in the Assembly were convinced that the most effective kind of army must be an army of volunteers, of young men whose passion for the nation and its Revolution would compensate for any lack of traditional tactical training. Although at this stage there was no suggestion that compulsion might have to be used, the law did contain some glaring ambiguities.[5] It described, rather tendentiously, a system of "voluntary conscription," and envisaged the creation of new battalions which would serve in a parallel capacity to those of the line. Volunteers were to be raised by each district in the proportion of one volunteer for every twenty National Guardsmen, and the assumption was clearly made that these volunteer soldiers would spring from the ranks of the Guard. They were to be equipped by their municipal authorities and would receive a rate of pay considerably above that of the line regiments. In practice, at least in the towns, they were often young men of some substance, active citizens of the sort who had already been admitted to Guard membership. They certainly represented a much wider cross-section of the local population than the men who had been drawn into the ranks of the line army, and they included many who were literate, educated, and politically aware.

The commitment of the Assembly to the voluntary principle seemed fully justified by the rush of potential recruits during the summer and early autumn of 1791. Indeed, in some areas of the country, recruiting offices were overwhelmed by the levels of enthusiasm displayed. Department after department could report with satisfaction that the government's appeal had been answered, that the young of their areas were burning with patriotic zeal and were offering themselves in satisfyingly large numbers to serve the patriotic cause. Local studies of these first volunteers tend to confirm this reassuring picture, even in areas which had never shown much enthusiasm for the career of arms.[6] The number of battalions which the Assembly had requested was quickly filled, then exceeded. Northern and eastern departments like the Vosges and the Meuse, the Ardennes and the Pas-de-Calais produced far more than their required quotas. In Paris and in many parts of the provinces such as the Marne, the Allier, the Charente, and the Puy-de-Dôme, the contingent was raised in a month or less— often in a matter of days. Some departments even asked for permission to form supplementary battalions rather than turn away men anxious to fight for the revolutionary cause. The first call for volunteers, by any standard of measurement, must be seen as an outstanding success, with more than one hundred thousand extra troops supplied for the revolutionary armies and an additional 169 battalions formed within two months of the Assembly's decree. The summer of 1791 marked the high point of voluntarism as fathers left their wives and children to volunteer, lads of fifteen and sixteen grew up rapidly through service with the armies, and local officials talked proudly of contingents leaving their regions wreathed in smiles and singing patriotic songs. It was the moment when fear of invasion blended most obviously with public indignation and revolutionary commitment, the moment when the émigré threat assumed a new credibility following the flight to Varennes. There was still an air of innocence and of optimism abroad on which the government could capitalize. Of all the waves of soldiers that would be produced by the Revolution, the volunteers of 1791 came closest to the ideal of the *soldat-citoyen*.

And yet there was already ample reason for circumspection. If one hundred thousand extra soldiers had come forward to serve in the new volunteer battalions, was it mere coincidence that at the same time the line regiments were suffering a shortfall of fifty thousand men?[7] This statistic was sobering because it suggested that the appeal of fighting, whether in the revolutionary cause or any other, was still strictly limited. The old line regiments had not succeeded in throwing off their tarnished ancien régime image after 1789, and the higher pay offered to volunteers merely ensured that the attraction of the line was still further diminished. Among the new volunteers were former soldiers who chose to desert from their regiments in order to join the new volunteer battalions, and it would be naive to expect that they all did so for reasons of revolutionary commitment. The volunteers were better treated, enjoyed greater freedoms as citizens, and were feted as heroes by their local communities, which often marked their departure with touching patriotic ceremonies. Most important of all, they signed on for a single campaigning season, after which they fully expected to be restored to the daily routine of civilian life.

In 1791, the lot of the volunteer still seemed glorious and faintly exotic, the once-in-a-lifetime chance for the village artisan or solicitor's clerk to escape from humdrum reality for a few carefree months in the service of the *patrie*. If many of the new volunteers did care deeply about the cause in which they had enlisted—and their journals and letters suggest strongly that this was so[8]—there were others for whom the volunteer battalions represented an opportunity to get away or a means of satisfying a thirst for adventure. There were so many possible reasons for enlistment. Some were rebellious spirits seeking a means of escape from parental authority; others were impoverished and hungry and were attracted by the relatively high level of income; others again were bored or were lured into volunteering by the bravado of their friends. Among the men of the volunteer battalions there were committed patriots, of course, especially in the ranks of the subalterns and NCOs, and their role was to be an important one in motivating their fellow soliders. But chance and boredom could play as important a part as political idealism or physical courage.[9]

In this first experiment in voluntarism, there was little sign that enthusiasm was confined to any particular class or section of the French population, although, as Jean-Paul Bertaud has shown, the response was most gratifying in the towns and most reluctant among the peasantry. If there was a group which threw itself more wholeheartedly into the battalions than any other, it was what Bertaud terms "le monde de l'échoppe et de la boutique," independent craftsmen and artisans, shopkeepers, and tradespeople.[10] Their officers were often drawn from the lower and middle bourgeoisie, or from soldiers of the line attracted into the volunteer battalions by the possibilities of rapid promotion. But the social basis of the volunteer battalions remained very much wider than that of the line; they were rarely dominated to the same degree by the rural artisans who were so prominent in the eighteenth-century military. At Aurillac, for example, in addition to the tailors and shoemakers who traditionally enjoyed a reputation for soldiering, were recruits from commerce and the liberal professions, including four of the clerks who worked at the town's Palais de Justice.[11] But it must not be assumed that the entire country was equally affected, or that—even in 1791—the recruitment was national in the strictest sense of the term. There were already clear indications that the traditional distinctions between regions of military tradition and those which resented any obligation to serve still exercised a certain sway. Paris responded enthusiastically, as was expected; so did the frontier departments of the East, like the Meurthe and the Marne. But there were also disappointments. The Breton departments did not produce the quotas expected of them; certain inland areas of Aquitaine and the Massif Central had to be exempted altogether; and in the West there were already indications that the religious issue was causing peasant resistance to the government's demands. And although the Ile-de-France responded well, as the wide prosperous plains around Paris had always responded in times of danger, even there enthusiasm tended to be limited to the towns and larger *bourgs* and to those rural areas where regular contact with Paris and urban markets was assured. Elsewhere the lists remained blank for weeks on end until persuasion could be exercised and men found who would be prepared to leave. Mayors also used sleight of hand to fulfill their military obligations, filling their quotas with men who had just recently moved to the area, men who had physical disabilities or who did not fulfill the basic height qualifications, vagrants and petty criminals, and those living on the margins of village society.[12] The battalions were duly filled, of course, and the government could congratulate itself on the levels of patriotism that had been demonstrated, but there were warning signs of severe difficulties ahead.

The shortcomings of the voluntary principle became evident within twelve months, when the government tried to repeat the exercise of 1791 in the changed political climate of 1792. It is true that recruiting officers were showing a greater degree of professionalism by 1792 and were refusing to take the boys of fifteen and old men of sixty-five who had been accepted on the previous occasion. It is true, also, that the circumstances that surrounded the levy had completely changed, with serious implications for popular enthusiasm. Whereas the 1791 recruitment was carried out in the dead season of the agricultural year, that of 1792 took place while the preparation of the soil was under way and farming was particularly labor-intensive. The *appel* of 1791 had been made before war broke out, when it was still possible to conceive of a short and glorious campaign, ending in victory and a triumphant return to the plaudits of one's fellow villagers. Such a dream was difficult to sustain a year later when the French army had been routed and humiliated, when families had sustained their first casualties, and when villagers had turned out to weep as the effects of the dead were returned. Besides, many of those most eager to serve had already left the previous year. Volunteers were not restricted to a narrow age group of the sort laid down by later conscription laws. They could come from the entire male population of the community between sixteen and forty-five, even if in practice the majority were young and single. But the effect of this was that only those teenagers coming of age since the previous levy could be said to form a new pool of recruitment, given that all the others were by definition men who had failed to leave in 1791. The political context, too, had changed, with events now dominated by the war, by the treason of the court, and by the new intolerance and extremism which marked revolutionary politics. For many, the dream of the previous year had turned sour, and recruitment inevitably suffered.[13]

As a result, the rush of eager volunteers which had so often greeted the first *appel* was rarely repeated. Areas of strong military tradition still succeeded in filling their departmental quotas, but elsewhere it was becoming clear that the simple act of publishing the government's decree and of opening a communal register in the local town hall would no longer suffice. Even in the district of Versailles, arguably the region of France that boasted the strongest military ties of all, it is noticeable how much the local battalions depended on former soldiers of the ancien régime regiments, even on former Swiss Guards, and on men who, in search of work, had drifted to Versailles from other parts of France.[14] Elsewhere the returns were patchy, with rural areas relying strongly on urban workers and artisans to fill their quotas, or reporting sadly that despite all their efforts, they had been unable to find enough able-bodied young men willing to serve. In some recalcitrant communes in the Auvergne, the demand for volunteers was met with rioting and violence: at Montsalvy, for example, an angry crowd stormed the town hall and seized the papers relating to the previous year's draft, thus rendering any serious attempt at recruitment impossible.[15] Everywhere the recruitment process seemed to be marked by a new mood of pragmatism far removed from the principled calls to the generosity of youth which had been so common in the previous year. Speeches and exhortations were no longer perceived as being a sufficient incentive to serve, a fact the soldiers themselves seem to have realized just as clearly as the politicians. The men of one battalion, who had themselves volunteered and who were reluctant to accept that others stay at home, urged the authorities to show a little flexibility. What was required, they suggested, was something colorful that could fire the imagination of the young, and they insisted that a few volunteers with a drum, some red, white, and blue cockades, and a bottle in their hands would do more for recruitment than all the speeches ever composed. The young patriots of Murat agreed, recommending that the government speak the language of ordinary people, the language of festivals and patriotic dancing, of free drink and ceremonial meals.[16]

The government was not deaf to such appeals. Where difficulties were encountered, towns and villages would often pay signing-on bounties in an attempt to stimulate patriotic sentiment. Substantial sums were handed over—the approved norms were eighty livres for infantrymen and 120 livres for the cavalry regiments—and some officials did not hesitate to pay in hard currency rather than in *assignats* if it was felt that such a gesture would produce the desired effect.[17] Desperate mayors, unable to stimulate voluntary inscription, were frequently forced to adopt some form of balloting in an effort to carry out their duty under the law, even though this necessarily implied the abandonment of the voluntary principle. Or they might play on the known weaknesses and miseries of the young men of their commune, like drunkenness or family quarrels, in order to fill their military quotas. There were cases where recruiting officers responded in exactly the way that had been requested by the lads from Aurillac: they toured rural communities, accompanied by drummer-boys, to *battre la caisse* and entice the patriotic or the desperate into their companies, just as they had done during the most desperate years of the ancien régime. The outcome of such effort was an intake into the armies that consisted massively of young and often callow recruits, three-quarters of them under twenty-five and many of these aged only sixteen or seventeen. Their officers might be sincerely patriotic, but the bulk of the soldiers would seem to have been the sons of the poor, many of them peasant boys who had had little or no formal education. [18] If they were volunteers, they were volunteers who in many cases had no desire to be in uniform and who felt no obligation to serve beyond the strict confines of a single year.

The principal effect of such a precarious recruitment exercise was to persuade the government that some form of compulsion was required if recruits were to be found in sufficient numbers to provide for the defense of the country. All too clearly the voluntary principle had failed. Yet it would be abandoned only gradually and with the greatest reluctance, not least because for many it had become synonymous with the revolutionary ideal. Besides, any suggestion of compulsion caused widespread repugnance among the population, especially in rural areas where it was wont to be equated with the hated militia of the ancien régime. For this reason the revolutionaries would cling to the fiction of voluntarism long after they had renounced its spirit, describing as volunteers men who had been drafted and coerced into uniform. In fact, the number of recruits continuing to present themselves voluntarily after 1792 fell off sharply; the need for some drastic new initiative was not in doubt. By the end of 1792, the military faced a crippling crisis of manpower as those volunteers who had survived the campaign all too frequently slipped off home to their farm or workshop. The Convention might appeal to them to stay at their posts, reminding them that although the law allowed them to retire to their farms, patriotism forbade it.[19] The officers might plead with their men in similar terms, emphasizing that no reason for quitting the ranks could possibly be legitimate as long as France remained threatened by foreign enemies.[20]

Appeals to patriotism had little effect, however. Few of the volunteers contemplated a career in the military, and many returned to civilian life proud to have played their part in defending and promoting the Revolution. As a result, the armies remained seriously under strength, to a degree which stopgap measures like the recruitment of special auxiliary troops—the *compagnies franches* of 1792, including a number of legions of foreign mercenaries—could not hope to solve.[21] At the beginning of 1793, the total strength of French regiments was around 350,000 men, a figure which seemed quite risible when compared to the 470,000 they had boasted in mid-1791. Government ministers and army generals alike doubted whether with such a depleted force France could fulfill her military obligations, especially since the new campaign season promised to be hard and exhausting. Far from achieving the peace for which many of the volunteers had hoped, the country was about to be plunged into hostilities with most of her European neighbors, while internal dissension in Brittany and the West would create new military fronts at home. A massive new recruitment effort was clearly required.

The government's answer took the form of a new departmental levy, the *levée des 300,000*, which was decreed on February 24, 1793. The armies required an additional three hundred thousand soldiers by the time of the summer campaigns, and the Convention was determined that the necessary manpower should be made available. But although the decree declared that all males between eighteen and forty who were unmarried or were widowers without children were to be placed in a state of permanent requisition, this was far from being a measure of universal conscription. The principal characteristic of the law, indeed, was the rather vague way it defined the obligations of the individual. In contrast, the duty of each department was clearly laid out—to produce the number of men allocated to it by central government, a figure that would be roughly commensurate with its population, although areas which had proved especially recalcitrant in the past sometimes found themselves more heavily assessed. Each department had its assigned quota, which it would then distribute among its constituent districts, again in proportion to their population. But there the guidance from the center stopped. The fiction of a voluntary army was not abandoned; the theory was maintained that the levy should be filled by calling for volunteers, although the law added that any deficit in voluntary enrollments must be made good by the recruitment of those who had been requisitioned. In practice, of course, this was very largely a fiction, except in the most patriotic areas of the East, and the vast majority of localities were obliged to resort to methods of coercion. Why should anyone wish to volunteer rather than leave his fate to luck or some form of chance? But therein lay the nub of the problem, for the government gave very little advice about how the choice of victims was to be made. The law stated rather confusingly that this choice should be left to local opinion in each commune, to the local people and their elected officers. They were obliged to carry out their recruitment process "by whatever means they found most suitable, by a majority vote." The government was far more interested in finding soldiers than in legislating for democratic practice.

It is perhaps surprising that they found as many as they did. Although they fell well short of their target of three hundred thousand new recruits, the recruitment had nonetheless produced around 150,000 by the end of July, and the serious shortfall in the strength of the armies was temporarily checked.[22] But the exercise had also revealed how limited was the Revolution's coercive power in an area where its ambitions ran counter to the instincts of a large section of the French population. In the spring of 1793, France was not equipped with the modern bureaucratic machine which an exercise of this kind demanded. In many of the more remote areas the practice of printing and circulating copies of decrees was still in its infancy, so information about the state of the law remained vague and sketchy. There were as yet no lists of those eligible to serve, no accurate records that could act as the basis for recruitment. Migrant workers and seasonal harvesters presented particular problems because no one was quite sure where their military obligations lay, and they frequently found themselves harrassed by every local town through which they passed. At the same time, communes did not know the extent of their authority, and their policing powers seemed largely restricted to appeals and exhortation. There was little guidance about where recruits should be sent once they had been enrolled: if civil administration was often confused, so were communications among local officials and the armies, which alone could inform the civilian population of military requirements. And the army itself was not always a model of administrative efficiency. Too often generals did not know who should and should not be attached to their companies or showed too little patience with the administrative problems encountered by local officials. The task of local *commissaires* was not made any easier when the men they had persuaded to leave for the armies were turned away from their designated battalions or sent home on the grounds that the units were already filled. In August 1792, for example, the district of Lille complained that confusion of this kind was vitiating the whole recruitment exercise, angering officials and causing consternation among the recruits.[23]

In country areas the success of the recruitment was further vitiated by a widespread suspicion that the levy was not equitable, that it did not weigh equally upon the entire community. In part this was due to the Convention's decision to authorize the use of *remplaçants,* a return to the traditional system whereby a man who was designated for service could buy someone else to serve in his stead. Many peasant communities viewed this practice with contempt and saw replacement as a basic injustice which ran counter to all the Revolution's pious words about the equality of man. Rural France was always ready to believe that the entire burden of recruitment was falling upon one class, the peasantry, and to believe that everyone else—the towns, the *gros bourgs,* the landowners, and the professional classes—was content to stand back from the recruitment process and leave the full burden of sacrifice to the poor. There were frequent allegations that local officials had conspired to excuse the sons of local notables or that mayors were bribed and corrupted by the richer landowners to exempt their sons and farm servants. Suspicions of the motives of others were never deeper than over the recruitment issue—suspicions that other communes would not contribute, suspicions that their own quota was unfairly high, suspicions, especially, of those with money or property or education, those who would know how to protect their own interests. And yet it was these very people who had often made the greatest gains from the Revolution. In the Sarthe, for example, popular anger was focussed on those richer peasants and townsmen who had bought national lands in the villages. They were seen as a class who had gained everything and contributed nothing to the Revolution, and the young men of the area demanded that they show an example of patriotism, that they pay back a little of their debt to society, by taking a lead in offering themselves for the army.[24]

Where suspicion gave rise to such animosities, seditious mutterings could easily lead to violence and rioting. This was especially true in the spring of 1793 because such a large measure of discretion had been left to mayors and municipal councils. They were the men who decided on the form of selection, supervised the recruitment process, and insisted that those designated should leave for the army. The fact that these men's august functions gained them personal exemption from service only added to the sense of grievance of the young, and their position as members of the village community—they were often small peasants who owned a few acres of land—only made them more vulnerable to pressure and to recrimination. Angry disturbances could be followed by threats, by the burning of hayricks or the mutilation of livestock; the mayor's position, far from being one of strength, could often verge on the untenable. Nor could the mayor necessarily count upon the support of the community at large, for it is clear that in many peasant villages, especially in the southern half of France, the young men enjoyed a wide measure of support and connivance from their elders. Those who were designated continued to benefit from that support. When they accepted to serve and were designated as soldiers amid a panoply of patriotic celebrations, they were village heroes whose glory was the reflected glory of the entire community. But by the same token, if they subsequently chose to desert, they could expect to be welcomed back into their families and hidden from the authorities. And if they preferred to evade the draft [as *insoumis*], hiding in the woods or watching cattle on the upland pasture, they would again be assured of the support of their family and friends. Like the calls for voluntary inscription of the two previous years, the *levée des 300,000* was couched in the language of patriotism and the imagery of national unity. But the levy was fraught with problems, and its implementation could easily have the effect of arousing passionate resistance to the state and reinforcing the bonds which united peasant communities against the outside world. [25]

It was not that towns and villages denied the need for some kind of military service, nor that the young of France were totally bereft of patriotism or martial spirit. Rather, it was the way in which the recruitment was operated that aroused such widespread opposition. Left to themselves, many communities would gladly have paid a tax or raised a public subscription with which to buy the service of others, whereas any form of involuntary personal obligation continued to be opposed widely. Yet, however vaguely the recruitment law had been drafted, it was personal service that was demanded, and in practice the choice which faced the mayor lay between some form of balloting (*tirage au sort*) and selection by public nomination (the so-called *scrutin révolutionnaire*). His designated task was simple—to provide the army with a fixed number of new recruits. The government did not as yet assume responsibility for either the method of recruitment or for its implementation. It was on the mayor and the municipal officers—and through them on the local community at large—that these highly delicate decisions fell, decisions which most intimately affected the welfare of every family in the local community.

Neither balloting nor public nomination was popular, and both were open to abuse. Of the two, the ballot was widely recognized to be the fairer, in the sense that far more was genuinely left to chance, and by the end of the summer the government would insist on balloting to decide the outcome of the *levée en masse*. But in the eyes of many villagers it was an intrusion into their liberties which recalled all the miseries of the ancien régime militia. Once again everything depended on the outcome of a single ballot—a young peasant's future, his standing within the local community, his ability to gain some degree of financial independence and to set up a family property of his own. For many young Frenchmen, indeed, the ballot became symbolic of everything that was most deeply resented about military service—its utterly arbitrary character, the feeling that one's future happiness lay in the hands of others, and the suspicion that those others were doing everything possible to protect those closest to them. It is no accident that it was on the occasion of the ballot, when the young men of the village were conveniently assembled together, that passive grumbling could most readily turn to violence and rioting. Gendarmes were attacked and ballot boxes overturned, and protection was offered to those unfortunate enough to draw a *mauvais numéro,* those designated by lot to serve. There was not much that the authorities could do to prevent such disorders, given the widespread support accorded to the new recruits. At Hesdin in the Pas-de-Calais, for example, in one of the most savage of these attacks, the government *commissaire,* Darthé, came close to being lynched by an angry, seething crowd of villagers.[26]

The principal alternative, that of selection by *scrutin,* was open to all kinds of cabal and chicanery—undoubtedly its main attraction for some communities. The principle underlying the *scrutin* was that the most patriotic boys in the village, the most respected and most politically reliable, would make the best soldiers for the Republic, and that only local people were in a position to choose the young men most suited to the honor of representing them in the armies. The reality, of course, was very different, with plots hatched and cliques formed to ensure that it was always someone else's son or nephew who was forced to serve. *Scrutin révolutionnaire* could serve so many diverse and ignoble purposes. It was a means of despatching one's rivals or personal enemies to the front, of satisfying the dictates of envy or revenge, and of choosing outsiders who did not impinge on village life. Migrant workers, sharecroppers, beggars, vagrants, and petty criminals were all highly favored in these popularity contests. So were the shepherds and cowmen who tended their beasts on isolated hillsides well away from the village community. In one village in the Cantal thirteen cowherds were designated for service on the same day— thirteen young men who all lived in far-flung mountain hamlets, who had little contact with the outside world, and who, on the day in question, had been left blissfully unaware of the recruitment exercise.[27] So widespread were abuses of this kind that departments and districts across France were moved to condemn the practice of *scrutin* as running counter to the spirit of the law, and the government forbade its use for all subsequent levies.

If the *levée des* 300,000 plugged the most urgent gaps in France's military defenses, it was hardly a glittering success. It had shown up some of the more glaring deficiencies in the administration, had revealed a significant spirit of resistance among the young, and had failed to come near its declared target. And if it is true that these difficulties stemmed partly from political setbacks like the defection of Dumouriez and the outbreak of the Vendean war, they did little to ease the manpower needs of the armies, which by the summer months were again facing defeat and the threat of invasion. Throughout 1793, the government was forced to turn again and again to the civilian population with repeated demands for recruits—a supplementary levy followed the main recruitment in February and March, then a special levy for the Vendée before the major recruitment of the autumn, the *levée en masse.* This *levée* was by far the most radical military recruitment law that the Jacobins were to pass, and it was how they sought to create the mass army with which revolutionary France could defeat the crowned heads of Euorpe. It was proclaimed in tones of high moral fervor reflecting the views expressed by radical politicians and *sans-culotte* militants during the previous months. And with the Jacobins now in power in Paris, the recruitment process inevitably became far more politicized, involving not only the administration, but also the Jacobin militants of the clubs and sections. An individual's attitude to military service was now seen as an integral part of his attitude to the Revolution, and a refusal to serve could readily be equated with a serious lack of political virtue.

This time the spirit of equality was to be respected more scrupulously, as there was no provision for replacement, no means by which the more fortunate could buy other men to fight on their behalf. The principle was accepted that the entire population was liable to make some sacrifice for the military effort, even if in practice the requisition was restricted to eighteen-to-twenty-five-year-old bachelors and widowers without family responsibilities. Others were to make what contribution they could; in the words of the Convention's decree of August 23, all Frenchmen were permanently requisitioned for the service of the armies until the enemy had been driven back and the territory of the Republic finally liberated: "Young men will go off to fight; married men will forge weapons and transport food supplies; women will make tents and clothing and will provide the service in hospitals; children will shred old linen; old men will be taken to the public squares to offer encouragement to the warriors and to preach the hatred of kings and the unity of the Republic."[28]

Carnot and his colleagues on the Committee of Public Safety believed that stirring language of this kind would inspire a strong patriotic sentiment among the population at large. They saw recruitment as a political as well as a military issue, and they took an intimate interest in the conduct of the war and in the success of the military levies. Of the twelve members of the Committee, several could claim a degree of expertise in military matters, and it was they who took responsibility for army reforms, who demanded new measures of surveillance, and who advised their colleagues of the more pressing needs of the armies. Saint-Just, a soldier's son as well as a committed Jacobin, took the most strongly ideological line, urging that recruitment measures must be equitable for all and that they must be enforced with draconian severity. Prieur de la Côte d'Or—who, like Saint-Just, made long and exhausting missions to the armies and devoted himself to the welfare of the troops on the ground—became the acknowledged specialist in matters of supply and provisioning. But it was Lazare Carnot who was the Committee's dominant voice on military questions. As a young officer he had come to understand the problems of soldiering at first hand; as a Jacobin he was committed to the ideal of a revolutionary army. But Carnot's great strength was his pragmatism, his insistence that the practical needs of the military must take precedence over narrow political dogma. He used his position on the Committee to achieve that end, helping to secure for the armies a degree of independence from political faction-fighting and to ensure that they were free to make professional military judgments when required. Even Robespierre appears to have listened to Carnot's opinions with respect; and contemporaries dubbed him, not without justification, "the organizer of victory."[29]

The new recruitment law was certainly what the more militant sans-culottes in the Paris sections and the committed clubists in provincial towns and cities had been waiting to hear: a requisition that would be truly national, that would affect rich and poor alike, and that would create an *armée de masse,* a force that could draw on the collected revolutionary strength of the entire nation. But what of less politicized opinion, of the kind which had already proved recalcitrant during previous attempts to recruit them for the military? Evidence of the recruitment returns would suggest that there was far less resistance during August and September than there had been in the previous spring, even in areas of the country which were notoriously refractory. Of course there were the customary regional discrepancies, with the eastern departments providing their battalions, armed and equipped, within a few short weeks, while the more recalcitrant regions of the South and Southwest registered a more muted response. Draft-dodging and desertion still sapped the strength of the armies, as they would continue to do throughout the decade. But they did not reach the epidemic proportions of February, nor yet the levels which would greet the first attempt at annual conscription in Year VII. There were occasional reports of mayors being threatened and harassed. There were isolated cases of rioting and of mass refusal to take part in the *tirage;* in one village in the Aude the young men overturned the recruitment stands, tore up the decrees which related to the recruitment process, and ceremonially trod them into the ground, singing the "Carmagnole" as a traditional mark of defiance to the Republican authorities.[30] But such instances were relatively rare, especially when compared with the outbursts of popular hostility that had greeted the levies of the previous spring. Even in departments not generally noted for their military enthusiasm, deputies-on-mission reported with pleasure that the young were leaving for the armies with unaccustomed docility.

How can this change of heart be explained? Given the ideological character of the Revolution, contemporary explanations tended to stress the impact of propaganda and the political commitment of the young men who were drafted. Although this may have played its part—in Paris and the major Jacobin centers especially—the extent of such politicization was still geographically limited, and there were large areas of the countryside where the patriotic message had little impact. The success of the *levée en masse* must be explained in more mundane terms. Everyday administration had become more efficient and more centralized. The lines of communication between the armies and the civilian administrations had been greatly improved. And the critical military situation of July and August 1793 made it easy for recruitment to be discussed as a short-term expedient to save the country in a moment of national emergency. By the end of the month, Mainz and Valenciennes had fallen, and Landrecies and Le Quesnoy, the last major fortresses between the enemy and the road to Paris, were under siege. Above all, perhaps, opinion was influenced by the fact that the new law was so much simpler, so much more obviously fair in its definition of who was to be included in the draft. No longer was the mode of practice left to local discretion and local skulduggery; balloting was now prescribed by law for all, and the supervision of the levy by deputies and political *commissaires* seemed to guarantee a greater measure of fairness in its operation. Threats of punishment and the beginnings of the terror were no doubt effective levers of persuasion, but the potency of the appeal of revolutionary egalitarianism should not be underestimated, especially in rural areas. In villages of the Seine-et-Marne, for example, those who drew low numbers in the ballot may have grumbled and accepted their lot reluctantly, but accept it they did in the knowledge that all were equal before the law and that recruitment was no longer an outrage to natural justice.[31] Local officials could even report from many parts of the country that the quotas had been rapidly filled and that the young men were preparing to leave amid scenes of gaiety and enthusiasm.

This is the image of the *levée en masse* which the Jacobins liked to paint and which Jacobin historians have tended to reiterate. The soldiers of the Year II entered revolutionary legend as being brave and selfless, cheerful and chivalrous, youngsters offering themselves with carefree generosity to the revolutionary cause. France's sons, in an image beloved of the popular press of the capital, were marching east to topple tyrants and to avenge Marat in a political crusade. It was important for the government that this image should win wide acceptance, and it became the subject of intensive propaganda, both in the armies themselves and in the community at large. The ideal of the nation rising as a man to defend its liberties was frequently repeated. So was the concept of duty, of the obligations of citizenship. Hence, when Carnot announced that there would be no provision for replacement, he was doing more than reversing a policy that had been applied to every recruitment pursued in France since 1758. He was doing more, too, than giving in to popular pressure from the clubs and sections. He was raising the issue of equality in its rawest and most politicized form.

> On the sacred territory of liberty [preached Carnot] in this same land where the rights of man have received legal sanction, human beings are being bought and sold; people speculate in this trade; it is conducted in shops and workrooms and in the streets. Not only has replacement deprived and denuded the battalions, but if the war continues it will prevent us from bringing them up to strength by recruiting more men. It has had the effect of spreading misery on all sides; wives have sold everything they own, even their clothes, to secure the replacement of their husbands; others have sold their small properties, the fruits of years of hard work; communes have sold their lands, their steeples, everything they own, to buy soldiers who are unworthy of the name, men who, by deserting from numerous battalions and selling themselves on a number of different occasions, have brought ruin to the Republic which they were supposed to defend.[32]

Once again the idealistic and universal lay alongside the most practical of political considerations. The system of replacement was being discarded because it was an affront to the spirit of the Revolution. It was also being abandoned as a policy that worked badly, that sowed discord and envy within communities, and was perceived as a major barrier to the achievement of the government's goal. The justification lay not only in ideology, but also in practical achievement: the *levée en masse* raised well over three hundred thousand new recruits for the armies and made significant progress toward the aim which had been set, the creation of a mass army three quarters of a million strong.

But how solidly founded was the Jacobins' claim that they were creating an army that was genuinely representative of French society, rather than an army of the poor and dispossessed? In February, there had been every reason to suspect that it was the more marginal members of society who were being sent to fight, but that had been a Girondin levy, and it was the Montagne which had always laid greatest store by ideals of equality. Available statistical evidence on the social origins of the soldiers is rather sketchy; once he was incorporated in the battalions, a man was stripped of all vestige of his social class or his profession in civilian life. However, there are highly suggestive indications. From his detailed study of the *registres de contrôle* of the army in Year II, Jean-Paul Bertaud offers a profile of the new recruits of the autumn of 1793 that was significantly different from that of their predecessors. Some departments even made it their responsibility to ensure that no distinction was allowed between rich and poor, between those with property and those without. They made a Republican virtue of finding a contingent that would reflect the social composition of their area. And although it would be difficult to demonstrate that the urban bourgeoisie played their full part in the recruitment—indeed, there is considerable evidence to the contrary—the sons of lawyers and notaries drew in the municipal ballots just like peasant boys, while men of property were to be found in the regiments fighting alongside apprentices and landless laborers.

Local statistics are quite clear on this point. Bertaud has found, for example, that in the district of Caen, 10 percent of the new recruits came from the families of lawyers and merchants, while in the district of Lisieux almost 13 percent had business backgrounds. In Parisian units, too, business and the professions were represented, as they were in towns as disparate as Abbeville and Avignon. That is not to say, however, that the revolutionaries ever achieved their goal of creating an army that was truly representative of society at large. Everywhere the conclusion is inescapable that the rich and educated could still find escape routes, often by taking appointments in the administration itself; their education, their understanding of the workings of the system, ensured that their role in the armies remained muted. But the *levée en masse* had other implications, too. In a largely peasant society, peasants were now present in the army in much larger numbers, although artisans and urban workers still made the greatest relative contribution. Even in Year II, there is little to suggest that equality of sacrifice was ever scrupulously imposed.[33]

Although the *levée en masse* won the approval of both generals and politicians, it was not followed up. Indeed, the army it raised remained the principal fighting strength of the Republic throughout the remainder of the Revolution. Neither the *levée des 300,000* nor the *levée en masse* made any provision for a limited term of service, so the young men drafted in the recruitments of 1793 were given no promise of an imminent release. Unlike the volunteers, they could make no claim to return to their farms after their first campaign, and the military had a vested interest in maintaining in the ranks seasoned warriors whose battle skills could be relied upon and whose experience could mold others. Besides, after some years in uniform, many of these men lost touch with their homes and families and ceased to be attracted by the idea of a life in agriculture. They became professional soldiers almost in spite of themselves, valuing the camaraderie of their fellows and dreaming of promotion and recompense in the context of the army. Many among them would serve the emperor just as loyally as they had served the Revolution; some would still be in uniform when the armies scattered in 1814 after the defeat of Napoleon.[34] What might seem rather more curious is that the revolutionaries should have made no effort to release them from service and taken no steps to see that they were replaced and rewarded. There was to be no further systematic recruitment before 1799; the men raised by the Jacobins were to continue to form the army of the Thermidorians and the army of the Directory, supplemented only by a few perfunctory and often localized *levées* that produced limited results. Any supplementary recruitment would seem to have been resented; in some departments the authorities hesitated to call the young men together lest they sparked off a violent reaction, and any hint of a new levy was accompanied by the spread of alarmist rumors through the countryside.[35] The product of such recruitment proved to be meager indeed—just over seventy thousand men from 1794 to 1797. As Gustave Vallée noted in his study of recruitment in the Charente, this was one of the greatest injustices of the revolutionary years because it meant that one generation, those unlucky enough to be between eighteen and twenty-five in 1793, should have been expected to bear the entire burden of war while those a year or two younger made no contribution.[36] The sacred principle of equality, it would seem, was not evoked when discussing the treatment of different generations; military interest was deemed to be paramount.

With the renewal and expansion of the war under the Directory, however, the strength of the armies was again drained away. If there were 750,000 men under arms in 1794, death, disease, and desertion rapidly took their toll, and the lack of new recruitment came to be felt more and more acutely with each year that passed. By *fructidor* of the Year III, strength had fallen to below half a million; by *thermidor* of the Year IV, to around four hundred thousand; by the end of Year VI to some 325,000, well under half the number considered necessary by the military high command.[37] It is true that the army by Year VI was more efficient and more professional than the battalions of young volunteers of 1791 or the Republican *demi-brigades* of 1794. They were better trained, tactically more astute, and had considerable battle experience. The majority of the soldiers still incorporated in the regiments had at least four years' service behind them, which meant that the French army consisted primarily of reliable veteran units into which new blood could be rapidly integrated. But the need for such new blood was overwhelming, and again the politicians had to decide upon the principles of selection which should be used. In this regard the change in the political climate of the Revolution was of the greatest importance. Whereas the Jacobins had been concerned to select an army that would not contradict the revolutionary principles of the Year II, by Year VI such niceties were largely forgotten. What was now needed was an army suited to the task of pursuing and winning a war of expansion against France's European neighbors. To recruit such an army, the Revolution dropped any pretense of voluntarism and turned for the first time to the notion of a systematic annual conscription.

Conscription was the principle of recruitment which would remain in force, with minor adjustments, throughout the Napoleonic years. It was by conscription that the exhaustive levies for the *Grande Armée* would be made in 1810 and 1811. It was by conscription that more than two million men would be found for Napoleon's wars of conquest, the annual levies reflecting accurately the state of confidence or anxiety that reigned in the high command. In the long term there was no doubting the capacity of the conscription machine to answer the demands of the military across a long and exhausting period of war. But in the immediate context of the Year VI it must be seen for what it was, as the latest in a series of devices for solving the recurrent recruitment crises of the revolutionary armies. The principle of a conscript army was first enunciated in the Loi Jourdan of 19 *fructidor* VI. By this measure the Directory sought to make good the losses in the armies in a planned and structured way—not by resorting to a once-for-all recruitment like the *levée en masse,* but by providing for a regular and smooth regeneration of the armies each year, as and when circumstances might demand. Those affected were men aged between twenty and twenty-five on the first day of *vendémiaire* each year, who were obliged to sign on in whichever of the five annual *classes* they belonged. There was no provision for replacement, although that would be revised in later years. All were required to present themselves for medical examination, all had to be available for service. But not all, of course, were expected to serve. The needs of the military would vary from year to year, and the armies had no wish to be encumbered with large numbers of untrained conscripts for whom they had no use. So it was foreseen that the level of demand would oscillate wildly, with all five *classes* being called up only in the most critical circumstances.

The youngest, in accordance of the law, marched first. In other words, the armies took those aged twenty and twenty-one in preference to their elders, leaving at least some of the able-bodied young men of the community to concentrate upon tilling the soil or otherwise earning their living. As a consequence, any young man who reached the age of twenty-five without falling to the ballot could breathe easily, secure in the knowledge that his military obligation was over. Whatever the final outcome by 1812 or 1813, the Directory had no intention of draining the countryside of its inhabitants or of putting agriculture at risk. Jourdan himself envisaged that in a normal year relatively few would be called upon to serve, seeing as the principal strength of his proposal the fact that a distinction could be drawn between obligatory conscription and actual incorporation.[38]

Each *classe* would be called upon in turn until the needs of the army had been met. Within each *classe,* lots would still be drawn to decide which of the young men should be forced to leave. In normal years it was envisaged that only those aged twenty or twenty-one would be required, thus ending any possible panic in the community and leaving sufficient manpower for the farm and the workshop. Above all, Jourdan hoped that the regularity of the procedure and the simplicity of the principle on which it was based would create a new mood of acceptance in the country, whereby annual recruitment would become a part of normal civic life, a routine procedure that would be seen as a simple *rite de passage* for young men on the threshold of their adult lives. A conscript army, he believed, would seem less unfair, less arbitrary, and hence easier to recruit. His purpose, there is little doubt, was brutally pragmatic. As with the structure of the revolutionary armies, so with their recruitment, political idealism had by the Year VI given way to the search for administrative efficiency.

That efficiency was not, however, to be achieved overnight. The conscription law was first applied, in Year VII, in the most inauspicious circumstances, as an emergency measure to solve a major crisis of manpower in the regiments. Not only were the first levies particularly heavy, but the fruits of the conscription of Year VII were also soon overtaken by the army's needs, and in that same year the recruiters would return for a supplementary levy of two hundred thousand men, then again for a further supplement on all five *classes*. It was a draconian introduction to the new system, which made it almost axiomatic that it would be bitterly resented. Besides, as with any major new initiative of this kind, it took time for people to appreciate its meaning and implication. Once again, as in 1793, the civil administration was frequently unequal to its task, as an uncertain and understaffed service battled to draw up accurate lists of the young men eligible to serve. In consequence, the law was met with widespread resistance and evasion; those areas which had proved recalcitrant during the *levée des 300,000* frequently took the lead in defying the recruiting officer. A good instance of this is the village of Escalquens in the Haute-Garonne, where four or five hundred villagers banded together to resist recruitment, and the gendarmerie had to be sent in to maintain a semblance of good order. In the undignified brawl which followed, the lieutenant in charge of the gendarmes was killed and five of his men seriously injured.[39] Here as in many other village communities, the tradition of antimilitarism had proved at least as strong as the determination of a succession of revolutionary governments. The degree of popular disobedience in 1799 merely reflected the scale of the sacrifice a new generation of young Frenchmen were being asked to make.

With such large numbers being called up, allegations of cheating and partiality were predictably common. Towns and villages complained that they were being unfairly treated compared to their neighbors; those designated denounced the seemingly large numbers of their peers who were excused service by some civil or bureaucratic function; and the old charges were again raised of favoritism and bribery serving the interests of the rich and well-connected. Already communes were finding that they had mislaid their birth and marriage registers, and mayors were charged with deliberately destroying their records to protect the sons of their closest friends. Frauds and subterfuges were commonplace in areas where the hostility to soldiering remained strong, and generally they were committed with the full knowledge and tacit support of the community. To gain exemption under the regulations on minimum height, families would send younger brothers who were not yet fully grown, trusting that their municipal officials would connive at their deception. Because bachelors were called first, young men of military age rushed headlong to the altar in the months preceding the draft; and as the Revolution had thought-fully legalized divorce, even widows of seventy and eighty could be called upon as temporary partners for reluctant recruits. There are even cases of village women who became professional wives for conscripts, offering themselves to a succession of young men living in fear of the draft. Technically they were within their rights. Although the authorities might denounce such ruses and deplore the fact that adolescents seemed to be opting for marriage at an ever-younger age, there was little that they could do to prevent it. Faced with a mixture of popular intransigence and youthful guile they were often forced to admit defeat.

Others sought to avoid the draft by inducing illnesses and feigning injury; in the Year VII, as in later years, rural France seemed to suffer epidemics of wounds that had conveniently turned septic. Self-mutilation—one of the traditional routes to safety in country areas—was again widespread, as army doctors resigned themselves to a rash of severed index fingers and painfully extracted teeth. The very desperate even hacked at their shins or sliced at their testicles in a bid to ensure that they were rejected as unfit, while wise women and itinerant quacks again pocketed the savings of the poor by recommending lotions and caustic unguents with which to deceive the military. Despite the law there were corners of France where money could buy a release from service, even in the Year VII, while all subsequent conscriptions allowed and even encouraged replacement. Those with adequate resources could therefore gain their exemption decorously. The many age-old deceptions were the resort of the poor—ways by which those with no hope of buying their freedom might hope to escape the regiment without actually breaking the law. For those unable to escape legally, there would always be deception. And where deception failed, there would be the illegal remedy of desertion.[40]

With the passage of time, conscription would come to be accepted with better grace by the population at large, partly through custom and habit, but primarily in response to the greater vigilance and greater cunning of the Napoleonic police. Over a period of years, it would not be difficult for the gendarmerie or columns of regular soldiers to spot and arrest on sight all the young men who seemed in the age range of the conscription and who could not produce papers to justify their presence in their village. By the end of the Empire, annual conscriptions, however much they were hated by an exhausted population and however damaging they had become to farming and to food supply, nonetheless achieved their principal aim. Resistance was gradually worn down, the principle of conscription imposed. But in 1799, much of rural France was still far from accepting the idea of an annual tribute of sons and brothers to the armies. Despite ten years of revolutionary propaganda, in many areas resistance was still endemic, and the prospect of the ballot and the high risk of actual incorporation spread popular panic and caused clashes between the police and the people. In villages in the southern Massif, deserters would be welcomed as cheap labor on the farm; in the Landes and along the marshy Gironde coast, they would be hidden by local fishermen; in the Pyrenees, they would blend easily into local bands of smugglers. Throughout whole regions, like the Roussillon, there were powerful psychological reasons for protecting young men on the run and for thwarting the best endeavors of the state.[41] The issue of recruitment showed, perhaps more clearly than any other, how limited was the Revolution's success in effecting real change in popular instincts and mentalities. The young men of the requisition were not interested in revolutionary politics or in the propaganda spread by local clubs and municipal councils. For as long as they remained civilians, protected by the comfortable traditions of their community, the Revolution had little means of educating them in citizenship, of instilling newfangled notions of civic obligation. It would be very different once they were incorporated in the armies.

4

REVOLUTIONIZING THE SOLDIERS

THE PRAGMATISM WHICH CHARACTERIZED THE REV-
olutionaries' approach to recruitment must not be allowed
to obscure their deeper social and political objectives. The
Revolution wanted to produce far more than a smooth bureaucratic machine; it was dedicated to the political education of its
citizens and the renewal of ancien régime society. For some revolutionary leaders, indeed, the terms *révolution* and *régénération* were
virtually synonymous, to the point where there could be no
renewal without the upsurge of enthusiasms and the unleashing of
political passions revolution implied.[1] French society, they believed, was ready for such regeneration, for a complete restructuring on new and untried foundations. Some regarded this process as
the inevitable outcome of the spontaneity of revolution; they
reveled in political disorder and violence and saw in that disorder
the genesis of their social dreams. Others, more cautiously, condemned disorder as a source of weakness and instability, believing
that genuine renewal could be brought about only through the
agency of the state. In either version of the regeneration of France,
however, the role attributed to the army was critical, not just
because a revolution needed an army in its own image, but also
because the army was such an ideal seedbed for revolutionary
ideas. The enthusiasm of the volunteers of 1791 and 1792 offered
an important revolutionary capital that could not be lightly dissipated. And the presence in the regiments after the *levée en masse* of

some three hundred thousand young men, wrenched from their families and their friends, offered an unparalleled opportunity for indoctrination. In the armies of the Republic, political education would assume its place alongside military drilling and lessons in tactics.

Crucial questions, however, remained. Which political ideals would prove most persuasive among the military? Would the troops become more politically conscious through their shared experience of war? Would ideologies be generated by individual groups of militants—like clubs and popular societies—or imposed by the revolutionary state? The political education of the armies began almost as soon as the Estates-General met, and it would continue throughout the revolutionary years. Every recruitment decree, every administrative reform passed in these years contained its element of self-justification, always couched in the politicized language the Revolution demanded. But the period when the greatest stress was placed on political education and political orthodoxy came in the summer and autumn of 1793, when the Girondins had been expelled from office and once Dumouriez's defection had focussed attention on the reliability of the military. The climate of that summer was particularly confused, the atmosphere in Paris more than normally thick with rumors of intrigue. There was certainly no single ideology that could be said to command a consensus. If the Jacobins were triumphant in the Convention, elsewhere political power remained dispersed and fractured. In the West, counterrevolution was rampant, and the Republic had to divert its troops to deal with internal insurrection; in the major provincial cities, the federalist interlude was only painfully being brought to a close; and throughout France, the balance of political power was changing with the increased use of terror and the greater imposition of control from the center. Even in Paris, the Revolution seemed in a constant state of flux. The politics of the Club was marked by bitter conflicts between moderates and radicals, while the Paris sections seemed uniquely placed to exert a radical and egalitarian influence over national policy. In the uncertain months that lay ahead control of the loyalties of the army would assume a decisive importance.

The *sans-culottes* took an especially active interest in the army. Many of the more radical sections, both in Paris and other towns, saw the soldiers as a valuable potential ally in their campaign for greater equality and greater resort to terror. They understood the power which control of the military bestowed and campaigned tirelessly to root out such vestiges of counterrevolutionary sympathy as remained in the regiments. But they wanted more than simply the exclusion and punishment of aristocratic officers. Increasingly they demanded the extension of political surveillance to all army officers and sought the removal of those of a moderate or Girondin persuasion. By systematic purges and the imposition of a clear political catechism they sought to ensure that the French armies reflected the political radicalism of Parisian politics; a reliable army, in the eyes of the sections, must necessarily be an army of *sans-culottes*. This offensive must, of course, be seen in context, for at around the same time the sections were mounting a separate but not unconnected campaign for a political force under their control to enforce requisitions and police the population at home. The idea of arming the popular classes against the rich, the *faubourgs* against the enemies of the people, had been gathering strength in the early summer. Robespierre had first championed the sections' demands in April; two weeks later the Department of the Hérault had petitioned the Convention to establish an armed force of five thousand men, paid out of public funds, to carry out essential policing, a force that would not be recruited in the normal way but would be selected "by personal summonses to those citizens recognised as the most patriotic."[2] By the summer the first battalions of this force, the *armée révolutionnaire,* were already being formed; by the late autumn and winter of 1793 the popular movement had acquired a powerful instrument of political vengeance, not just in Paris but in more than half the departments of France. And although the *armées* were in principle quite separate from the military battalions, in the confusion of a civil war that distinction was not always clinically respected. By a subsequent decision of the Committee of Public Safety, those detachments operating in the same zones as the regular forces were to take orders from the military commanders. In Normandy, for example, the *armées* would be assimilated into units manning garrisons and could even be ordered to march to the frontiers if required.[3]

With the Jacobins in government in Paris, the *sans-culottes* sought to extend their political influence by a sustained campaign of radical propaganda. The soldiers, not surprisingly, figured among their principal targets. Both the sections of the larger towns and local Jacobin clubs throughout France took it upon themselves to provide political surveillance for the troops, reporting on their conduct, their public spirit, and on the reputation of their officers. Letters from local volunteers and despatches from the commanders of locally recruited units were read out proudly at club meetings. Some clubs and sections sent emissaries to the armies with the express mission of spreading political tracts and patriotic propaganda among the men of their local companies. More commonly, they set up correspondence committees to keep in regular contact with the armies in the field, thus maintaining valuable links between the military and political militants in the local community. Virtually every club took some kind of initiative. Some kitted out volunteers with uniforms and equipment, an act of patriotism for which they expected to be kept abreast of their soldiers' performance once they had been incorporated. Others made financial contributions to encourage recruitment and took a leading part in stimulating obedience among those eligible to serve.[4] Others again helped raise collections or forced loans to provide comforts for the soldiers; or they interested themselves in their welfare, lobbying for better rations, denouncing corrupt suppliers, or trying to obviate the worst defects of military hospitals.[5] With recruitment such an integral part of the life of the nation by 1793, popular societies could scarcely avoid taking an active interest in matters such as these, but their interest often spread to more ideological aspects of army life, to questions of internal discipline and to measures guaranteeing the democratic rights of the troops. At Lille, for example, the club spent a great deal of time discussing military maneuvers, and when Custine was appointed to command the Armée du Nord, it immediately denounced him to Paris for his political opinions.[6] In the same way, the Jacobins of Blois listened to soldiers' complaints against their officers with evident sympathy, conducted campaigns of denunciation against unpopular officers, and showed their determination to police every unit of the army that visited the town. So persistent was their interest that the government felt compelled in 1791 to rebuke the Blois society for its interference in army affairs.[7]

Because soldiers had been granted all the benefits of citizenship, their role in political clubs and societies could not be restricted to a passive compliance in the initiatives of others. On the contrary, they were given every encouragement to lead an active political life, either by forming popular societies within their regiments or by joining civilian clubs in the towns where their units were stationed. That decision was taken as early as 1791, when indiscipline threatened the armies after the imprisonment of five soldiers who had attended a *société populaire* at Wissembourg without the permission of their superiors.[8] Soldiers were quick to profit from their newfound freedoms. Late passes were issued for those wishing to attend popular societies. Special military clubs were to be found on all the major frontiers by 1793, and reports from deputies-on-mission spoke approvingly of their Republican principles and of their determination to root out the errors of federalism. Some of these clubs affiliated immediately with the Jacobins in Paris and took advantage of the communication network this gave them; the sense of isolation, of being cut off from the mainstream of revolutionary politics, could be intense in these regimental societies.[9] But others remained as clubs for soldiers, dealing almost exclusively with military matters, and it was against them that accusations were leveled of extremism and *hébertiste* influence. Military clubs, especially those attached to the Armée du Nord, were deeply influenced by the writings of the Père Duchesne. They conducted their own purges, excluded the more moderate Jacobins from membership, and sought their officeholders among *sans-culottes* from the more radical Paris sections. They quickly developed a reputation as meeting places for discontents whose real quarrels were with their officers and who sought an outlet in political organization.

The number of military clubs remained relatively small, however, even during the winter of 1793–94 when Hébert's influence was at its height. It was much more usual for soldiers wishing to keep abreast of current politics to join the local Jacobin Club in the town or village where they happened to be encamped or garrisoned. Often they joined for reasons that were only mildly political—to read the Jacobin press or to find companionship outside the narrow confines of the army. Soldiers who found themselves hundreds of miles from home yearned for the familiar and anxiously sought communication with the outside world. One of their first actions was frequently to make contact with the popular society in their home town and to send news of the war. Typical were the volunteers from Bar-le-Duc, who joined their local society in Belgium late in November 1791, got themselves elected to its *comité de correspondance,* and wrote to the Jacobins in Bar expressing the ardent wish of their new society to establish mutual ties of affiliation.[10] But others were more devotedly political, using the clubs as vehicles for the causes they held dear. From Bitche, for example, one soldier from the Armée des Vosges wrote back to his popular society in the Faubourg Saint-Antoine in Paris denouncing the pernicious influence of nobles and clergy, of "cette clique nobiliaire et sacerdotale" whom he regarded as so damaging to the cause of liberty.[11]

In the patriotic mood created by the war, soldiers could generally be assured of a warm welcome in the popular societies of the towns where they were stationed. Clubs, indeed, went out of their way to seek new members from among the military, sending deputations to address the troops and recruiting whenever a new regiment arrived to man the garrison.[12] Even clubs in towns far removed from any war front—like that of Libourne in the Gironde—would expressly welcome troops who were passing through, treating them like conquering heroes and bestowing largesse upon them.[13] Quite apart from any element of prestige or reflected glory which military members might bestow, the more radical clubists rightly assumed that the arrival of soldiers in a town guaranteed an infusion of patriotic sentiment. Their contribution could often be a vital one. At Maubeuge and Sédan in the Ardennes, members from the armies were able to dominate the local societies and turn them to specifically military ends; the club at Colmar already numbered some 150 soldiers among its 400 members by the end of 1791; and at Wissembourg, the society was referred to as a "société patriotique et militaire."[14] In the Nord, there was a significant military presence in the clubs of all the major cities close to French battle positions, like Cassel and Bailleul, Cambrai and Lille.[15] As a percentage of the military personnel engaged in the region, their number was, of course, small, but they included men of extreme radical views, many of them exiled from the sans-culotte politics of the capital, who had no scruples about using the provincial societies for their own ends. They could use them as channels for political denunciation; they could influence the very bodies entrusted with the surveillance of the armies; and during Bouchotte's term at the War Ministry, they could hope to catch the minister's eye. Bouchotte was himself deeply committed to the cause of the Jacobin and Cordelier clubs, and he endorsed the calls of Robespierre and Hébert for a much more radical approach to the army command. During his period of office he not only supported the clubs' demands for a more rigorous purge of aristocratic officers, but he also actively encouraged club membership as a means of political education in the armies.

Although ordinary soldiers would on occasion make use of the clubs to denounce their commanders, more commonly it was politically committed officers and members of the military administration who played the most important role. At Le Havre, the most prominent figures from both the army and the navy were to be found at the local Jacobins, ranging from the general in charge of the garrison to one of the ships' captains in the port. Just as important, however, was the indirect influence of the rank and file, especially of the men of the Paris requisition, who turned out en masse to the patriotic festivals organized by the club and involved themselves in its political debates. [16] The Lille club could also lay claims to being a "société militaire." Listed among its twelve hundred members was the wherewithal for an impressive regimental line-up: in addition to two ministers of war and two future marshals of France (Mortier and Macdonald), the club boasted nine generals, six colonels, five lieutenant colonels, and a rich sprinkling of other senior officers. [17] Just as significantly, it included many leading figures from the administration and support services attached to the Armée du Nord—*commissaires des guerres*, surgeons and doctors from the military hospitals, officials of the military postal service, and those employed to organize supplies of fodder and military transport. In the Nord, it is clear from the club's registers that these civilian administrators played a very prominent role, especially in the powerful committees through which the society operated. They, like the military themselves, could be counted among the most radical agitators in the club's affairs.

The Jacobin Club of Lille provides an interesting, if rather extreme, case study of the effect which an invasion of soldiers could have upon the affairs of a provincial society. [18] Because of its proximity to the frontier, Lille was particularly prone to military influence: it had suffered a long siege and hosted a garrison throughout most of the period. The club had, quite properly, welcomed members from the armies and had an honorable record of support for soldiers' interests. It had also shown a radical streak over military matters from an early date, identifying with the cause of the Swiss of Châteauvieux in the months after the Nancy mutiny, for example, and sending money to those serving long sentences in the hulks at Brest. But in most respects it had been a typical provincial club, whose officeholders had been professional men or constitutional priests. In the spring and early summer of 1793, however, there was a sudden incursion of new members from the battalions, primarily supporters of General Lavalette and the *sans-culotte* politics he championed. Lavalette was the former commander of the battalion of the Parisian Section des Lombards and a prominent radical in the days leading up to the Tenth of August; a close friend of Ronsin and other leaders of the Paris sectional movement, he was one of several Paris radicals to win rapid promotion in the army under the patronage of Bouchotte.[19] By late 1793, the society's most sensitive committees were packed by Lavalette's supporters, almost all of them soldiers and outsiders to Lille, and the society changed dramatically in character to become terrorist and arguably *hébertiste.* One of these men, an officer in Lavalette's army, even dubbed himself the Père Duchesne of Lille.[20] This was the phase when the society founded its *armée révolutionnaire* under Lavalette's closest ally, Dufresse, whom the club, on its own authority, raised to the rank of general, an elevation confirmed by the compliant Bouchotte. It then proceeded to purge all those whom it suspected of moderation, from the garrison to the municipality and the clubs of surrounding towns. It purged its own members, too, expelling many of the Lillois who had previously been displaced from office. It attempted to stamp out hoarding and speculation by the most intensive surveillance, ordering the closure of the city gates and the interruption of all trading for a period of twenty-four hours. And, driven on by a strongly anticlerical military clique, it ordered the arrest of priests and the closure of all churches in the city.

If the two deputies currently on mission to the Nord gave legal sanction to the establishment of the Lille *armée,* the organization and recruitment of the force were largely handed over to the clubists. And the clubists who mattered—the president and secretaries, the *commissaires* who were chosen to carry out policy, the

trusted lieutenants who packed the most sensitive committees—
were all Parisians and men of the Lille garrison. The same familiar
litany of names and military ranks appears again and again:
Lavalette and Dufresse, of course; Favart, *général de division;* Nivet,
chef de brigade; Target, *colonel;* Agut, *adjudant de la place;* and many
others. [21] They selected the patriots who should serve in the new
terrorist force, they chose the political priorities that should be
pursued, and they appointed their close associates to all the
positions of authority within it. Richard Cobb is quite justified in
his claim that the role of the deputies, Châles and Isoré, was quite
"minimal" in the whole affair, and that the exercise of terror in the
Nord was left to the *sans-culotte* militants from the army. [22] Lavalette and his military friends had made themselves the undisputed masters of Lille, holding far more authority than the
moderate municipal council which had been cowed into impo-
tence, and determined to rule by terror and to wreak vengeance on
their opponents. In the words of the club's minutes of October 7,
1793, they were united with all the *sans-culottes* of Lille in a state of
all-out revolution, and they would remain in that state until the
last enemy of the public good had been destroyed. [23] Their power
seemed unassailable, at least for as long as they continued to enjoy
the confidence of the Committee of Public Safety in Paris. But that
appearance was deceptive; the risk of political isolation was never
far removed. To the Lille Jacobins, the military members would
always remain intruders, "foreigners" as the doctor, Fauvel, called
them, who did not understand the true interests of Lille. [24] Even
Dufresse recognized that their power base was too narrowly Parisian and that they enjoyed little support locally. As a result of their
political extremism, moreover, the Lille Jacobins had few allies in
the smaller towns of the region, in clubs like those at Douai and
Saint-Omer which they had bullied remorselessly. [25] Their cavalier
treatment even of the Jacobin deputies sent on mission to the
Nord led to their denunciation and eventual dismissal, to the
obvious satisfaction of the local community.

The infiltration of the popular society in Lille by the military demonstrates less the political education of the soldiery than the abuse of power by a small, tightly organized group. *Sans-culotte* politics lent itself to such factionalism, and the armies of the Year II were a useful political vehicle for *sans-culotte* extremists, many of whom came into the military after an apprenticeship in the more radical Paris sections. Among the volunteers of 1791 and 1792, in particular, there were men, driven by a fierce political idealism, who had joined the army to save the Revolution and preach the virtues of the Republic. Young and headstrong, without family commitments or a stake in civilian society and nurtured in the hothouse atmosphere of military politics, they were often impatient of routine and intolerant of compromise, the kind of Jacobin activists easily attracted by the ideas of Hébert or the Enragés. Such men were in a very real sense a by-product of a revolutionary army; they would continue to flourish in the regiments long after the execution of Robespierre and the overthrow of Jacobinism in France itself. Although the presence in the War Ministry of a committed radical like Bouchotte—who lent his support to Dufresse and Lavalette even when they challenged the authority of the Convention's own deputies—helped ensure the dominance of the *hébertiste* faction in Lille, the episode also demonstrates the dangers incurred in using the clubs as an instrument of political education. Despite the appearance of tight central control, local Jacobin clubs could easily develop their own political aspirations, and, with attendances at humdrum daily meetings predictably low, it was not difficult for small factions to build up a local dominance. By their enthusiasm and their radical ideas the military impressed the less active clubists, by their organizational skills they infiltrated their friends and took over the clubs' principal offices. As a result, the clubs provided an extremely flawed method of exercising political control over the armies or of imposing revolutionary discipline.

What did the government intend to achieve through the political education of the armies? Was it primarily concerned with control and discipline, with ensuring that the military restricted themselves to executing the wishes of the political arm? Or was it seen in more ideological terms, as the active encouragement of political activism among those who were to fight in the name of the Revolution? These are quite distinct and different aims; it is even arguable that they are incompatible—the one leading to a force of soldiers who accepted the political will of others and carried out their orders loyally and promptly, the other producing an army of committed Republicans, of men who had thought about politics and who were ideologically bound to their government and its principles. The first option would result in an army which understood its duty to the state, an army which could be relied upon to support any regime without question. The second, in the context of 1793, would produce an army of committed Jacobins, reading newspapers and political speeches, following events in Paris, and fighting less out of duty than out of commitment. It would be a truly revolutionary army, fighting with all the passion that term implied. But for the leaders of the Revolution it would always contain an element of threat, the threat that comes from armed men imbued with a sense of mission, risking their lives for a cause. The army's support for every twist in revolutionary policy and for each succeeding regime in Paris was not something that could blithely be taken for granted.

Yet revolutionary politicians saw no contradiction between these two aims. The danger of a military putsch was never far from their minds, and it was considered vital that the army should be answerable at all times to civil government and should be prevented from having a political will of its own. Although the revolutionary state depended on the army to win its wars and to defend its territory, it would be no exaggeration to say that the state lived in fear of the army it had created. It feared the parallel power of the military, and many Jacobins shared Hébert's belief that military control was the very essence of dictatorship. Hébert had expressed this fear succinctly on March 8, 1793, when he asked for the recall of all the political intriguers who were currently at the head of the Republic's armies. If such a step were not taken, he warned, the Republic would be finished, and so would liberty; "we shall have created nothing more than a dream."[26] Soldiers constituted a social body open to subversion: spies and enemy agents, recruiters for foreign armies and for counterrevolutionary causes, aristocrats, honeyed tongues urging the troops to desert, all presented very real threats to the nation's security. For that reason the armies were specifically listed as a sensitive area from which political suspects were to be banned. For that reason, too, it was deemed necessary that the armies should be bound tightly to the political leadership of the capital, and the politicization of the troops was intended to create bonds of political empathy between soldiers and politicians. An effective revolutionary army had to be an army of revolutionaries who believed in the justice of the cause in which they were fighting. And that in turn meant that a constant stream of propaganda had to be directed toward the military, propaganda originating in Paris and reflecting the current concerns of the government. Unlike the membership of clubs, it was not a voluntary matter, the result of the whims of individuals. Revolutionary propaganda was for all, an element in the preparation of the armies as crucial as any training in the use of arms or in tactical maneuver. Under the Jacobins, especially, it was to prove unremitting.

The purpose, of course, was to create a new kind of army, spiritually and intellectually prepared for the rigors of fighting a revolutionary war. In his study of the biggest of the revolutionary armies, the Armée du Nord, John Lynn has shown the degree to which political instruction was a necessary element in building up morale and creating battle effectiveness. Although the part played by politics is slight in a conventional army, in a revolution, Lynn argues, this necessarily changes, and "to the extent that troop motivation depends on the belief of the rank-and-file that its sacrifices are appreciated, there is every reason to argue the propaganda campaign contributed to the high combat effectiveness of the Armée du Nord."[27] The political consciousness of the revolutionary armies was complex and at times diffuse. In the Nord, the army's regional character contributed to its sense of identity and pride; so did the oaths the troops were repeatedly made to swear, oaths to die for their country and to fight for liberty and fraternity. The revolutionary concept of fraternity, indeed, arguably rather vacuous in civilian society, assumed a rich and evocative meaning in the ranks of the army, where young men did feel like brothers, dependent on one another in the face of shared danger, mutually dependent, too, inasmuch as they had no one else to whom they could turn.

Political propaganda came in so many shapes and forms. The watchwords used by the different units spelled out a simple and unequivocal message: "Rois, tyrans, vaincrons" (Kings, tyrants, let us triumph over them) and "Révolution, convention, obéissance" (Revolution, convention, obedience) were typical in their directness.[28] Even the explicitly revolutionary tactics adopted by the military quickly became assimilated by the propaganda machine. Although the French infantry fought both in close order lines and in dispersed formation as skirmishers, it was their dash, their élan, that entered revolutionary legend. Despite the undoubted quality of French artillery, it was the simplest of weapons, the bayonet, which came to symbolize the spirit of the armies of the Year II. To the propagandists of the time, the army was composed of peasant boys armed with bayonets and pikes—the famous *arme blanche*—fighting and winning through reckless courage and bravura. Throughout the revolutionary wars, however much French tactics might be adapted and improved, it was this image which continued to capture the popular imagination. In Lynn's phrase, "only the cult of the bayonet approached the level of a military doctrine."[29]

Speeches and polemical tracts, decrees and military ordinances all spoke the same revolutionary language. Over time, it is true, the tone and emphasis altered, the injunctions to the soldiers reflecting the political mood of the moment and the priorities of those in power. The Girondins preferred calls for patriotic endeavor and heroic self-sacrifice; the Jacobins stressed the defense of the Republic and the pursuit of virtue. But there were certain recurrent themes aimed at improving the morale of the troops and reminding them of their revolutionary purpose.[30] The ideological character of the war was emphasized continually, as a war of liberty both for the French people themselves and for the subjects of kings and emperors. Their enemies were stigmatized and caricatured: the foreign tyrants and their lackeys; the terrible two-headed monster of Pitt-Cobourg, always preparing to crush the Revolution and to bribe the French into acts of treason; the "mangeurs d'hommes" who sent their troops to kill and maim the youth of France; and the motley crowd of aristocrats and refractory priests, hoarders, and speculators who preyed on the generosity of spirit that was the hallmark of the *sans-culotte*. These enemies became even more numerous as the Revolution passed to its more exacting phase, because even moderate Republicans and those who played no part in politics risked being identified as agents of the enemy. In contrast, revolutionary propaganda was full of praise for the people, those ordinary Republicans whose sacrifice would be rewarded in the victory of the revolutionary state. And if in a civilian context Jacobin speeches contrasted the virtue of the honest artisan with the ambition of the rich bourgeois, in the armies these same stereotypes emerged kitted out in uniform. The ordinary soldier is the pure Republican, motivated only by his love of France; his officer the man of property, who may be corrupted by vanity or by personal advancement. By 1793, Republican discourse came to emphasize more specifically political symbols: the maintenance of the gains made in the Revolution, the unity of the nation, the evils of federalism, and the protection of the Constitution and the Convention. Political virtue had become the undisputed goal of the true Republican.[31]

This message was communicated to the soldiers in different ways and in different registers, some subtle and subsumed, others open and blatant. The government was constantly at pains to impress on the troops that political authority was paramount and used every means at its disposal to convert and proselytize. Politi-

cal emblems and symbolic gestures entered even the most hack-
neyed of ceremonies, and in the army, far more than in civilian
life, the government had a captive audience. It resorted to symbols of the nation and of the Republic almost as much as it relied
on the printed word—a wise move in view of the high levels of
illiteracy among the *soldats-citoyens,* and a tacit acceptance that
much could be gained from the traditional attachment of the
military to gesture and ceremonial. All references to kings and
symbols of seigneurial privilege were, quite naturally, effaced,
whether from military escutcheons or from uniform buttons.
Official papers, including letters of promotion, which bore any
trace of monarchy, were to be returned and reissued in Republican
form. New flags and banners were designed carrying explicitly
Republican motifs. Decrees and proclamations bore those ubiquitous emblems so evocative of the Republic and its purifying
creed—the tree of liberty, the red Phrygian cap, the cleansing
blade of the guillotine. Uniforms, too, rapidly developed political
connotations as all associations with the Bourbons were erased, the
blue of the volunteers replacing the white of the line to become the
unquestioned uniform of the nation. In 1793, indeed, the Convention ordered line officers to abandon their white coats and
adopt the blue tunics of the volunteer battalions, a gesture which
implied a rejection of aristocratic prejudice as well as a determination to impose a potent symbol of the Republic. Officers could
defy these orders at their peril. Those who refused to wear the red,
white, and blue cockades issued to the regiments opened themselves at once to surveillance and political investigation.[32]

If blue uniforms and tricolor cockades were constant reminders
of the soldiers' ideological affiliations, the politics of the Revolution was also imparted in the course of their mundane daily
activities. On the long trudge of the day's march or around the
campfire after the evening meal, the men would, like armies from
time immemorial, entertain themselves by singing songs, some
amusing and scurrilous, others defiant and fiercely patriotic.[33]
The political opportunities this presented were not lost upon the

politicians, nor was the emotive power of the song underestimated. It was not, of course, a particularly subtle vehicle for
propaganda; the song was not the place for detailed political
analysis. In a few easily memorized verses it was difficult to do
more than encourage and exhort, cheer up flagging spirits, and
entertain those weary after the effort of war. Few songs of the
revolutionary period did more than evoke Republican courage,
denounce traitors and hoarders, or pour scorn on France's enemies.
But they did so memorably, economically, and with considerable
verve. Songs like the "Chant du départ" and "Ça ira," the "Carmagnole" and the "Marseillaise," became the battle hymns of the
Republican armies. Lesser ditties could both entertain and instruct with a simple and reassuring patriotic message. The value
of such songs lay precisely in their ability to combine these two
functions, reminding the men of their patriotic duty while helping them to relax, to enjoy the companionship of others, and to
forget for a few brief hours the miseries and deprivations of army
life. "The people still sing much more than they read," wrote
Thomas Rousseau, who worked with Bouchotte at the War Ministry; "I think that the best way to instruct them fruitfully is to
present them with a lesson in the attractive form of pleasure."[34]
The editors of newspapers would often print songs specifically for
their military readers, and Bouchotte put aside 80,000 livres from
his department's budget for printing and distributing songbooks
to the troops.

The soldiers' leisure was supervised in other ways, too, as the
government sought to turn hours of pleasure and relaxation into
periods of practical gain for the Revolution. Leisure could prove so
dangerous, so damaging to virtue! Hence the leisure pursuits of
the troops had to be closely policed, and the men's contacts with
undesirable elements in local society reduced to a strict minimum.
Off-duty hours were fraught with perils. Like all soldiers, those of
the revolutionary armies flocked to bars and wayside inns whenever opportunity and cash allowed, in the hope that they could
escape for a few hours from the discipline and the monotony of the

barrack-room. There they could enjoy a sociability of their own making, where the values and high spirits of the young could be given full rein. But for the authorities, that very freedom was a source of danger. The soldiers were not only freed from the ambiance of army life and the surveillance of their officers, but they were also beyond the frontiers of political orthodoxy. The inns where soldiers congregated were also the favored haunts of enemy agents and those counseling desertion, just as drinking dens around garrison towns always attracted recruiting officers from enemy armies and those seeking to profit from the trade in substitutes. In bars, too, soldiers might be lured into the ready embrace of local prostitutes, whose charms could not only distract them from the defense of the Republic, but could also result in the spread of venereal disease throughout entire regiments. And drink could easily lead to license and excess. Military authorities viewed bars in military towns with alarm because in them all the rules of army life suddenly ceased to apply: they offered the young recruit a whole counterculture to the culture of duty and obligation that was central to military discipline.

So with theater and public entertainment: the government's approach combined a wish to prevent the moral corruption of the troops with a desire to use the stage for political education. All over France the theater was subjected to new controls and censorship, whether by municipalities, popular societies, or deputies-on-mission. The pressure for control, indeed, came as much from militants in the clubs and sections as it did from the center. On 16 *frimaire* II the Jacobin Club in Lille devoted much of its session to a discussion of the moral effect on young soldiers, on boys of seventeen and eighteen who had only recently left home and who were for the first time exposed to the attractions of city life, of the kinds of entertainment that were currently on offer.[35] The programs proposed to counter immoral influences were predictably didactic, with more than a sprinkling of plays in praise of specifically military virtues. In Bordeaux, the Grand Théâtre gave over its stage to edifying performances of such pieces as *La Plantation de l'arbre de la Liberté* and *Le Départ des volontaires villageois pour la frontière.* Soldiers attending the theater in Metz could warm to the proud welcome that awaited one of their own in *Le Retour du Père Gérard dans sa ferme;* in Paris they could enjoy *Le Siège de Thionville* at the Opéra National or *Agricol Viala* at the Opéra Comique. At Besançon it was even claimed that patriotic plays were proving the most popular with theater audiences—plays like *Bara* and *Viala* which praised the child heroes of the new France, or eulogies of revolutionary morality like *La Parfaite égalité* and *L'Epouse républicaine.* Theater was no longer to be judged as entertainment. It was a place where spirits could be refreshed by being steeped in republicanism, where political ideology could be expressed without fear of contradiction or demurral.[36]

However ideologically correct individual plays might be, and however respectful of political niceties the actors employed, theater could never aspire to be a means of mass politicization in the armies. It would always remain a strictly minority taste, limited by price in the first instance and also by class and cultural tradition. In practice it was among the officers that the theater found its customers, which in the puritanical atmosphere of the Year II could lead to charges of political elitism. In the eyes of some Jacobins, theater would always be a form of privileged culture, its actors indistinguishable from the powdered fops and dandies of the ancien régime. Although it might contain a healthy political message, there remained the suspicion that for a soldier it was an unworthy and rather effeminate form of entertainment which implied self-gratification and even dereliction of duty. Officers who were in the stalls at the *comédie* were, by definition, not in the camps; they were choosing to isolate themselves from their troops in pursuit of pleasure, and the purists saw in such conduct an element of frivolity they could not condone. Saint-Just, for example, while on mission to the Armée du Rhin, ordered the arrest of officers found wandering the city streets or emerging from brightly lit theaters when they ought to be under canvas, sharing the rigors of their men. He had little time for the culture of elites, reserving his enthusiasm for forms of politicization directed at the army as a mass. [37]

Perhaps the most effective of these forms was the patriotic festival, the *fête patriotique* which was such a regular feature of French political life during 1793 and the Year II. Fêtes were unashamedly propagandist in both content and format, presenting a theme (like childhood) or a revolutionary hero (Marat or Le Pelletier) in a pictorial and easily assimilable form to which the public at large could relate. The fact that the fêtes were local community activities made it relatively easy to involve the people in the work of the Revolution, and also to explain to a wide audience the terribly elusive concepts which so entranced the politicians of the day: the Nation, or Unity, or Fraternity. Ever since the first festivals to celebrate the *fédération* of July 1789, the revolutionaries had shown a predilection for lavish public spectacles at which revolutionary achievement could be celebrated in a stylized and symbolic manner. By the Jacobin period the entertainments were established as an important part of the propagandist armory of the state, a ceremonial round of celebrations and symbols that marked the passing of the seasons as predictably as the old harvest festivals and Church rituals. Ritual, indeed, was central to the success of these occasions, with the same pedagogical images—trees of liberty, Phrygian caps, tricolor cockades, the altar of the *patrie*—recurring again and again, and with evocative drawings and caricatures helping to engrave the symbolism on the popular mind. [38] By instituting and regularizing fêtes, and by tying them firmly to a familiar Catholic calendar, the Revolution sought to remind, to cajole, to implant certain basic ideals, and to keep these ideals fresh in the minds of the people. [39]

With the advent of war these revolutionary festivals became more military in tone. In almost every festival the army would be represented, providing the martial music that accompanied the ceremony, marching in solemn respect for the unity of the nation or for the new constitution, mingling with civilians in a symbolic demonstration of the complementary roles which they played in the creation of revolutionary France. Drummer boys would lead the processions, veterans would be honored, and the child prodigies to whom the Jacobins were so attached—youngsters like Bara, killed by the Vendeans at the age of fourteen, or Joseph Viala, who at thirteen served and died for Republican Avignon against the federalists of the Midi—would again be paraded to public adulation. The spirit of the fête also entered the process of recruitment, with the new recruits from each town or village being treated to a patriotic ceremony on the eve of their departure for the regiments. Here, as elsewhere, soldiers and civilian officials were both represented; none of these popular fêtes, even those held to celebrate Republican victories, was ever allowed to become a purely military affair that might seem to separate the military effort from the wider political revolution. The avowed focus of these festivals varied widely. At Strasbourg, for example, there were nine major fêtes between the Jacobin seizure of power in June 1793 and the fall of Robespierre at Thermidor. Besides festivals dedicated to the Supreme Being and to celebrate the Fall of the Bastille, they marked such diverse revolutionary achievements as the arrival of the new constitution, the anniversary of Louis XVI's execution, the retaking of Toulon by the Republic, and the destruction of the power of priests. Volunteers from the armies would turn out on the Place d'Armes to participate in the ceremonial and to enjoy the free ball that followed.[40] Likewise, at Abbeville, celebrations united soldiers and citizenry both in the solemnity of the occasion and in the subsequent revelry. The evenings would end with communal singing and dancing by torchlight, involving the town council and the local club as well as troops from the garrison and members of the general public.[41] Festivities of this kind were intended to portray the soldier in two very different roles—as a defender of liberty, young, selfless, and heroic, and also as a man of the people, sharing popular tastes and popular pleasures.

If fêtes proved an excellent means of spreading a general revolutionary commitment and a sense of shared involvement, they could not communicate precise information or sharply focussed ideas. At best, they could provide a simple and uplifting message, dividing the world into the good and the bad, the enlightened and the benighted. At Dunkerque, for example, a fête was organized in *thermidor* of the Year II to mark the defeat of France's enemies and to indicate the contempt of local people for the plot that had been uncovered to flood the country with forged currency. Puppets were used to depict the central characters, and the fête had much of the simple power of a morality play:

> A corps of musicians, followed by drummers, marched at the front of the procession, followed by members of the town council wearing their sashes of office; then followed the municipal banners of Dunkerque, and the members of the Club, arm-in-arm with Americans and with Batavian patriots in a gesture of fraternity. The procession ended with puppets representing the kings and emperors being dragged in chains on an open cart, along the sides of which was inscribed the caption, "Crowned counterfeiters." Each despot also had fixed to his chest a statement of the charges brought against him.[42]

Like the other symbolic approaches to propaganda used in the armies, fêtes of this kind lacked the flexibility of the printed word, yet the government had increasing need of such flexibility as it sought to explain its actions and priorities to the military. Besides, the soldiers themselves demanded more than slogans and uplifting tales. In the citizen army of the Year II, men were crying out for news—news of home and family, of course, but also news of political change, of social progress, of the fortunes of war. They thirsted for information and sought comfort in any hint of victory, any suggestion that peace was about to be proclaimed. They wanted opinion and explanation as well as the bald diet of information the generals might see fit to supply. Many of them had become accustomed to a France where news and debate were available in abundance, where editors and pamphleteers had been bursting to inform and persuade. In the regiments, where news was scarce and the sense of isolation widespread, the demand for newspapers was overwhelming.[43]

Some means had to be found to satisfy this demand. The movement of units from town to town and the frequent loss of contact while on campaign made it well-nigh impossible for soldiers to rely on subscriptions to political papers at home, while the existing military press, papers like the *Journal militaire,* had a limited and rather technical appeal. Under the Convention, however, when ministers were more conscious of the need for information, policy changed dramatically, and newspapers came to be seen as an important element in the battle to win the minds of the troops. The Ministry of War began to distribute papers to the troops. In December 1792, Pache initiated this policy by organizing the distribution of the *Bulletin de la Convention Nationale.* And in May 1793, the Convention voted 50,000 livres to the new minister, Bouchotte, "to provide for the despatch to the armies of newspapers capable of enlightening and motivating patriotism."[44] The content of these papers was not chosen cynically for sycophancy or blind obedience, nor were they aimed solely at the officers. While Bouchotte was at the War Ministry, indeed, it was government policy to distribute—at considerable cost—some of the most radical titles from the Parisian press, papers like Vatar's *Journal des hommes libres,* Laveaux's *Journal de la Montagne,* Hébert's *Père Duchesne,* and, for a short period, Marat's *Publiciste de la Révolution Française.* From Bouchotte's accounts it has been shown that in the period up to *thermidor* more than seven million papers were distributed in this way, at a cost of some 435,000 livres. Hébert alone received some 118,000 livres from public funds, and more than 1,800,000 copies of his paper were ordered for the armies.[45] But in Bouchotte's view it was money well spent because the papers would serve not only to entertain the troops, but also to inculcate an element of revolutionary discipline. The Committee of Public Safety agreed and made specific grants for the purpose, particularly in the early period of Bouchotte's ministry, before

Jacobin suspicions of popular radicalism became aroused and government policy was turned against extremists and *exagérés*.

The Convention did not, however, restrict its activity to distributing the civilian press; it also encouraged the publication of military papers, both nationally and within individual armies, whose readership was largely limited to the troops themselves. These were very different in kind from the polemical *sans-culotte* tracts that arrived in bundles from Paris. They were generally produced for one single army, and they varied considerably both in content and in political leaning. Often poorly produced on local presses, they depended on the patronage and inspiration of individuals, usually generals or deputies-on-mission with the armies, who used them either to radicalize military opinion or, in some instances, to counteract the effect of the more extreme Parisian papers. Their economic foundation was often shaky; a number of them appeared only irregularly and were predictably short-lived.[46] Some were official in tone, like the *Bulletin de l'Armée des Côtes-de-Brest,* which devoted more than half its space to army or government announcements, gloating in its somewhat rhetorical style about victories over the Vendean rebels and the frightful outrages the brigands perpetrated in reply. Defeats were reported, although more soberly; after a rout suffered near Nantes, the paper concentrated on raising morale, printing excerpts from political speeches, urging a spirit of emulation among the various armies, and preaching homilies about the need for discipline in the face of adversity.[47] An earlier venture, the *Bulletin de l'Armée du Midi,* published in September 1792, had similarly restricted horizons, containing nothing that could heighten tensions within the army and giving little more than a heavily factual progress report by the commanders.[48] But not all the military press was so prosaic. The *Argus* in the Nord—"L'Ami Jacques" to its regular readers—devoted much of its space to political matters of interest to the region; unlike most of the military papers, it could be bought freely in the towns along the northern frontier, and it tended to take a fairly conciliatory, pro-Girondin line in its editorials. Perhaps the most appreciated feature of the *Argus* was the free expression it encouraged from its readers, for it was in its correspondence columns that the most committedly Republican sentiment could be found. One such letter praised the paper for its resolute stand against counterrevolution and urged further vigilance, encouraging "L'Ami Jacques" to pursue religious fanaticism into its darkest hiding places, to sap its strength, and "exterminate this hydra that is the root of so many ills."[49]

Of the six army papers that appeared between April 1792 and the end of 1795, Marc Martin has pointed to two that were more radical than the rest. On the Channel coast, the *Journal de l'Armée des Côtes de Cherbourg* was far more than a military bulletin; it maintained close links both with the local Jacobins and with central government in the person of the deputy-on-mission to the army at Caen, Robert Lindet. During Lindet's mission, indeed, the paper regarded him as a political mentor and unfailingly turned to him for advice and guidance; it even seems likely that he was one of the main inspirations behind the paper's publication.[50] And at the other end of the country, in Perpignan, the *Avant-garde de l'Armée des Pyrénées-orientales* played a similar role, printing political comment more than factual news, and using its columns to create among the military an opinion receptive to radical reform. Here the encouragement of that most Jacobin of generals, Dugommier, is very evident, while the editor, Romarin Bussat, was a member of the local political elite, doubling as public prosecutor at the military tribunal in Perpignan. As an example of a paper with an avowedly political purpose which also carried the sort of news the soldiers wanted to read, the *Avant-garde* was a model of its kind. Eschewing long, dreary reports of maneuvers and exaggerated accounts of enemy losses—the stock-in-trade of the duller scions of the military press—it told its readers about victories on other fronts, especially against the Prussians and Austrians in Belgium; it commented on the supply situation in the Roussillon, a matter of intimate concern to the men bivouaced along the Spanish border; and it reported the more significant judgments handed down by the local courts. But just as welcome to the troops reading it were the more polemical items in the paper: the patriotic songs for communal singing, the accounts of the ideas being discussed in the local Jacobin clubs, or the authoritative dismissal of dangerous rumors which had been sapping the soldiers' morale.[51] Bussat possessed that most critical gift in a journalist, the ability to entertain as well as to instruct.

Although newspapers of this kind, written specially for a military audience, could play a significant part in the political education of individual armies, their impact was necessarily very localized. Whole armies, among them some of the most important like the Rhine and the Sambre-et-Meuse, had no military press of their own; others had papers that did little to raise political consciousness. What was still lacking even at the height of the terror was a national military newspaper that could give voice to a Jacobin vision of France, both of its political achievements and of its military targets. This was the gap Carnot sought to fill when he created, in July 1794, a political newspaper for all France's armies, *La Soirée du camp.* Published in an edition of ten thousand, it could aspire to make some impact on military opinion. Like Hébert, Carnot and his collaborators used the device of an imaginary character to speak to the men, in this case an old, retired soldier, Va-de-bon-coeur, a man who had been born into the line and who had served there all his life, losing a leg along the way, then an arm and an eye in America. He was a sergeant, a man of the people, who drank and laughed with the common soldier, who spoke his language, who shared his fears and his ambitions and his devotion to the Republic. He warned his readers from the outset that they would find no pretty phrases in his writing, no well-turned political concepts; instead, he would talk of patriotism and gaiety, courage and loyalty, what he described as the essential attributes of the French soldier.

Va-de-bon-coeur, in short, would not bore them with politics in the way that politicians do; he would chat to them exactly like those battle-hardened veterans whose stories they like to hear around the fire of an evening. Carnot used this clever device to press home the political orthodoxy of the day. In the very first number he distanced himself from Hébert, angrily denouncing the Père Duchesne for having tried to restore the institutions of the ancien régime: "From time to time he was amusing, that Père Duchesne; he sometimes made me laugh as much as anyone. But that's because at the beginning I didn't have doubts that he wanted to spread counterrevolution and blacken the reputation of the French soldier. But that was one of his ways of taking us all back to the Ancien Regime. How many times, once I had begun to see clearly, did his papers lacerate my heart! For I'd as soon swallow a barrel of gunflints as see the soldier's good name reviled."[52]

In his thirteenth issue, dated 14 *thermidor,* he tried to explain to the soldiers how the man they had been told to revere only a few days before, Maximilien Robespierre, had deceived them all through his well-practiced hypocrisy: "Why, you will say, was this infernal plot not discoverd earlier? Why did the energy of free men not rise earlier against a tyranny that was a thousand times more odious than that of oriental despotism? . . . My friends, it is because this monster was above all a hypocrite; it is because he knew how to seduce the people."[53]

After Thermidor, the political tone of the paper would fall away as news from the front was featured more prominently, and Va-de-bon-coeur became a more unambiguous instrument for raising army morale. But for a few short weeks the Jacobins had in *La Soirée du camp* that most valuable asset, a means by which politicians could speak directly to their soldiers.[54]

By means of this wide range of persuasive techniques the Revolution sought to politicize the individual soldier, to form him into a disciplined patriot willing to make the ultimate sacrifice for the cause of France. A thousand eulogies painted an idealized picture of the soldier; he was a citizen first and foremost, a citizen who understood the laws of the land and who accepted the alienation of some of his own rights in the cause of the

Republic.[55] From the soldiers' own diaries and letters it is clear that this propaganda bore fruit, that the soldier of the Year II, more than his counterpart under the Directory or in the line army of 1789, did think politically and had at least some basic inkling of the nature of the cause in whose name he was enlisted. He was encouraged to show an intelligent interest in public affairs. He was even encouraged to petition the Convention on political as well as purely military matters. But he was not expected to support any sort of Republic or to deviate from the political instincts of the government of the day. The army had become an *école du jacobinisme* capable of turning peasant boys who had never traveled beyond the nearest town into citizen-soldiers who understood the basic elements of the revolutionary catechism. The army, in other words, was itself a form of education, and one which placed a premium on political orthodoxy. It should not be imagined that the process of education was gentle, or that the lessons were optional, reserved for those with the wit and interest to read newspapers or to interpret the nationalistic symbolism all around them. Inside the armies political terror was used just as ruthlessly as in civilian society as a means of conversion and constraint. The soldier of the Year II was under constant political surveillance, and the politicians would brook no denial.

This surveillance was largely the work of the political agents who were sent out to the armies from Paris, and who exercised a very real control over their day-to-day activities. During the revolutionary period, indeed, there was a constant flurry of political visitations—by deputies-on-mission from the Convention, *commissaires* sent by the Ministry of War, and agents of the Committee of Public Safety—all of whom were concerned with the political reliability of the troops as much as with their performance in the field.[56] Through these various agents the government sought to ensure that the army remained at all times answerable to political control. No new principle was involved; military intendants had been used in the ancien régime for very much the same purpose, and where conflicts had arisen it was always the civil authority that had the last say. What changed with the Revolution, as Jacques Godechot has shown, was the urgency with which the problem was perceived: the 1791 constitution failed to define the relationship between the government and its military commanders, and circumstance, in the shape of the Nancy mutiny, led to regular and anxious surveillance. The Convention, as has been shown, was even more distrustful of the military, and especially of the officer class, and this distrust was rapidly translated into more far-reaching political controls. The practice of sending out deputies became the norm rather than the exception, until in April 1793 it was decreed that three deputies should be on duty at all times with each of the major armies on the frontiers. Their powers, too, were considerably extended. The Committee of Public Safety demanded that they live in the camps with the soldiers, receive their complaints, and maintain a tight check on the activities of their commanders. From September 1793, they were empowered to suspend all officers and civilian administrators who seemed inadequate to their task; by the end of December they were ordered to dismiss and arrest any general deemed to be betraying his responsibility. Yet it could not be assumed that such wide-ranging authority would be respected by the military, many of whom were impatient of the pretensions of the state. Generals were still wont to question the value of civilian interference in military strategy, and political agents were often tolerated rather than respected. As Danton remarked to the Paris Jacobins, Dumouriez's troops in Belgium had mistaken him for the general's secretary.[57]

The importance the Committee of Public Safety attached to these missions can be judged from the caliber of the deputies they used, front-ranking Jacobins in many cases, like Milhaud and Soubrany in the Pyrénées-orientales or Saint-Just and Le Bas in the Nord. Nor is there any reason to doubt their effectiveness in restoring morale and imposing the government's will; their powers were almost limitless, and they made full use of the authority vested in them. Whereas generals like Custine risked denunciation if they tried to implement a strict code of military discipline, deputies could not only do so with impunity, but could also justify their measures in the name of the Revolution. Saint-Just's missions to the Rhine and the Nord are often regarded as models of their kind. Unlike some of his colleagues, Saint-Just refused to accept that his brief was limited to the affairs of the armies themselves. He did, of course, concern himself with the serious interruptions in supply which were the scourge of the armies on the frontiers, and he showed little mercy to those found guilty of speculation at the expense of the troops. He also took desperate measures to prevent the total disintegration of military morale which threatened to result from unchecked looting and pillage, ordering exemplary punishments for those convicted but insisting that treatment be equal for all regardless of rank. And he took special care to reform the local structures of the army, not just to conform with the law, but as a response to the problems he encountered on the spot. But the impact of his mission did not stop there. In Strasbourg, for example, he sought to revolutionize the local authorities, and his purge of the army was matched by an equally ruthless purge of civilian officials, a step which served to appease the men in uniform and make them more willing to accept a severe military regime. He looked beyond the organization of victory to the ultimate success of the Republic; that, in Saint-Just's view, must be the aim of all policy, whether economic, social, or military, and he made use of the powers he enjoyed on his missions to take a decisive step toward the accomplishment of that long-term goal.[58]

Saint-Just's task was made possible by the extension of political terror to the regiments and by the imposition of a severe code of military justice. When he found that discipline had all but collapsed in the Armée du Rhin, for example, he promoted the revolutionary tribunal into a military commission against which there could be no appeal. Sentences were carried out within a matter of hours. A man who had been found guilty of profiteering out of army supplies was shot in front of the troops; other death sentences were imposed for royalism, emigration, passing supplies to the enemy, and abandoning a fort when under attack.[59] Because pillage was such a threat to morale, military courts could, and did, ensure that looters were firmly and publicly dealt with, as a reminder to others of their duty to obey the law. And where lack of discipline threatened the stability of the armies, or where desertion reached intolerable proportions, savage and exemplary punishments could again be sought to limit the damage to the strength of the regiments.

If this approach to justice was in a sense somewhat opportunistic, reserving repression for those offenses which seemed to do most harm to the fighting strength of the armies, Jacobin sentencing policy also contained a highly moralistic streak. Tribunals weighed the gravity of the offenses they were judging, and the distinctions they made reflected something of the high moral tone of Jacobin politics. Whereas purely military offenses were often treated with relative leniency, certain categories of crimes were singled out for harsh and repressive punishment. Crimes which smacked of moral laxity, for example, persistent drunkenness and debauchery, licentiousness, and especially rape, automatically incurred heavy sentences; officers admitted to military hospitals and who suffered from venereal diseases were liable to be cashiered and declared unfit to serve the Republic. Even thefts were graded according to the degree to which they were an outrage to Republican virtue. Whereas taking property from the rich might be condoned at times when the armies went hungry, stealing from the state or from other soldiers was judged much more harshly, and thefts of grain or livestock from local peasants could result in summary execution.[60]

The operation of such justice was deliberately very public, a part of the shared experience of military life. The judgments handed down by the tribunals were published and displayed prominently in both the camps and nearby towns. To be effective, such justice had also to be exemplary. Milhaud and Soubrany described how a former general, denounced for treason, had been dealt with in the Armée des Pyrénées-orientales. The man had been executed, they explained, in the middle of the Camp de l'Union at Perpignan, where all the soldiers could see him. He had been judged there, and the guillotine had been transferred for the purpose: "You should see how such examples give energy and confidence to the Republican soldiers. One single cry—'long live the Republic, long live the Montagne!'—could be heard, uttered from twenty thousand throats."[61] In similar vein, Ruamps reported the exemplary value of capital sentences among the garrison at Landau. When panic threatened to spread through the garrison, he told the Committee in Paris, he had acted promptly, seizing a number of soldiers who were talking of the need to surrender and having them summarily shot in front of their fellows.[62] In all the armies, indeed, deputies looked to the courts for help not only in the punishment of misdemeanors, but also in the education of those who looked on. This was especially true of the show trials held to punish commanders deemed to have betrayed their men or to have lost battles through culpable incompetence. The Armée du Nord alone lost three of its generals, Luckner, Custine, and Houchard, to the guillotine, in Houchard's case for his poor judgment in failing to follow up the retreat of the enemy and turn a creditable but limited victory into a rout.[63] Again, it would seem, the main purpose of the sentence was educative rather than judicial.

The Jacobins demanded more of their citizens than passive acceptance; indifference and apathy became crimes that could be punished at law. In their eyes citizenship implied positive duties and commitments, the sublimation of selfish ambitions in the pursuit of a shared political goal. In that sense they sought to spread revolutionary idealism throughout French society, to politicize the French nation. And the army, whether as a reflection of society at large or as a sort of political academy for the nation, had necessarily to share these political goals if it were to be an effective instrument of the Jacobin Republic. After Thermidor, the political climate would change, and with it the role which the army was expected to play. As the Thermidorians dismantled the structures of revolutionary government, abandoning the emergency laws and special jurisdictions of the Terror, retreating from central economic controls, and seeking efficiency less through ideology than through the construction of a permanent bureaucracy, so the demands they made of their soldiers were also transformed. And the importance which had been attached to political education throughout much of 1793 and the Year II was reduced rapidly. The army had now to reflect a new set of political imperatives.

The change was, of course, one of degree. The Thermidorians and the Directors had no wish to relinquish the powers which ideological control of the military had offered. They, too, saw themselves as the leaders of a revolutionary society whose existence depended on its ideological base and where royalism and reaction had not ceased to threaten. Besides, Jacobin sympathizers were still to be found in key posts in the French army. They could ill afford to neglect the political opinions held among the military. But political education ceased to be the obsession it had been under their predecessors. The quality of the army was again seen less in terms of its opinions than of more traditional virtues like firm discipline and tactical competence. Military courts became less concerned with the repression of political offenses and more single-minded in their pursuit of obedience and authority. Deputies-on-mission were still sent out from Paris, although they were now referred to as *commissaires aux armées,* but their unlimited powers were removed, their financial resources controlled, and their right to overrule generals and to appoint to military offices withdrawn. They were there to encourage the zeal of the officers rather than to give them orders; the political arm was no longer supreme.[64] Likewise, the flow of political tracts was quickly staunched, and the Republican symbolism of the armies became more unambiguously patriotic, more part of the tradition of soldiering, and less imbued with political ideology. The troops were no longer given access to the radical press, and the papers that continued to be produced for the armies became dull digests of information, devoid of political ideas or stimulation.[65] The recruitment exercises of 1792 and 1793 were not repeated, and men already in the armies were encouraged to think of their trade in an increasingly professional way.

Jacobin influence in the armies did not die out overnight. Indeed, because their activity in civilian society was so closely circumscribed, those Jacobin or neo-Jacobin clubs which continued to operate after Thermidor were increasingly inclined to look to the soldiers as potential allies in a common struggle. Soldiers were seen as men ripe for conversion, men whose years of service and sacrifice would make them open to egalitarian ideas, and Jacobin societies were eager to make contact with them, to petition in support of their claims, and to induce them to become involved in the Jacobins' own battles against local officials. The same pattern was to be observed all over France, in Nice and Orléans, in Clermont and Perpignan. Clubs and *cercles constitutionnels* desperately sought to involve the military as a means of escaping from the isolation to which they had been condemned. They fraternized with local regiments and offered hospitality to army units passing back and forward to the front. They took up soldiers' perennial grievances and made them their own. They involved themselves in campaigns to improve the conditions in which soldiers were billeted and took up the soldiers' greatest cause, the campaign for a guaranteed veterans' bonus. Jacobin petitions and pamphlets emphasized a commitment to greater equality—greater equality in land distribution, for example, so that returning soldiers could aspire to be small farmers in their own right, and greater equality of sacrifice for the war effort, to be achieved by high rates of tax on the rich. After the upsurge of royalist activity in the Year V, when the government was more alarmed by the threat from the right than by that from the left, such activity increased dramatically, with Jacobin cells active in the armies and Jacobin pamphlets circulating among the troops. As radical leaders like Marc-Antoine Jullien recognized, the military had become a particularly rich seam for political activity, containing as it did men who had never come to terms with Thermidor and who had sought shelter in the armies from the persecution of the White Terror. Committed Jacobins among the soldiers followed Bonaparte in Italy and Egypt, and neo-Jacobin cells were still to be found in the regiments of the First Empire.[66]

But if Jacobinism continued to command an audience in the armies, it posed little threat to the regime. It could even be regarded, with some justification, as a political safety valve for a government that was less and less interested in achieving greater equality at home. Despite the understandable fears conjured up by the specter of an army out of sympathy with its political masters, the truth is that ideological propaganda among the soldiers had never posed any real threat to the government of the day. The mutinies of 1790 belonged to another era. Even in the Year II, when Jacobin propaganda was at its most intense, the soldiers accepted the coup d'état of 9 *thermidor* with surprisingly little protest. They allowed Robespierre to be deposed and guillotined without attempting to intervene. This in turn might suggest that the real impact of Jacobin political education on the armies can be exaggerated. Soldiers who read eulogies of Robespierre in one issue of the *Soirée du camp* seemed unperturbed when a subsequent issue reviled him as a usurper and a tyrant. Likewise, those who had fought with apparent fervor for the principles of the Year II offered their services without demurral to the very different regimes which replaced the Jacobin Republic. The Constitution of the Year III occasioned no outrage among the military, and the historian is entitled to ask why. Why, if they really believed in the Jacobin Republic, did they passively allow it to die, when they alone had the armed strength that could have prevented its demise? Why, when political training had been such an integral part of the discipline and motivation of the revolutionary armies, did they respond with a whimper rather than with a bang?

In part the lack of any unified response could be explained by the geographical dispersal of the armies, which would have made effective political action against the new government difficult to orchestrate. But to explain their inactivity in these terms is to assume that there was a political will to oppose in the first place. There is very little evidence for such a claim, and that in turn must lead us to question the nature of the political faith the troops had acquired during the Jacobin months. Were they really won over to the ideals of Jacobinism, as seemed apparent at the time, or should the acquiescence of the majority of soldiers not be seen as simply another aspect of the obedience to authority engendered by life in the regiments? Because their first loyalty was to the Republic, that loyalty could be transferred without great difficulty to the Thermidorian regime. Indeed, a failure to effect such a transfer would leave individual soldiers and army units in open rebellion against the Republic, in clear breach of all the lessons inculcated by revolutionary discipline and revolutionary justice. It was a case where discipline and ideology, never the easiest of bedfellows, were seen to be in conflict. But if discipline won—and there is little doubt that it did—doubts must surely be cast on the effectiveness of the Jacobin campaign to raise the political consciousness of the soldiers. Did this supposed politicization amount to much more than the assimilation of a few slogans on the eve of battle and the playing out of stereotyped republican rituals? After all, independent thought was not really what the Jacobins were seeking. The soldiers were expected to participate and encouraged to involve themselves in political action—but only the political action that was prescribed from the center. Like political clubs and municipal councils throughout France, their role was to follow rather than to lead: they were spear-carriers in a much wider political drama.

5

PROVIDING FOR THE SOLDIERS

F THE EFFORT OF RECRUITING ARMIES OF THE SIZE which the Revolution required served to test the administrative capacities of the state, so did the task of maintaining and servicing them. It was an enterprise that had no parallel in the armies of the ancien régime, when an annual production of fifty-five thousand rifles had been sufficient for all eventualities.[1] But the vast scale of revolutionary warfare ensured that supply would pose daunting problems for the government and its administrators, calling for new laws and a new emphasis on planning and on direction from the center. It was an area in which ideology and enthusiasm would prove no substitute for careful planning and painstaking administration. To be effective, an army required far more than manpower and tactical training. It had to be clothed and armed, fed and watered. Supplies had to be moved into position in the field. Transport had to be assembled, and convoys organized. When soldiers fell sick or were wounded in battle, sufficient medical services had to be prepared so lives would not be squandered needlessly. Provision had to be made for those maimed in the service of their country and for the dependents of those killed. And money had to be found to pay for it all, at a time when the regulation of the assignat and the harnessing of a reluctant economy were presenting massive problems in their own right. The supply issue would not only place severe strains on the economy, but it would also place a severe strain on popular tolerance.

For the individual soldier, questions of supply loomed very large indeed. It was not just his honor or his comfort that was at stake, but his very survival. The fear that supplies would be lost or stolen, and that units would be left without food, the fear that soldiers would be abandoned shivering from cold in the Pyrenees or on some Alpine pass, these were everyday cares about which soldiers needed reassurance. But they were also important cares for the state and its agents because such matters were just as vital in the creation of an effective army as questions of political control or the maintenance of strict discipline. Regular supply and good discipline went hand in hand. Without serviceable weapons, troops risked losing heart before battle was even joined. Without basic foodstuffs, soldiers had no alternative but to loot and pillage. Deprived of firewood and clothing, they were tempted to turn to theft and destruction. In Belgium, for example, long delays in bringing in supplies encouraged a rapid escalation of looting and disorder and left soldiers more concerned to acquire booty than to win battles. Not only were crops ripped out from the fields and farmyards pillaged of livestock, but sheets and shirts were also stolen by troops left half-naked to face the winter, and kitchen utensils disappeared to service the soldiers' canteen. Even the fish were removed from village fishponds.[2] Garrisons at Reims and Verdun, threatened with a reduction in their bread ration, rioted to the point of insurrection, refusing even to listen to the orders of their commanders.[3] The lesson was not lost on the revolutionary leadership. Without assured supply, military morale slumped badly and even the most elementary discipline was lost. Likewise, shortages could undermine men's political loyalties because empty bellies and rusting bayonets could lead to a more generalized sense of grievance, and it was all too easy to think that life had been less onerous in the days of the monarchy. Provisioning was not an issue of secondary importance. Discipline, political education, and supply played a complementary role in molding a modern military machine.

The Revolution willingly accepted these responsibilities, recognizing that it had a duty to ensure that its "braves défenseurs" were adequately supplied with the necessities of life. Because soldiers were citizens who had voluntarily made a considerable personal sacrifice in the interests of the Revolution, this was the only response possible. The government owed them such basic comfort and amenity as it was able to provide, as it repeatedly acknowledged in countless addresses to the troops and in the preambles to decrees on supply. In *ventôse* of the Year III, for instance, it accepted that it was the state's duty to look after all those spheres of a soldier's existence which had to do with his everyday survival, all those aspects of military life divorced from training and discipline. The state had to care for the welfare of the armies, "their pay and their food, the upkeep of their uniforms, their lodging, health, and their ease of movement from one place to another."[4] The sentiment was an honorable one, reflecting both a recognition of mutual responsibilities and the implications of its own ideology. It was also a practical necessity if the war was to be waged successfully. But it is easy to underestimate the enormity of this undertaking, to forget that France in the 1790s was still a largely artisanal economy ill-equipped for the scale of economic mobilization required, or that the French state still lacked much of the administrative capacity that is taken for granted by all modern governments. Because the early economic reforms of the Revolution had been aimed at reducing state restrictions on free trade, the government exercised less direct control over individual producers and merchants than had the governments of Louis XV or Louis XVI. In the summer of 1791—in many ways the high point of economic liberalism—all price controls on bread and meat were removed, and military provisioning was handed over, at least temporarily, to private enterprise.[5] Nor was there the sort of control over clothing suppliers which could guarantee that the soldiers would be adequately clad. The first volunteers, indeed, often left for the front in the spirit of national guardsmen, with uniforms bought by relatives or sewn together by proud mothers and with rifles produced by fellow villagers as their contribution to the war effort. Although such makeshift arrangements were rather picturesque and would furnish the theme of many nineteenth-century woodcuts and caricatures, they were no substitute for a national system of supply. As the scale of the war increased, they provided a salutary warning that France still lacked the infrastructure necessary for a modern army.

By the autumn of 1793, after the *levée en masse* had created a mass of more than half a million men spread across fourteen separate armies, the full enormity of the question of supply had to be faced. Whereas municipal levies might produce the men required by the state, they frequently failed to arm and equip them as the law demanded. Recruits turned up without shoes or with only the wooden clogs they used on the farm; uniforms were often a cruel approximation of the real thing, as families desperately used any cloth they could find which vaguely approximated to the national blue; the young soldier was as likely to be handed a defective hunting rifle as a weapon of war. Drawing on the reports sent in from towns and villages all over France, Jean-Paul Bertaud has shown how precarious the supply situation was for many of these young recruits, who risked being thrown into battle armed only with pikes or with firearms intended for hunting rabbits. From these reports it becomes clear how desperately many local communities had sought to conjure up weapons from their own resources. In the District of Sainte-Menehould, for instance, they organized a collection of hunting rifles from among the local peasants; at Boulogne, they disarmed the National Guard in order to equip the volunteers; at La Rochelle, they sent off their recruits armed only with sticks. When distressed mayors turned to the departments or to deputies-on-mission for advice, the replies they received were an eloquent testimony to the government's helplessness in the face of penury. "Arm yourselves with pikes," advised Elie Lacoste, "and failing that with swords, axes and even pick-axes."[6] It was a bleak reply, in many ways a counsel of despair. Lacoste and his colleagues knew very well that the supply situation in the armies was lamentable, that soldiers could not forever be expected to fight with makeshift weapons and wear patched and threadbare uniforms, and that the call to local communities to furnish arms and equipment could be nothing more than a short-term expedient to overcome a period of crisis.

Under the Jacobins, the free economy of the early Revolution was rapidly subjected to greater and greater state control—the insistence on the use of assignats rather than coin, the close regulation of local markets, the move toward mandatory price control over a wide range of everyday commodities. From May 1793, the Convention moved back toward the regulation of grain prices; from September, the law of the maximum was applied nationally to sales of grain and flour. In part, this about-turn was a by-product of the Jacobin alliance with the Parisian sections whose militants pressed the state to protect the poorer members of society from the worst abuses of market economics. But there is also a strong case for seeing the move toward control as a necessary corollary to the crisis in military supply. With hundreds and sometimes thousands of men deployed within a single region and moved from town to town on their way to the front, it was no longer feasible to depend on local farmers and the local market. Requisitions and compulsory purchases were required, often at very short notice, and they would remain a central part of governmental strategy right through the revolutionary decade. In the early months of the war the government had tried to leave supply to private contractors, then it had used state agencies before finally it vacillated between a reliance on the state—the *régie*—and direct provisioning by individual battalions.[7] Grain shortages, unchecked inflation, bad debts to local peasants, and the reluctance of local people to accept payment in paper all aggravated the crisis and forced both peasant and military quartermaster to turn to the black market if the troops were not to starve. In that regard, government regulation could add to the problem of supply, especially in areas of the country where the tradition of smuggling and tax evasion was deeply rooted. And while some *commissaires* and deputies-on-mission stubbornly insisted that the letter of the law must be respected at all times, others would close their eyes to the flouting of the maximum if it were the only way of ensuring that the men were adequately fed. In extreme cases even deputies-on-mission could find their instructions overruled.[8] The feeding of the armies was too important and too immediate a task to be subject to severe legal constraint. No policy drafted in Paris could hope to meet the needs of requisitioners in Alsace or the Pyrenees. This applied equally to the measures taken by the Directory; if Jacobin controls caused supply to dry up through self-interest and resentment, the lifting of such controls in the Year III simply resulted in a free-for-all in which the military was often ill-equipped to compete.

While the armies were fighting on French territory, supply problems centered on the competition of soldiers with local people for resources made artificially scarce by the army's arrival. Because military transport was never sufficient for the soldiers' needs, requisitioning generally affected only those departments immediately behind the armies' lines. Thus the two armies engaged in the Pyrenees restricted the major part of their requisitioning to the immediate hinterland—the Pyrenean departments themselves, the Roussillon, Pays Basque, and Béarn—while the Armée du Rhin limited its attentions to seven departments of Alsace and the East. Local people understandably felt that they were being expected to shoulder a disproportionate share of the military burden, especially when the military insisted that they accept payment in the long-discredited assignats. In certain instances, indeed, the scale of that burden was such that it could not be supported by local markets without causing misery and deprivation among the villagers themselves. In the one department of the Pyrénées-orientales, for instance, there would be at any one time between ten and forty thousand French troops competing for bread with a local population of only 125,000; it was one of a number of areas where the sheer density of the military presence placed insupportable strains on the balance of the local economy.[9]

With the expansion of the war on to foreign territory, the

problem of supply was simply exported. By 1793, there was no way that French agriculture could feed the men fighting in the revolutionary armies, even had the government wished it to do so, and in September, the Committee of Public Safety ordered its commanders to procure the food stocks they needed, as well as supplies of clothing, arms, equipment, and transport, from the peoples of the occupied territories. As far as was possible, the war would in future be fought and paid for by the defeated nations, and it would be their responsibility to maintain and supply those of the armies deployed outside France. Victory, in short, could be turned to profit, and the crisis could, in the short term, be alleviated. Within days of entering Brabant, for instance, orders and requisitions for the military were widely imposed, and local peasants, like their French counterparts, were subjected to the constraints of the maximum. For the Belgians, the bill would be a heavy one. In the six months from October 1794, the requisitions demanded by the French totaled some 27 million livres, and in *vendémiaire* of the year Year III, the *commissaire-ordonnateur général* in Belgium, Sabin-Bourcier, ruled that half of all the grain produced in Belgium and the occupied territories—the term was defined to include not only wheat, but also rye, oats, hay and straw—must be requisitioned for the use of the French armies. [10]

To regulate military supplies and requisitions on such a scale, the revolutionaries required a sizable administrative apparatus. As with matters of recruitment and strategy, they were reluctant to leave these questions to the military themselves because Jacobin suspicions of the probity of senior officers died hard. Supply questions did, of course, fall within the brief of the deputies sent on mission to the armies, and they were called upon in moments of crisis to intercede with local authorities or to make an example of recalcitrant merchants. But on a day-to-day basis, the provisioning of the armies was controlled by the supply officers attached to the battalions, the *commissaires ordonnateurs* and their staffs. They worked closely with the specialist bodies set up to oversee food and fodder supplies, hospitals, and military transport. But theirs was the ultimate responsibility, both on foreign territory and in the military divisions within France itself; they had to arrange for food supplies, pay the suppliers, exercise quality control, verify the standard of lodging, and generally ensure that the soldiers were not being abused or ill-treated. It was a powerful post, intended to act as something of a check on the generals' freedom of action and thus one that could bring charges of meddling in military affairs and incur the wrath of the high command. In the context of the Revolution, the job almost inevitably became highly politicized. There was nothing new about the post itself; ancien régime armies had had to be supplied, and they, too, had been serviced by *commissaires*. But both the scale of the wars and the political importance of the soldiers' welfare changed the role and the status attributed to the administration of military supply. Those who had served the ancien régime were immediately suspect for jobs where the nation's interests were so intimately at issue. In the words of a published pamphlet on war provisioning in *brumaire* of the Year II, the eighteenth-century *commissaire* had been at the beck and call of the generals and had enjoyed little standing either with the armies or with the government: "During the reign of the despots, when the armies were the property of kings and the regiments of their courtiers, these courtiers were sufficiently adroit to appoint as *commissaires* their secretaries, stewards and other creatures, who, out of gratitude to their former employers, would help them to steal army property in return for a share of the spoils while taking every opportunity to depress the lot of the ordinary soldier."[11] Under the Revolution, their functions would be repeatedly reviewed, the size of the service greatly expanded, and the ancien régime personnel purged.

The *commissaires* to whom the Revolution turned in 1793 were genuinely independent of the generals alongside whom they served. They did, however, share a common military background, which was essential if they were to understand the complexities of supplying armies that might be constantly on the move. In practice, the 390 *commissaires* appointed by the Convention in

April 1793 were chosen from carefully designated groups. The law was very precise on this point: a *commissaire* had to have relevant military experience, either as a *commissaire des guerres* in the old line army or as a serving soldier with firsthand knowledge of supply problems, usually a sergeant-major or quartermaster. [12] The evidence available suggests that the spirit of the law was closely observed: in the Sambre-et-Meuse, for instance, all the *commissaires* were former soldiers. Many of them were men in their twenties or early thirties whose service dated only from the revolutionary years, but the group included a substantial proportion of veterans who had served long years in the ancien régime regiments. They were generally men of some accomplishment, with personal experience of both administration and accounting; in civilian life they had been notaries' clerks and government officials, lawyers and teachers, many of them employed in various sectors of public administration. [13]

The intention was clear, to create an expert service that would be politically responsible instead of being answerable to the army high command. But the difficulties *commissaires* faced in carrying out their duties were daunting, even for the most seasoned administrator. They had to cope with sudden influxes of troops and with the crisis in supply which that necessarily entailed. And in moments of crisis they could feel terribly solitary and vulnerable. From Avignon, for instance, the *commissaire* pleaded with his departmental authorities in the Year VII for some practical measure of help. He had just received 650 men and 200 horses, passing through to the armies in Italy; he had heard that another 580 men and 240 horses were to descend on him the next day; and he had been told to expect a further fifteen hundred artillery horses in the immediate future. Without assistance from local officials, he said, he had no way of preventing disorders from breaking out, with troops going hungry and valuable horses consigned to the knacker's yard. [14] What made the *commissaire's* job even more difficult was the fact that he had no guarantee of the resources which he required. In *floréal* IV, the supply situation in the lower

Rhône valley had been just as desperate, with the troops unpaid, the military hospitals denied food and medicines, and meat supplies withheld by local butchers. Again the *commissaire* in Avignon, Sartelon, had had to throw himself on the mercy of the Department, explaining that since his treasury was completely empty he found himself unable to fulfill even his most basic duties. [15]

Because military supply was such a sensitive issue, it was only too easy for a *commissaire* like Sartelon to fall foul of his political masters. There were so many potential conflicts of interest in which he might become embroiled, with peasants angry at the sight of their harvest being removed, with local authorities more interested in their own supply crisis and unsympathetic to the demands of outsiders, even with rival *commissaires* trawling in the same limited markets to supply their own regiments. And denunciation during the revolutionary years could seem such an easy option. Writing in the Year II to a colleague who had just been promoted to Lyon, the *commissaire-ordonnateur* of the Twenty-first Division Militaire saw fit to warn him of the perils which his post would entail. Because of the nature of his work, he could never be on the spot to ensure that abuses did not occur; he would have to trust the integrity of others. Yet he would surely suffer from the gossip and machination with which the service was riddled. He would receive countless denunciations and complaints, all of which he was bound to investigate, although he knew very well that the vast majority were false and malicious. He could not afford to take chances, or to work other than by the book. His colleague's advice was sobering: as a *commissaire* he should keep a complete set of laws and decrees by him at all times, and in his dealings with his staff he should consign everything to writing so that he could demonstrate his own probity and justify his conduct. [16] It was advice which he would have done well to follow because allegations of theft and self-aggrandizement had to be counted among the hazards of the profession. The Robespierrist paper, *L'Antifédéraliste,* claimed that the supply administration was contaminated by "a band of brigands who had previously spent their time in the antechambers and the stables at Versailles and in the brothels of the Palais Royal." Even more threatening was the accusation leveled by Saint-Just in a famous speech of October 1793, when he alleged that the Republic was being undermined by its own administrators, by the twenty thousand fools and hangers-on "who corrupt it, battle against it, and bleed it of resources."[17] Incompetence and corruption went hand in hand.

Although graft and corruption did aggravate the problem of military supply and did on occasion place the welfare of the troops at risk, the Jacobin emphasis on *vertu* should not detract from the difficulties the *commissaires* faced or from the extent of their achievement. Theirs was in so many ways a thankless task. They were obliged to treat with local authorities and assuage local opinion, to find food and fodder at short notice, to billet soldiers on unwilling villagers, and all without the financial support or administrative knowledge necessary to the task. Advance planning could never be easy along a war front, where units might retreat without warning, convoys be cut off, or sources of supply lost. At any moment the scale of the problem could be changed utterly, as new units were moved into the battle zone or as new recruits arrived to join their battalions. The needs of hospitals and military ambulances were impossible to predict with any measure of accuracy. The number of new recruits who would be joining a given regiment was not always communicated in advance. And the persistent shortage of money, the failure to pay the soldiers, and the debilitating falls in the value of the currency all added to the difficulties of supply. Although there is no reason to doubt the serious intent of the government in building up the authority of the *commissaires des guerres* and in backing that authority with the full rigor of the law, they needed a measure of good luck if their reputation were to survive intact. When things did go wrong, their failure was so very public. In the Year II, for instance, there were serious failures of provisioning, both in food and clothing.

Among the men of the Drôme, fighting in the Army of the Moselle, were many who were ill-shod, reduced to tattered rags, and attacked by vermin.[18] Under the Directory there were frequent reports of poor-quality food dumped on the armies by unscrupulous suppliers: gangrenous bread at Ax, rotting meat at Epinal.[19] In every case it was the *commissaire* who was held to be responsible. Whereas his successes passed relatively unnoticed, failures of supply led to shrieks of denunciation and torrents of abuse.

Foodstuffs were, of course, the most pressing priority, the area where a failure of supply led to the most obvious hardship, to begging and looting in the surrounding countryside, to damaging disputes with the local community, and to disillusionment and desertion from the ranks. In order to guarantee the smoothest possible flow of provisions, the government gave its *commissaires* sweeping powers; they could buy supplies away from local markets, wherever they could find them; where the owners expressed a reluctance to sell, *commissaires* could, on their own authority, order the goods to be forcibly seized; and when no transport was available locally, they were authorized to requisition sufficient horses and carts to get the food to its destination. Defective convoys could be rejected and the produce confiscated; suppliers who tried to cheat the armies by offering short-weight or spoiled merchandise could be severely punished by the courts.[20] But the problem of supply stretched far beyond the provision of basic rations. It was the duty of the *commissaire,* for instance, to ensure that the men in his care were kept warm so that they might avoid the illnesses and fevers which so often decimated the ranks of eighteenth-century armies. Hence, tents had to be waterproof, adequate quarters had to be found for those who were billeted at private homes, and stocks of firewood had to be available when they were required. For villages which had troops imposed on them, the consequences could be very serious. At Tournoux in the Basses-Alpes, for example, the establishment of a military camp proved a source of endless squabbles with the army authorities. A communal forest was near where the army was encamped, and the villagers had depended on the forest for generations, not only for wood supplies but also for protection against possible avalanches. But the troops, too, had need of the wood to provide them with a strong defensive position and to serve as a source of heating. Their interests and those of the villagers were incompatible.[21] And however much the government might be sympathetic to the villagers' case, it could not ignore the needs of its armies or risk arousing the soldiers' resentment against local people. Cold and demoralized troops were not just ineffective soldiers, they were potentially undisciplined and dangerous. At Avignon in the Year V, a shortage of wood led to rioting and disorder in the barracks, as the men burned and looted the building, ripping out anything that would burn and leaving around them a scene of utter devastation.[22]

Weapons were constantly in short supply. No army could fight without arms and ammunition, but in 1793, France's armories were small, artisanal units of production which were poorly equipped to supply the Republic's soldiers. The productive capacity that had sufficed in the ancien régime could not hope to cope with the demands of the *levée en masse*. Besides, France could not even rely on all its old arms factories because the invading forces had destroyed the armory at Maubeuge and threatened to put Charleville out of action, while the federalist revolt in Lyon led to the temporary loss of the Saint-Etienne Armory. The desperate situation left French troops without the weapons they required for their defense, and the Jacobins resorted to desperate solutions, amounting in fact to the nationalization of the arms industry.[23] The Committee of Public Safety itself took over the organization of arms production in Paris, making use of the scientific skills of men like Monge and Berthollet and the organizing capacity of the clubs and sections to construct open-air forges in the streets and squares of the capital. New foundries were established in a score of provincial towns and cities, and several thousand workers, selected from among the married men who had been excused military service, were requisitioned for the manufacture of weapons.

In the field, too, *commissaires* and deputies commandeered local foundries both for the supply of firearms and for their repair. Even small gunsmiths in provincial towns risked being taken over, family firms like Rougier's workshop in Gap, which was employed to mend guns and bayonets for the Armée des Alpes. In the Year II, Rougier found that he had become an employee of the state and that his workers had been requisitioned for state service; when five of them wanted to leave to return to their homes, the army withheld its permission, arguing that they were forbidden to leave without military authorization.[24]

The provision of powder for the army's muskets was equally urgent because the supplies in the government's magazines at the beginning of the war dwindled rapidly and there was considerable alarm lest they run out altogether. Again, the Committee handled the shortage as a national emergency which put at risk the success of the armies and the lives of the men. Because there was no chance of importing saltpeter used for making the gunpowder France required, an act of national mobilization was necessary if sufficient supplies were to be found.[25] The powers of the state administration responsible for munitions—the *régie* established by Turgot back in 1775—were substantially increased, the law of August 28, 1793, placing at its disposal all the soil in the country which might contain deposits of saltpeter and encouraging exploration and research. The results were encouraging; new deposits were discovered in departments from the Indre-et-Loire to the Vaucluse, and individual householders responded to an appeal to search their cellars and outhouses. To encourage their zeal, the government paid for the saltpeter brought in to its depots; to educate the people in the best means of extraction, salaried agents were sent into the popular quarters of Paris to hold informal classes in the techniques involved. Once again the Jacobins were relying heavily on the patriotism and revolutionary commitment of the *sans-culottes,* as both individuals and sectional committees threw themselves enthusiastically into the task of searching cellars and separating the precious substance from damp and rotting earth. In all, some sixty sectional workshops were established, producing fifty thousand pounds of saltpeter every ten days for the nation. The armies were thus able to surmount what could have been their most critical area of shortage, largely by ad hoc measures of popular mobilization. Such enthusiasm, of course, was of short duration; it did not survive the fall of Robespierre. By the Year VII, the minister of finance was complaining that saltpeter supplies were again falling below the army's requirements, and he blamed the shortfall on the cupidity of the *salpêtriers,* the low price paid by the state, and the unprecedented levels of demand which had been created by an extended war.[26]

The supply of uniforms presented the government with an equally severe challenge, especially once the original tunics and breeches provided by local communities as part of the recruitment process had become ripped and worn. The armies' difficulties stemmed partly from inflation, but in any circumstances enormous costs would have been involved in issuing new uniforms to several hundred thousand men. In 1792, indeed, communes kitting out volunteers had frequently complained that the uniforms placed an insupportable burden on local taxes, and many had recourse to forced loans from their more prosperous citizens. For example, a little village in the Seine-et-Marne had to find more than 236 livres in order to clothe a single soldier.[27] Once they were incorporated into their units, the men became, of course, the responsibility of the Ministry of War, which had to find both the funding and the sources of supply for hundreds of thousands of jackets and trousers, shoes and stockings, shirts and collars. Suppliers were not always easy to find: there was no precedent for state orders on this scale, raw materials were themselves scarce or of poor quality, and, unlike arms manufacture, there was no attempt to nationalize the clothing trades. And although firms were invited to apply for a share in the military market, the government's reputation for poor payment, and its insistence that manufacturers accept paper currency, meant that military supply could appear a somewhat unattractive proposition. Under Bouchotte, much of the work was channeled through public workshops set up in the sections of Paris, an arrangement which had a clear political appeal for the Jacobins, but which also allowed for greater control and accountability. Work was allocated through *commissaires* appointed by the sections, who distributed orders so that each seamstress registered in the section could be guaranteed her share. It was a solution that was seen to be fair, and one which took account of local political pressures. It had less to do with guaranteeing effective supply.[28] Still the complaints flooded in—of· political favoritism by the sections, of idleness and disorder in sectional workshops, and of poor-quality garments which caused discomfort and misery to the troops. They, as always, were the ones who suffered, from uniforms that did not permit easy movement in battle, from rough cloth that tore easily, and from supply failures that left them dressed in rags, exposed to the elements, and unable to change their clothing for months at a time. Damp and fetid uniforms merely added to the dangers of fever and to the rampant spread of scabies.

The provision of uniforms proved a recalcitrant problem, one which was still far from solved when the first conscription dramatically swelled the ranks of the armies in the Year VII. But at least regular channels of supply had been established, and government *commissaires* knew to whom they could turn. The more desperate expedients of the early years, like the reuse of garments taken from the bodies of those who had died in hospital, were thankfully surpassed.[29] So with the supply of footwear for the troops; the most serious shortages threatened in 1793 and the Year II, when the first mass armies were assembled. Again, the government could not contemplate nationalizing shoemaking and had to rely on the good will of individual *cordonniers* up and down France, a good will that could not be assumed while payment was made at the rate laid down by the maximum. Leather was expensive and in short supply, and the army soon discovered that many of the boots that were delivered to them were of poor quality and unable to stand up to the rigors of military life. In 1793, the situation in many of the armies was critical: stocks were running out, and the rate of consumption of footwear was alarming even the government's own agents. Replying to Duquesnoy, on mission with the Armée du Nord, Carnot could offer little but sympathy, suggesting that the troops might be asked to wear wooden clogs—the traditional footwear of the peasantry in many parts of France—until fresh supplies of boots could be found.[30] But, once again, the Jacobins showed that they were prepared to take a highly interventionist line to alleviate the misery of the soldiers. In *brumaire* of the Year II, Bouchotte ordered that every shoemaker in the country must supply his town council or section with five pairs of boots every ten days for each journeyman and apprentice in his employ; the boots would be paid for, and the leather for them supplied, at the price established by the maximum. For a limited period during the winter months of 1793–94, as a crisis measure to ensure that the troops were decently shod, Bouchotte further demanded that cobblers work only for the armies, devoting their entire productive capacity to the needs of the war. It was a valiant effort to deal with an insuperable problem. In *ventôse* of the Year II, Cellier was still writing from the Nord that the shortage of footwear was causing outrage among the men. "Most of them still go barefoot, they do not even have clogs; there are angry murmurs in the ranks, and they are afraid that they will still be in this state when the campaigning season begins."[31]

In each area of supply, it would seem, the revolutionaries offered two distinct solutions: stopgap measures to overcome the immediate crisis and a more considered administrative solution which alone could serve the needs of a long campaign. The collections of hunting rifles and family trips to the cellar which characterized 1792 and 1793 soon gave way to forges and mines; collections of shirts and bedding from the richer members of the community or the use of property sequestrated from émigrés were replaced by more secure sources of production. Whereas enthusiasm could resolve an immediate problem, it could not be maintained over a period of many years, and the government recognized the need for a regular supply service staffed by squads of specialist workers selected and requisitioned for the service of the armies. Like the soldiers themselves, workers in key industries were given no choice, as the armies requisitioned large numbers of metalworkers, gunsmiths, and locksmiths to man the new workshops established in the rear of the armies. Such requisitions were largely local affairs. At Saint-Gaudens, for example, all the workers and artisans living in and near the town were called up in June 1793 to man a repair depot that had been set up for the rifles and muskets of the Pyrénées-orientales.[32] Likewise, the Revolution called up large numbers of transport workers—carters and bargees, drivers and ferrymen—who were given charge of military transport and placed under military discipline for the duration of the war. Although recruiting officers were always suspicious that draft-dodgers would actively seek jobs in the transport industry as a means of avoiding active service, the government quickly accepted that transport workers were just as necessary to the success of the armies as those who fought in the ranks. The fear that the armies would be cut off without essential supplies was too intense, the specter of famine and deprivation too devastatingly real. From March 1793, the Convention specifically exempted from service all carters and drivers who could provide evidence that they were engaged in military provisioning, an indication of the high priority given to their work.[33]

Military transport required more than men, however; it also required large numbers of animals. Horses were already in short supply because of the needs of the cavalry; in *vendémiaire* of the Year II, the Convention ordered a requisition of forty thousand cavalry horses, holding town councils responsible for finding animals of adequate size and strength. Horses were invaluable; too, for military transport, but the government quickly found that they were in terribly short supply. Besides, any attempt to requisition horses was met with recalcitrance from peasants, who deeply resented having to part with their most treasured possession. It was not only horses, of course, which the army desperately

required. Moving bulk supplies behind army lines, carrying
weapons to the front, evacuating the wounded from the battlefield—these tasks presented considerable logistical problems, especially in the mountain territory of France's Alpine and Pyrenean
frontiers. Carts had to be requisitioned from peasants whose living
had already been made more precarious by the loss of sons and
farm servants to the army. Mules were more valuable than horses
in mountainous terrain, and oxen were in regular demand for pull-
ing heavy loads. These, too, had to be requisitioned, and practical
considerations dictated that once again the full weight of these
requisitions fell on the departments closest to the war fronts. In
the Hautes-Alpes, for instance, a detailed commune-by-commune
census of farmyard animals was drawn up, listing each peasant by
name and enumerating each individual animal and piece of equipment. For the canton of Ribiers—one rural canton chosen at
random from the census return—there were "thirty-nine horses or
mares and 201 mules used for work in the countryside and usually
also for ploughing, 322 donkeys for transporting manure, wood
and soil, and thirteen carts used for the same purposes."[34] Peasants
could ill afford to lose their animals, and the requisition of livestock was often far more bitterly resented than the recruitment of
their sons; in acts of individual or communal defiance, many
horses and mules were hidden from the authorities. Yet the army's
need for such animals was overwhelming. Rations had to be cut,
and soldiers went hungry when draught animals were unavailable.
In the Spanish war it proved impossible to evacuate the wounded
because of a shortage of carts, and the army was reduced, in
desperation, to asking its own soldiers to provide animals from
their family farm in return for an immediate period of leave and
the promise of a job in military transport when they returned.[35]
Again, a desperate supply crisis required desperate solutions.

Although the government devoted much money and effort to
ensuring that the armies were adequately fed and clothed, its
concern for the welfare of its soldiers extended into other fields,
too. In particular, the physical health of the troops was a matter of

consuming interest both to legislators seeped in the philosophy of the Rights of Man and to political leaders appalled by the devastation caused by infections and fevers in eighteenth-century regiments. It is true, of course, that army doctors were under strict instructions to prevent and report malingering; just as young men often sought to avoid service by claiming imagined ailments or by inflicting self-mutilation, so illness was a favored route by which a soldier might seek a break from the armies and gain a few weeks at home with his family. But most of the illness that doctors encountered was all too horrifyingly real, as fevers and dysentery scythed through the battalions in the Nord and on the Rhine. Few members of the Assembly in 1791 disagreed with the premise that the debt society owed to its soldiers was "le plus sacré" of its many obligations, or that it was the government's duty to provide the best available medical care for those who were wounded or who fell ill in the nation's service.[36] For the sick, this involved the guarantee of a hospital bed and medical attention. For those so badly wounded that they could not remain in the army, it implied the provision of a pension or some other form of security for their old age. And for all soldiers, for all who risked their lives in the revolutionary cause, it meant security born of the knowledge that the state would offer an assured level of support for their widows and dependents. These ideals were widely shared by revolutionary politicians, who believed that as a citizen, the soldier was entitled to the care as well as the gratitude of the nation.

Although these noble sentiments seemed at times to stand in glaring contrast to the fate which actually befell sick and wounded soldiers, massacred on the battlefield or left to die on carts by the side of mountain roads, there is no denying the concern of the revolutionaries to improve the standard of care available. The scale of the war quickly outstripped the existing capacity of France's military hospitals, making new initiatives a matter of considerable urgency. But what new initiatives? How best could the state cope with thousands of wounded and dying soldiers? How could it conjure up medical services sufficiently close to where they were required? The solution which commanded the widest support, both among generals and politicians, was for the state to build or designate special military hospitals, for the use of the army alone, in which military discipline could be maintained and desertion discouraged. But that was also the most expensive of the options available, requiring the expenditure of millions of livres on new or converted premises. A second solution was to allocate a proportion of the wards or the beds in ordinary civilian hospitals for military use, a cheaper remedy and one which had the advantage of providing care locally for the sick and wounded. The soldiers themselves generally preferred this, not only because they could enjoy a more relaxed regime while they were recuperating, but also because it eliminated a tiring and sometimes deadly journey of many miles to the nearest *hôpital militaire.* The convoys carrying the injured back from the front line were known to be an added source of death and misery, as men weakened by wounds and numbed by pain were tossed around on open carts. When two sick soldiers died on such a convoy near Rethel in the Year II, for example, both the local people and their comrades from the Armée des Ardennes accused the army of neglect and called angrily for vengeance.[37] For those less seriously ill, there was a third possibility. The army accepted that, where the strain on hospital beds was too great, those men whose homes were less than sixty miles away might be allowed to return to their families to be tended. Although there was always a risk of desertion, their chances of making a full recovery were higher in their own homes.[38]

Many of the military hospitals opened during the Revolution were former monastic buildings seized as *biens nationaux* and hastily converted for the use of the soldiers. Among the local population they did not enjoy a very high reputation, for the institutions were seen as a dangerous and unwelcome source of contagion that had been artificially dumped on their community. Although all eighteenth-century hospitals were viewed with suspicion and mistrust, military institutions seemed particularly sinister; they were shut off from the rest of society, rather like prisons; they often appeared to have a tragically high death rate, particularly in towns close to battle zones; and some among them were dark and pestilential breeding-grounds for disease. At Mâcon, for instance, inspectors found the former abbey of the Carmelites to be "insalubrious, inconvenient, and cramped," and so recommended its closure and the transfer of the wounded to the town's civilian hospital.[39] More graphically, Dugommier described to the Convention the pitiable conditions that prevailed in the military hospitals at Perpignan. Disorder reigned everywhere he looked; the wards were not closed, the spaces between the beds were unwashed, and the administration and staff seemed incapable of looking after the building. He reported that "the most revolting filth, on sheets, on nightshirts, on the bodies of the patients, breeds disease instead of destroying it." And he concluded that in such conditions the most robust health would be ruined in a matter of days, and that "the unfortunates who went there in the hope of restoring their health simply languished and ended up leaving behind what small part of their lives remained."[40] Further back from the frontiers conditions were often better, the work of the hospital staff more relaxed. At Limoges, for instance, a town well removed from the battle zone, the local *hôpital militaire* treated ordinary ailments as well as war wounds, and although most of its patients were seriously ill, their recovery rate was very high.[41] There was a sense, indeed, in which military hospitals could even be regarded as privileged institutions in what was a perilous period for the hospital service in France; unlike their civilian counterparts, military hospitals enjoyed the right to requisition the linen and equipment they required from local monasteries and from the properties of émigrés. In the straitened financial climate of the revolutionary years it was a concession that proved invaluable.

There remained, however, a yawning gulf between the intentions of the legislators and the conditions which applied in military hospitals up and down the land. Many of them complained of staffing problems, pointing out that they were overwhelmed by the number of patients whom they were being sent. The qualifications of those who did work in military hospitals are not in doubt: the records of a hospital like Verdun show that the senior medical staff—physicians, surgeons, and apothecaries—were men of considerable experience who had devoted their lives to military medicine.[42] But they suffered serious shortages, especially of qualified chemists, which led the government to place all pharmacy students, as well as doctors and surgeons between the ages of eighteen and forty, in a state of requisition for the service of the armies.[43] There were also constant complaints of a shortage of trained nursing staff, the *infirmiers* without whom they could not function. The recruitment law did not exempt *infirmiers* from service and drained the military hospitals of good workers who were just as necessary to the armies as the soldiers they became.[44] As the demands of war increased, so the resources of the hospitals became more and more stretched, with serious problems of supply reported on all sides. Everyday consumer goods like vinegar and olive oil were impossible to find; drugs and medicines were not delivered; there were shortages of sheets and linen, beds and mattresses. At Gap, for instance, where many of those turning up for treatment were so ill that they could barely survive the journey, the hospital was forced to turn them away because it had no mattresses and no straw. Weeks passed before the straw was delivered, and the efficiency of the hospital was seriously undermined.[45]

For the army, the greatest advantage of special military hospitals for its men lay in the degree to which it could still control their lives. Soldiers remained under strict military discipline; their freedoms were curtailed, their diet regulated, their visits supervised. The regime in some of these hospitals took controls to exaggerated lengths, with sick soldiers waiting in line outside the administrator's office in order to be allocated a bed.[46] But, to the army's obvious relief, they remained soldiers during the period of their treatment, soldiers who could be called to account if they abused the confidence placed in them. In civilian hospitals, by

way of contrast, few constraints could be imposed, with the result
that some of the troops earned a reputation for drunkenness and
horseplay that destroyed the smooth running of the institutions
and put the men's recovery in doubt. Wards were turned into
wrestling arenas and gambling dens by troops relieved to be freed
from the ardors of the army, and where large numbers of men were
billeted on a hospital—as happened frequently in cities close to
the frontiers—public order could be placed at risk. Venereal
patients, in particular, earned a reputation for causing wanton
disruption in the hospitals to which they were sent, whether by
acts of high-spirited hooliganism or by their debauched behavior
with local prostitutes.[47] Putting troops in civilian hospitals was
hardly an ideal solution, either for the army or for the local
population, who in many cases found themselves excluded from
their own town hospitals as a result of the huge influx of patients
from the regiments. It was, however, a necessary solution in that
it was often the only way that medical attention could be obtained
at short notice, and the government spent large sums of money to
refund local hospitals which had cared for the military. Payments
might come late and in devalued currency, but at least soldiers
remained a higher priority than the civilian sick, and the hospitals
which cared for them had more chance of recompense.

The concern shown for the physical welfare of the troops extended also to their psychological well-being because the army
was well aware of the damage to health and morale caused by
mental depression. The problem of depression, of homesickness
and nostalgia sufficiently serious to be seen as a medical condi-
tion, was common to all eighteenth-century armies, but the vast
numbers of men involved and the huge distances covered by
individual regiments ensured that the damage inflicted by *mal du
pays* reached unparalleled proportions during the revolutionary
wars. Even the generals recognized that there was a difference
between nostalgia, gnawing at men's souls and destroying their
previously robust spirits, and other, lesser ailments. As Marcel
Reinhard has shown, epidemics of nostalgia could do incalculable

damage, not only to isolated individuals, but also to whole battalions of recruits. Men fell sick and wasted away; they lost all
appetite for life; they became a prey to fevers and debilitating
contagions. To make matters worse, it was a difficult ailment to
treat because doctors were unsure what proportion of it was
physical rather than mental. Like all exiles, soldiers easily became
homesick, especially because so many of them were young lads
away from home for the first time in their lives. Periods of
boredom and inactivity could bring on fits of nostalgia, as could
the everyday sights and sounds that revived memories of familiar
landscapes: the sight of terraces of vines along the Rhine, or of
mountain pastures in the Alps; a first glimpse of the Mediterra-
nean for Breton boys for whom home was the sea; a day's march
under open skies with scudding clouds that recalled one's childhood back in the Ile-de-France. An hour spent over a bottle with a
cousin or a brother as garrisons changed, or the sound of a half-
forgotten patois somewhere deep in Central Europe, and young
men who had shown every concern for the defense of the Revolution would turn their thoughts to home.[48]

Contemporary medical opinion was agreed that the character of
the war made the problem worse, especially the insistence on
personal service from young men who had no taste for soldiering
and the abolition of the regional character of the units in which
they served. As for the armies, they did what they could to meet
the reasonable requests of their men. They recognized that young
peasant boys were particularly prone to miss their families and
friends, and they fully understood the degree to which soldiers
were deprived of female company. As in most armies, therefore,
official attitudes to prostitution were more than a little ambivalent. The political leaders might speak in high moral tones of the
damage caused to French fighting strength by the "plague" of
prostitutes that followed the armies. The Convention even tried to
clean up the camps in April 1793: "useless" women were to be sent
home immediately, including soldiers' wives who were given 5
sous per mile to see them on their way. Battalions were limited to

four laundresses to wash the men's linen.[49] But such draconian measures had little effect on the ground. In practice, the armies tolerated the presence of prostitutes and camp followers, at least until they became nuisances to the community at large or threatened to unleash syphilis epidemics among the troops. And when controls were introduced to restrain the gaggles of women who were such a feature of garrison towns, these controls were generally motivated by fear of disease rather than by any puritanical revolutionary concern for morality. Military commanders had every interest in ensuring that their soldiers were given a modicum of creature comforts wherever this was compatible with the basic discipline of regimental life. In the same vein, they listened to many of the requests to serve with other lads from the same village. When soldiers in the Basses-Alpes in 1792 asked to be reassigned to the same regiments as their friends, for instance, the generals agreed, on the grounds that "the force with which the request was made led us to fear the consequences of a refusal, of which the least would have been large-scale desertion."[50] And they recognized the seriousness of the disease, treating sufferers with unusual care and attention. In 1793, when Jourdeuil was trying to reduce the rate of desertion in the Armée du Nord, he forbade all medical leave except for one single illness, "nostalgia or *mal du pays*."

There were other aspects of military welfare which no government of the revolutionary period could afford to ignore. Most notably, they had to face the problem posed by large numbers of war veterans, men too old or too broken by war to be easily reintegrated into civilian life. If the state had an obligation to the young who were engaged in the service of their country, that obligation could not stop when a soldier was killed or seriously wounded. Veterans demanded fair treatment, and the new status attached to soldiering made it difficult for the government to refuse. At the same time, those still serving in the battalions in Spain or Germany pressed for assurances about the security of their dependents back in France. After so many wars during the eighteenth century, the problem of sick soldiers and impoverished widows was not a new one: what was new was the demand that the state should equitably and evenhandedly treat those who had died or lost limbs in its service. If there had been military pensions under the Bourbon monarchy, they had been grossly weighted in favor of the higher-ranking officers, who had often enjoyed inflated gratuities while ordinary infantrymen had been reduced to begging and vagrancy. Revolutionary governments could not allow such blatant injustice to continue unchecked. Pensions rapidly assumed a new importance among the priorities of the state, and from 1792, a series of new and radical measures were taken to try to ensure that those who had suffered in the cause of the Revolution were not condemned to new suffering and neglect on their return to civilian life.

From 1793, the basis on which military pensions were paid was radically reformed. The sums to be paid to those wounded in action and forced to give up soldiering were now calculated in proportion to the degree of incapacity which they had suffered rather than to the rank they had occupied. Although inflation soon overtook the actual sums allocated, the principle that underlay pension policy was clear to all: those soldiers who were rendered unfit for further action were to receive 15 sous per day; those who had lost a hand or an arm were to receive 20 sous; those who had lost the use of two of their limbs were to get 500 livres per year.[51] Widows, too, were guaranteed pensions at a level determined by the length of their husband's service, but from *prairial* of the Year II, the law was rewritten to give them and their dependents flat-rate pensions that would guarantee a basic level of wellbeing to all. Throughout the period the Convention showed enormous interest in the plight of its servicemen, issuing law after law to take account of new circumstances or to care for those who had previously been excluded from the pension provisions. From June 1793, for instance, in cases in which a man's career was ended by serious wounds, where he had been blinded or had suffered amputation, it was decreed that he should be given an honorary promotion to the rank of *sous-lieutenant* and rewarded with a lieutenant's pension.[52] Of course, those engaged in active fighting were not alone in suffering wounds and incapacities in the cause of revolutionary France. In *nivôse* of the Year II, the same benefits due to volunteers and their dependents were extended to those who worked for the armies in an ancillary capacity, as carters and grooms, blacksmiths and armorers. For many, such a measure meant the end of a long period of insecurity. On 27 *nivôse* II, for example, the rule was used to pay pensions to the wife and child of the unfortunate Mergé, critically injured while working as a carter for the Armée de la Moselle when he was kicked in the stomach by one of the horses in his charge.[53]

The reformers turned their attention, too, to the residential care offered to veterans, to those too ill to return to civilian society, or those who found themselves on their discharge without either a home of their own or relatives prepared to look after them. Again the Revolution sought to remove privilege from the few and open up such care to those who most needed it. The Hôtel des Invalides in Paris was transformed from its ancien régime function as a center of noble privilege into a model community that would cater to some four thousand veterans chosen in accordance with need rather than rank. The regime in the hospital was reformed to be equal for all, and from 1793, men pensioned off after serious injury were offered the choice between a pension and a residential place in the Invalides.[54] The aim, once again, was to match provision with need and human suffering, and that in a country where social policy was still in its infancy. It was a highly laudable objective, and if it failed to achieve all that the revolutionary leaders hoped it was not for a lack of effort. In the Jacobin months alone, some twenty-five laws and decrees ordered and redistributed aid to soldiers and their dependents. But the size of the pensions bill became too unwieldy for the faltering economy of the 1790s, and obligations that had been solemnly entered into could not always be honored. Nor was the administrative apparatus always equal to the task of collecting and adjudging thousands of individual applicants, each with very different personal circumstances. Even the raised expectations created by new laws and decrees could cause distress: the opening of the Invalides, for example, resulted in an unbridled spate of optimism, with local councils all over France dispatching sick, crippled, and half-starved veterans to seek their fortune in Paris.[55] Under pressure of inflated numbers and deflated resources, the Directory struggled to keep the system afloat. Pensions remained a high state priority, as they were bound to do after several years of war; but the concern to be fair to all was progressively sacrificed to economic realism.

If Paris were to secure and maintain the loyalty of the troops, these measures were the least that could be offered, the least that would suffice to calm the doubts and quell the anger of the men. For government was obliged to demonstrate its continuing commitment to the welfare of the troops and its understanding of their legitimate fears. This was especially true of the many peasant boys incorporated in the armies, whose strength and youth were sorely missed on the family smallholdings and who risked poverty and proletarianization if they were deprived of the opportunity to build up small farms of their own. It was for this reason that much of the revolution's social policy focused on the special problems of the countryside. The grant of assistance payments in the *grand livre de bienfaisance nationale* of the Year II was specifically linked to the problems of agriculture, with charity reserved for country dwellers and denied to their urban counterparts. And in September 1793 young men serving in the armies were encouraged to think that they could hope to gain landholdings even though they were absent for long years from the village community, since the law gave the families of serving soldiers special priority in the distribution of émigré property. In practice this measure often ran into crippling problems of communication and bureaucratic muddle. But at least it was testimony to the goodwill of government, to the determination to ensure that the sacrifice of a generation of young Frenchmen did not pass unrewarded.

Of course there was an element of political calculation behind all these measures to improve the quality of life in the ranks. Provisioning and pensions were vital in raising military morale and in cementing loyalty; in this respect the social legislation of the Convention can be seen as an integral part of its programme of military reform. The work of the *commissaires des guerres* was also, in its way, political, part of a diffuse campaign by the government to demonstrate to the men some of the more palpable benefits of the cause for which they were fighting and dying. The fact that the ordinary infantryman would be given medical care for his wounds in the same conditions as his officers had a profound propaganda value in an eighteenth-century army, just as the soldier who knew that there was a pension to save his wife from poverty or his children from degradation might be expected to fight more single-mindedly for the national cause. Like changes in tactics, like reforms to restructure the armies, like the distribution of political newspapers, measures aimed at improving the lot of the troops had a distinct political purpose. It could never be forgotten that the men in the French battalions were also individuals whose hopes and grievances must be listened to. As long as soldiers were citizens, capable of holding and expressing opinions, their views and their concerns would remain matters of considerable consequence for those in government.

6

THE SOLDIERS AND THEIR WORLD

H OW DID THE MEN WHO SERVED IN THE REVOLU-
tionary armies react to the reforms carried out in their
name? How closely did they correspond to the idealized
image of the volunteer that government tracts and military man-
uals painted? How far, indeed, did the French succeed in their
avowed aim of changing the fundamental psychology of the individual soldier? These questions are central to any assessment of the
character of the army during the revolutionary years; yet they are
difficult ones to answer because they involve some appreciation of
the mentality and everyday attitudes of men whose very presence
in the armies necessarily reduced their freedom of expression.
More, it is true, is known about the views of the officers: it was
they who tended to write journals or leave memoirs, and it was
they who were most likely to leave some record of their activities
in the clubs and popular societies of the towns through which they
passed. Of the rank and file, however, far less is known. Drawn
principally from the popular classes of French society, they were
often illiterate and seldom left records for posterity. Few wrote
journals of their travels, and those who did were often unrepresen-
tative in their Republican zeal or their enthusiasm for army life.[1]
The majority would never have considered that their feelings or
reactions could be of the least interest to others.

Many of them, however, did send letters home to their families,
letters which for most soldiers provided the only link with the life

they had left behind. These letters are not the perfect means to grasp the soldiers' mentalities, even if there was little army censorship and few seem to have felt seriously restricted in criticizing the army's routines. Conditions were not ideal for encouraging a regular and lucid correspondence. Many of the letters were written in conditions of great discomfort, in moments snatched from guard duty or in the cramped surroundings of a hastily constructed encampment. Literacy rates were low, and mail services infrequent. Often the letters were dictated to one of the few men in the regiment able to read and write, who would become a public writer for the others, rather in the manner of those scribes who still set up their stalls in the markets of the Balkans. The others would pay him for his services, generally by buying him drinks, and a crisis would ensue if he were subsequently to be killed or wounded in battle.

The letters themselves were often stereotyped, relying on the same standard formulas, for soldiers had little experience in letter writing and would often become tongue-tied with embarrassment when the moment arrived. Where they gave details of battles and military maneuvers, they tended to repeat blindly what they had been told by their officers. Or else they would wildly exaggerate their own role, or their bravery, or the dangers they had faced. For the military historian, seeking to recreate the details of a particular encounter, they provide little of value. But for the historian interested in mentalities, trying to understand the feelings and responses of ordinary soldiers, they can be an unexpected source of interest because they discuss with an all-consuming passion the routine and the banal, the quality of everyday life which was of only passing concern to politicians and military reformers. The letters dwell at length on the soldiers' fears and anxieties, on those reactions they dared not divulge in the regiments but which they knew that their parents would understand and often share. Most important, they were the only means of direct communication between the frontier and the village, allowing for the exchange of views—and sometimes for bitter altercation—between the soldier and his family, between military values and those of civilian society. Hundreds of these letters survive, both in printed collections and in the archives, and in a direct, often rather innocent way they allow us to enter the psychological world of the soldier during the revolutionary wars.[2]

The picture that emerges is satisfyingly diffuse, littered with admissions of human weakness as well as with declarations of loyalty and Republican valor. The Jacobin portrayal of the soldier of the Year II was not a purely propagandist invention: there are among these letters repeated declarations of faith by men deeply committed to the ideal for which they were fighting. They wrote with conviction about the justice of their cause, describing the courage of their fellows in battle and taking pleasure in the scent of victory over the armies of tyrants. The attitude of Joliclerc, a peasant boy from the Jura, is typical in this regard, his ardent patriotism underpinning his entire approach to the fighting. As he pointed out to his parents, his life and his faculties belonged not to him, but to the Nation; and he urged them not to shed any tears for him, not to regret the day when he left to join his regiment. Rather, he explained, they should rejoice, for "either you will see me return bathed in glory, or you will have a son who is a worthy citizen of France who knows how to die for the defense of his country."[3] In similar vein, a volunteer from the Indre, Gabriel Bourguignon, wrote in the Year II that he thanked heaven for the victory which they had just been granted. He would, he exclaimed, "rather die a hundred times over than concede an inch to the enemy. Our cause is just; and we shall defend it as we have always done, to the very last drop of our blood."[4] These are just two of many examples of an ardor that went far beyond what was expected of young soldiers being blooded in their first campaign. Of course they had listened to the ritualized propaganda offensives launched at them, and the language of that propaganda found an echo in their writing. But such repeated and effusive declarations of patriotism cannot all be dismissed as stereotyped conventions. Among the first volunteers, in particular, were many who relished the role in which they had been cast.

Others demonstrated their zeal through idealized accounts of the military engagements in which they had taken part, battles in which the enemy had been made to learn a sound Republican lesson. Often these have less to do with the details of the battles than with the sheer, undiluted pleasure of finding oneself on the winning side. One volunteer from the Deux-Sèvres, recounting a recent victory over the Prussians on the Rhine, made no attempt to disguise his pride in the achievement of his unit. They had, he crowed, fought "like lions. . . . Our brigade, unaided, has raised the siege of a fortress defended by five thousand Prussians and nine cannon, a fortress perched on the side of a mountain, up which we had to crawl on all fours."[5] Even the prospect of embarking on a campaign that might lead to victory could result in a mood of excited anticipation. In *messidor* of the Year II, for instance, Louis Godeau, a schoolteacher from the Loir-et-Cher who was passionate in the revolutionary cause, reported that 150,000 men were about to be sent to invade England. The invasion, he felt sure, would be the turning point of the war, for the civilian population would be certain to rally to the cause of liberty, and the fighting would be over after a short and decisive campaign.[6]

If such letters are deeply imbued with patriotism, they must also be read with a certain caution. Men like Godeau believed inherently in the justice of their cause, but they also believed what their officers told them, especially on tactical matters, and they could be terribly naive. Besides, even in the Year II, there were reasons other than patriotic fervor for applauding victory on the battlefield. Like any eighteenth-century army, the soldiers of the Republic dreamed of the booty and plunder which they assumed as their due, and victory could also be assessed by the treasures it uncovered. Writing from Valenciennes in 1792, the volunteer Alexandre Ladrix took pleasure in the defeats French forces had inflicted on the enemy in the Nord, but what pleased him most was not the 142 prisoners they had taken, but the booty they had acquired: grain and foodstuffs and army horses which would be auctioned for the benefit of the troops.[7] For some, the hope of victory could be directly equated with the expectation of food and drink. One soldier, encamped at Landau, looked forward eagerly to the rich pickings which would come with victory. They were, he said, just waiting for the Army of the Moselle to make a strategic breakthrough in order that they might march in themselves, "when we hope to harvest the corn of the Palatinate where we have in the past drunk such excellent white wine."[8] Or again, an apparent enthusiasm for the war could conceal an even greater enthusiasm for peace; the same treaty which imposed a revolutionary victory on Europe would also release the troops from the continued fatigues of army life. Many of these men had signed on in the optimistic belief that hostilities would be over after a single campaigning season, and as the war dragged on, they found it harder to conceal their longing for a return to a normal civilian existence. A French victory would mean security, the comforts of family life, the end of a long nightmare. Some wanted more, most notably a vestige of vengeance for the loss of the best years of their lives. Godeau, for example, gleefully reported in the Year III that a peace treaty was imminent and that he now wished to see those who had bayed for the shedding of innocent blood brought to justice in their turn.[9] He would be bitterly disappointed, but so were the many soldiers who thought that a peace treaty would automatically end the war and lead to their own liberation. When peace came in 1797, it meant little more than months of aimless waiting in muddy, unsanitary camps. As Ladrix wrote from Treviso, "We are finally enjoying peace, but we are enjoying it so little that we would rather have war; at least in war you only have to die once."[10]

Some of the soldiers were, of course, more single-minded in their devotion to the Revolution and all its works. Their loyalty stemmed from more than simple patriotism; they were committed Republicans, worthy pupils at the army's *école du jacobinisme,* and they exalted in what they saw as the essential morality of their cause. "The war which we are fighting," wrote Pierre Cohin from the Armée du Nord, "is not a war between king and king or nation and nation. It is the war of liberty against despotism. There can be no doubt that we shall be victorious. A nation that is just and free is invincible."[11] Such men accepted at face value the army's propagandist accounts of enemy maneuvers. The enemy was perfidious and ruthless, burning French villages and putting civilians to the sword. And woe betide any French soldier who fell into their hands. In August 1792, Favier, from Montluçon in the Allier, explained to his parents that the Austrians were trying to terrorize the soldiers as well as the civilian population of the East. "Volunteers who are captured bearing arms are hanged. The monsters think they will frighten us by such means, but they are mistaken, we shall merely do our utmost to prevent them from taking us alive."[12] But of all their enemies, the most ruthless and unprincipled were, of course, the Vendeans, whose cruelty knew no bounds and who showed no respect for the most basic rules of war. Louis Primault, from the First Battalion of the Deux-Sèvres, had the misfortune to be sent to the Vendée in 1794. He described to his sisters, at home in Parthenay, just what fighting against them implied: "The brigands are not the sort of men who will fight a war as we do; they gather in groups of ten or twelve and follow a main road from the protection of trees by the roadside. If they see three or four poor volunteers who are unarmed or who are coming back from hospital . . . they appear and try to kill them to take what possessions they have; that is the sort of master-stroke we expect of them."[13]

Those who served in the Vendée and who suffered from Vendean attacks were soon persuaded that Vendeans were not as other soldiers. Joliclerc, like many who fought against them, described the aftermath of treachery and massacre when the troops found their comrades butchered by the wayside. Anger mingled with Republican indignation: "We shall go in with a rifle in one hand and a torch in the other. Men and women, all will be put to the sword. All must perish, all except little children. These departments must serve as an example to others that might wish to rise in rebellion."[14]

The view was widely shared that those who took up arms against the Republic should expect no mercy. In the Vendée, Turreau, the general in command of the Armée de l'Ouest, proclaimed to his troops in January 1794, that because they were in rebel country, they had orders to raze villages to the ground, burning all property and putting all living souls to the sword. It was a draconian command, sparing neither women nor children, and some of the soldiers did have qualms about carrying out a policy that involved such needless slaughter. Girardeau, a sergeant with the First Battalion of the Gironde, expressed the feelings of many when he wrote that, amid the burning and killing, "what was saddest was those poor little children."[15] But others carried out Turreau's instructions with a relish that smacked of blood lust. At Les Epesses, after having all the men shot, Amey ordered that the ovens be lit, and the women and children of the village were thrown to the flames. As the gendarme Graviche reported, "the cries of these miserable souls so amused the soldiers that they wanted to carry on this game. Once there were no more Royalist women to throw, they turned to the wives of true patriots."[16]

The desire for vengeance was not confined to the rebels of the West. It extended also to those implicated in the various federalist revolts which threatened to plunge France into civil war during the summer of 1793. There could, for instance, be no excuse for the leaders of the revolt in Toulon, who had handed over the city and its port installations to the enemy and had patently weakened France's position in the war. Hence when Toulon fell to the Republican forces in the autumn of 1793, the armies followed—with interest and often little tolerance—news of the repression which ensued. The Toulonnais were traitors who had put the armies' safety at risk, and they should expect no more indulgence than the Vendean insurgents. In the opinion of one young Savoyard, the betrayal of Toulon was simply a symptom of the visceral royalism he has encountered throughout the south of France. "The further we progress into the Midi," he opined, "the more we find that public opinion is rotten to the core; down here they don't speak of patriotism any more, it would seem rather that they want to see the return of the King, and the red-white-and-blue of the Republic are replaced by the yellow and green colours of Artois' livery."[17] Others were less interested in explanations than they were in retribution. When Toulon fell, one of the Republican soldiers described the scene that followed, with his general lining up the population and demanding to know which of them had "sold their city and betrayed their country." In all, he said, there were around two hundred "who were immediately shot."[18] More vengeful was another soldier who had taken part in the siege, Jean Sallé, a corporal from Auxerre. He reported approvingly that "at present we are occupied every day with the task of shooting the aristocrats; not a day passes but fifty or a hundred of them are executed. They fall to shouts of "Long live the Republic!"[19]

In like manner defeats could be explained by the prevalence of treason in high places, in the general staff or among those counter-revolutionary officers who had been subverted by Lafayette or Rochambeau. Especially in the months following Dumouriez's well-publicized treason in the North, the more rabid Republicans in the army were bent on a veritable witch-hunt among their commanding officers. When their lines were almost overwhelmed at Landau, one volunteer from the Indre explained that the traitors had been uncovered at the very last moment, that disaster had been averted only because "the Supreme Being unmasked their crimes."[20] For many Republican soldiers, indeed, the Dumouriez affair marked the political turning point in the war, the moment when they realized the need for eternal vigilance in the ranks of the army itself. Favier, deeply shocked by what he had heard, believed that the mentality of the soldiers had undergone a marked transformation in the wake of Dumouriez's defection, for Dumouriez had been regarded as one of the saviors of France. "Whom can we trust now?," Favier asked in some despair. "I no longer have any doubt that our defeats, the indiscipline that reigned in our army, the disorder, the most frightful looting, the panics that made our soldiers run away, that all our misfortunes have been provoked by him and by him alone."[21] It was a convenient fiction, and one that helped promote political education in the ranks. The trial and punishment of officers who failed in their duty left a particularly sharp impression on the minds of the soldiers under their command. When, for instance, a cavalry officer was condemned to death at Perpignan for dereliction of duty in 1794—he had allowed fifty of his men to be taken prisoner in Spain—he was guillotined in front of the entire army. Jean Massip, a young soldier from Saint-Ybars (Ariège), wrote a graphic description of the execution. "We were," he told his father, "assembled around the guillotine, some twelve thousand of us, to see him beheaded, but it was soon over, both the execution and our thoughts on the matter."[22]

Some soldiers sang the praises of revolutionary policies, not just as they affected the armies but in other spheres as well. They wanted change in every area of public life and were impatient to see the enemies of the Revolution dislodged from positions of influence. Thus the sight of the former seigneur returning to dine in what had been his château filled one volunteer with revulsion; while another complained that the region where he was posted "is full of aristocrats of all kinds, while priests are encouraging a high degree of fanaticism."[23] Priests were sometimes singled out for denunciation, although generally for specific offenses which outraged Republican morality. Leclerc, for example, a sergeant-major stationed in Strasbourg, related with great venom the story of a refractory priest who had been corrupting the citizenry. The priest had been discovered disguised in women's clothing, clutching the paraphernalia of his former office. Both he and the two women who had been sheltering him, added Leclerc with a certain relish, had been guillotined for their crimes.[24] The disdain in which émigrés were held would seem to have been fairly widespread among the troops, especially inasfar as they were seen to be aiding the cause of the enemy. And there was a certain rather Jacobin enthusiasm for using terror as an instrument of state against the Revolution's enemies—or at least against enemies that caused particular offense to the troops. Not surprisingly given the vagaries of supply, those who were suspected of hoarding foodstuffs or of cheating the soldiers of their rightful rations were savagely denounced. Likewise, the troops showed an understandable anger when local peasants and shopkeepers refused to accept the assignats with which the men were paid. In Metz, one soldier told how a currency market had grown up around paper money, how he and his comrades, on their arrival in the city, were accosted by Jews offering to buy or to sell assignats for a 20 percent commission. In the eyes of the troops, this contemptible form of commerce speculated on their poverty and their vulnerability, and they wanted tough judicial measures to stamp it out.[25]

But such opinions were scarcely widespread, even in the summer of the Year II. Indeed, expressions of strongly Republican views are very rarely articulated in the personal correspondence of the troops; they were primarily restricted to Jacobin militants who joined the army with political as well as military ambitions and to some of the young officers who made a career in the revolutionary battalions. If large sections of the rank and file shared these opinions, they were discreet in doing so. And certain points of Jacobin dogma clearly caused widespread unease, even among those who were fighting in the revolutionary cause. For each soldier who denounced the treachery and fanaticism of the clergy, for example, there were several to express their private reservations about the wisdom of a policy of out-and-out dechristianization. Boys from deeply Catholic backgrounds found it very hard to understand the Revolution's obsessive crusade against the Church and were reluctant to associate themselves with acts of gross impiety and sacrilege. Young Oriot wrote from the hospital in Reims to his father in Colombey-les-Deux-Eglises expressing his distaste for the profanity he saw around him. In the cathedral of Reims and in all the churches in the town, he noted disapprovingly, saints were taken from their niches and thrown to the ground. Saint Rémy, the patron saint of Reims, had been seized from his reliquary and—the emphasis is Oriot's—*buried;* impious hands had ripped off his garments, "which were as fresh as the day when he died, but which fell away to dust as soon as people sought to grab hold of them."[26] In contrast, there is a note of joy in this letter from Sergeant-major Dumey to his mother at Verlinghem, near Lille, written when he discovered that the period of religious persecution was over: "The holy religion which our forefathers have professed for so many centuries is beginning to restore its altars, struck down by the impious and wicked hands of those monsters who overwhelmed the human race with their iron yoke. Already a large number of towns have dismissed the lying priests who have been deceiving them, to bestow their confidence on more worthy ministers of the Almighty."[27] For Dumey, like many others, there was no longer a conflict between his duties as a citizen and his beliefs as a member of the Catholic Church.

If few of the soldiers were themselves highly politicized, many appear to have been influenced by the example of others—of their commanding officers, or of the deputies sent on mission to the armies, men whose exploits and personal courage often left a deep mark. The new spirit of equality within the army allowed officers and men to come into regular contact, and the soldiers were often positively impressed both by the bravery of their commanders and by their unexpectedly approachable demeanor. In some ways the troops' response was the traditional response of ancien régime armies. They would identify with their units and would defend the honor and reputation of their leaders. One soldier wrote of the poor morale which resulted from having three different generals within the space of a few months; another of the uplifting effect on spirits of their commander's speech on the eve of battle; and when the commanding officer of one battalion left to take up a post elsewhere, sixty of his men promptly deserted.[28] There were even instances of feuding among the soldiers of different regiments, leading to animosity, violence, and, on occasion, to murder. A good example of this is the bitter feud which erupted between two regiments serving with the Armée du Nord in the Year IV. The insults and provocations rapidly multiplied: a volunteer had received a saber cut following a drunken brawl; an officer had been ambushed by men from the other regiment; a captain had had a large sum of money stolen; finally, a soldier from the same regiment had been set upon and left to drown in the Yssel. It was all terribly traditional, a feud about identity and honor that could have happened at any time during the eighteenth century. And it is a salutary reminder that once men had been incorporated in their units, traditional rivalries and competitive instincts could prove more powerful than all the political education in the world.

Nor should it be imagined that all the young men who found themselves in uniform accepted their fate with courage and fortitude. Many, of course, did, and the carefree bravura of the revolutionary troops was to become one of the great clichés of military historiography. But not all approached their first hail of bullets with equanimity; not all were the gallant, swaggering heroes of military legend. Very often the letters they wrote to family and friends—as opposed to the public statements the politicized few sent to their clubs and town councils—told a very different, rather faltering story. The first experience of battle could be deeply traumatic, and the more honest among the men were not afraid to admit the fear and panic they had felt. A young soldier from the Meuse wrote, after a day-long battle in which the French had taken the town of Arlon, that when he had seen the first troops fall dead and wounded around him, he had been terribly afraid. "Our sergeant then gave us some brandy; he told us not to be afraid, to take our courage in both hands; but when I then saw him fall to the ground, I was not singing; I waited my turn, I saw the shells and the bullets coming straight at us."[29] Death was ever-present in the battalions, and it would have been a foolish man who pretended that the sight and smell of death did not affect him. As

the war intensified, indeed, soldiers recognized that their continued good health, even their continued survival, was very much
a matter of luck. Many of those who looked forward to returning
home to see their parents or to hold their newborn brothers and
sisters added that this milestone assumed that they would not be
killed in the meantime. Their units often took heavy casualties,
and these inevitably included boys from their own villages, deaths
that affected the survivors most deeply. The loss of a friend—of a
fellow villager who shared the same culture and spoke the same
comforting dialect—was almost as personal as the loss of a brother
or a cousin. René Jendry, from Simplé in the Mayenne, was
himself in the hospital when a close friend died. He did not spare
his parents the gruesome and heart-rending detail. "He died,"
said Jendry, "the most terrible death you can imagine, for he
suffered dreadfully; for more than a week he could neither see nor
talk, and he was unable to recognize anyone."[30]

Some admitted quite frankly that they hated army life and that
they bitterly rued the day they had signed on. As campaign
followed campaign, weariness and exhaustion took their toll. Or
they dreamed of settling down in civilian life and regretted wasting their best years in the military, dismissing their initial enthusiasm and flush of patriotic fervor as the passing follies of headstrong youth. Nostalgia, the *mal du pays* so rightly feared by army
commanders, sapped their sense of commitment just as it undermined their physical health. Thus soldiers would enquire about
the crops and the family vineyard, their memory jolted by the
sight of peasants toiling in the fields of the Rhineland or Northern
Italy. They asked about the flocks and about the success of the
annual lambing. Or their thoughts turned to the village church,
and they expressed the hope that mass was still being said as it had
been when they had left or that the church bells were still in their
customary place.[31] In short, the men wanted reassurance that
there would still be a familiar landscape for them to return to, if
indeed they did return, and a role which they might fill within
village society. Jean Dascin was one volunteer who quickly had

second thoughts. After a year in the army he admitted that he had taken an unwise decision; he found he had no taste for soldiering and wanted, above all else, to settle down in his native Ariège. For him, the decision was doubtless made simpler by the fact that he had found a girl whom he wanted to marry, and he was naturally anxious lest the army deprive him of all chance of a normal family life.[32] Dascin's was a common enough experience during the campaigns of the Year II and the Year III, but it was by no means universally shared. With the passage of time there would be others who acclimated to army routine, becoming accustomed to military discipline and gaining much-needed reassurance from the male sociability of the mess. After eight years of soldiering, for instance, Louis Godeau felt that he knew no other life. He explained to his parents that although he very much wanted to see them, he had no desire to leave the army for good, even after all the suffering and carnage he had lived through; the prospect of being unemployed in civilian life frightened him, and even the possibility of a job, a teaching post in the local school, was not sufficient to offset the feeling that civilian life would be strange and distant, without the safe, familiar norms which gave meaning to his daily existence.[33]

The unhappiness experienced by many of the soldiers shines through in their concern for the future of their younger brothers, lads one or two years younger than themselves who would in their turn have to submit to the lottery of the *tirage*. Some, it is true, delivered moral homilies about patriotic duty and urged their siblings to find the heart for war. But they were, from the government's viewpoint, disturbingly few. The numerous enquiries about the following year's levy and about the numbers demanded in local villages concealed a touching concern for the welfare of younger brothers and childhood friends. And even those who, whether from patriotic instincts or from a desire to reassure their parents, declared themselves well satisfied with military life, would often advise their brothers to find a stable job in the local community or to look for a replacement. Joseph Rousseau, from

Châteauroux, expressed relief on learning that his brother had found a job in the town, not just because it would bring some money into the household, but because he had convinced himself that, with the recruitment season around again, the brother too would have been taken by the military.[34] It was a natural enough reaction from men who had lived through so much misery and degradation. Even those who had accepted to serve as *remplaçants* might go to considerable lengths to dissuade their brothers from following in their footsteps. When one such man, Bardin, wrote to his brother from the Armée des Côtes-de-Brest in the Year II, he had two urgent questions on his mind. First, had his brother received the payment due to him from the family of the man whose place Bardin had taken? And second, very tellingly, what papers should Bardin fill in to ensure that his brother would not have to follow him into the army?[35]

This ambivalence toward the life they led is also shown in the mixed attitudes of many soldiers toward those of their fellows who had avoided the draft or who subsequently deserted from their regiments. Some, like Joliclerc, were openly contemptuous of young men sheltering in the safety of administrative postings or living openly in their villages, free from any harassment by the gendarmerie. The inequity of the situation offended and outraged them.[36] But others were reluctant to condemn. They recognized the risks involved in the deserter's way of life and painted a bleak picture of the fate that awaited them if they were caught. Some were honest enough to admit that they, too, had toyed with the idea of slipping off home or had been tempted by the freedom which desertion seemed to offer. Where they had been stopped by the authorities, like three lads from the Meuse in the Year II, their response was not to express contrition, but to imply that next time they would take more careful precautions.[37] Desertion, in the eyes of many soldiers, was not a crime to be condemned out of hand, but a viable means of escape, and one which had been the resort of discontented troops from time immemorial. Besides, few parents rushed to condemn their sons for seeking to return to the farm, and the men who did escape detection were usually assured of a warm welcome when they arrived. Some parents, seeing other youngsters walking about freely in the community and angered by the sacrifice still expected, went rather further, putting moral pressure on their sons to defy the law and return home. This could leave the young man in an impossible dilemma because parents often resorted to emotional blackmail, implying that a failure to desert meant a lack of concern and filial piety. Louis Godeau was one soldier who resisted such blandishments, but it was not easy. "Each letter that you write to me breaks my heart," he replied to a particularly insistent request that he desert. "You cite the example of several boys who have returned to their homes by fleeing from their units, living in fear of recapture. As soon as they return home, they are continually harassed and forced to hide in the forests." Was that, he asked plaintively, the fate that they really wanted for him?[38]

Many of the young soldiers in the French regiments were away from home for the first time in their lives, and the pull of family and friends was very strong. Letters from home were read with an all-consuming passion, and long silences between letters brought cries of protest and occasionally of recrimination. Yet the postal services to and from regiments that were constantly on the move were unavoidably accident-prone, so many of the men lost contact with their families, sometimes forever. And the growing reluctance of the generals to grant home leave added to the sense of abandonment and isolation prevalent in the battalions. It was so terribly easy to lose touch, and when no letter arrived, the sense of disappointment could turn to hurt and open resentment. Some blamed the influence of aristocrats in the military postal administration; others, more obviously, assumed that they had been forgotten and written out of their parents' lives.[39] In like vein, family problems—a serious illness, a bereavement, or, especially during the Terror, the arrest of a father or an elder brother—could lead to feelings of despondency and to a hollow sense of helplessness. The soldiers were so very far away, unable to help out on the farm or to bring their daily wage to eke out the family economy. They often expressed anxiety about their families' material conditions, the lack of money and the high cost of food, conscious of the fact that they could no longer play their part in staving off hunger. The very precariousness of their own existence, living from hand to mouth without any assurance of what the next day would bring, would seem to have led many of these youngsters to show a touching understanding for the problems experienced by their parents.[40] Their own insecurity merely underlined their dependence on those whom they had previously taken for granted.

That same insecurity made them seek the reassuring company of their *pays*, of the other boys from home whom they ran across in the regiments. Often they would expressly choose to serve in the same units as their boyhood friends, and even after months of soldiering their closest comrades would be drawn from their own narrow locality. In the unfamiliar world of the camp or the barracks room, other villagers were a rare source of solace. Their talk was of the same fields and the same economic problems, and they were a source of common information, a channel of shared news of people back in the community. A letter to any one of them from a mother or brother would be listened to with keen attention by the whole group, all anxious to hear what had been happening in their private corner of France. And when any one of them wrote home, his letter would be passed from hand to hand within the village and searched for any news it might hold about the welfare of his peers. Within the army, too, such contacts were jealously guarded. When regiments changed over, or when they passed close to one another in Germany or in Italy, soldiers would seek out their friends and break a bottle together; and when the new levies were announced they would enquire which of their fellows had been designated to join them. Even in sickness and death it was more than likely that it would be a friend from home who would care for the victim, inform his parents, and carry his sad little bundle of possessions back to his grieving family. There was a comfort and reassurance to be gained from such camaraderie which went far to offset the miseries of army life, and even the military authorities were reluctant to break up groups of soldiers who showed such obvious cohesion and fellow-feeling. It was a major impediment to the smooth working of *embrigadement* in the Year II. As one young man from the Ariège wrote in the Year II, they were imbued with a real sense of solidarity, a desire to stay in one another's company. "They have left all of us, our whole company, together, and it is only the officers and the captains who are out of place."[41]

Companionship of this sort helped the individual to reestablish his identity amid the collective anonymity of the army: hence the importance soldiers attached to writing letters, to singing songs, and to those long bouts of story-telling and reminiscence which recalled the traditional *veillées* of French rural society. Their desire for news and the intense curiosity which they showed about one another's affairs were natural enough concomitants of the boredom so many suffered. Life in the regiments during long periods between campaigns could be quite stiflingly dull. Men complained of the long hours devoted to the same routine exercises designed to instil a sense of discipline and to provide an acceptable level of physical fitness. No doubt, as a somewhat demoralized Gabriel Noel readily conceded, the exercises were well designed to achieve those limited goals. But what was their effect on the spirit of men subjected to the same drab routine every day of their lives? Looking at his own lieutenant, Noel found that military training had done nothing to widen his horizons; the man had always been a soldier, knew the training schedules to perfection, but "he knows nothing in the world except that."[42] Likewise, the long march to the front, or the solitary journey to join one's regiment, or months spent in the inactivity of winter quarters, all were periods of emptiness and boredom that increased the danger of homesickness in the ranks. The more imaginative and the more educated among the troops could, of course, make their own entertainment: they could read, they could write to others of their experiences, they could indulge in the simple pleasures of tourism. But for many these were pleasures quite foreign to their peasant upbringing, or activities which were ruled out by an inability to read and write. They dreamed of military action and prayed for the arrival of the new campaign season as the only possible means of breaking the awful monotony of their daily existence.

The boredom and attrition of military life were greatly exacerbated by the physical discomfort the men were expected to suffer. Heat in summer brought lice and vermin, while unsanitary conditions in the camps made for almost permanent epidemics of diarrhea and vomiting. Yet winter could bring extreme cold and deprivations of a different sort; as Claude-Joseph Gillet wrote from winter quarters in Piedmont, soldiering was a hard and unyielding profession when you had to spend hours on guard duty with snow up to your waist.[43] The lack of decent clothing, and especially of fresh linen, added to these deprivations as the troops were forced to work and sleep in the same damp garments. Uniforms became worn and tattered on their backs, the same jackets serving for years on end; shirts and trousers were often stitched together out of rags or patched with whatever cloth came to hand. The men's health inevitably deteriorated. Jean Cordelier, for example, a soldier from Avallon in the Yonne, wrote to his daughter to describe the tribulations of everyday life. It was six weeks, he said, since he had had a change of clothing; for six weeks, he had been forced to sleep in readiness for action, fully dressed and with his kit bag on his back.[44] In such circumstances disease and fevers were inescapable, especially in those camps where men were forced to pile on top of one another for warmth and to sleep two or even three to a bed. Joliclerc, who talked insouciantly of the pair of trousers he had made out of an apron he had found in the Vendée, scoffed at those who asked, somewhat innocently, whether the troops suffered from lice. Was it possible, he asked, not to have them, when the regiment was billeted in a church, three hundred men sleeping in the same building in the most insalubrious of conditions?[45] Some of the soldiers would even have envied Joliclerc the roof over his head to keep out the worst of the rain and cold. Often they had to pitch camp on whatever flat land they could find within range of their battle positions. "We are encamped on ploughed land, in the mud," complained one soldier from the French camp at Longwy in the Year II. More graphically, Gilbert Favier reported that the night they had just spent had been the most unpleasant of the entire campaign: "We were sleeping on a ploughed field which incessant rains had made as soft and clawing as the mud in a pit."[46]

Yet in the opinion of most soldiers it was not cold or even disease which sapped their strength most damagingly, but the shortage of food and nourishment. Nothing was more likely to create unrest in the ranks than the threat of starvation, and the soldiers' letters made constant reference to the rigors and shortages they were forced to undergo. In distant provinces of France, especially abroad, familiar foodstuffs were scarce or seemed unbelievably expensive. Bread, meat, wine, and beer were the necessities of life for the young men of the regiments, and the staples about which they were most prone to complain. High cost led to a steady rumble of dissatisfaction, and shortages were less easy to bear in view of the arduous physical routine the troops' life-style imposed. In the mountains, in particular, the men often found themselves reduced to a single meal each day because rations ran short. "We don't live, we struggle to stay alive," wrote one soldier from the army encamped outside Mannheim. "We are reduced to a daily ration of two pounds of potatoes which have completely rotted and three ounces of dried peas that have been gnawed by weevils."[47] The quality of life was not much better for those troops sent to the Vendée. In a letter from Saumur in September 1793, one man complained that appetites were never assuaged and that the men were always hungry, despite devouring horses, dogs, cats, and even rats.[48] Sieges imposed added strains on soldiers' diet. In the Year III, Pélerin Goiseau, a vineyard worker's son from Auxerre, wrote to his parents from beneath the walls of Mainz that morale had slumped badly and the men were suffering serious deprivation: "For four days we have eaten nothing but vegetables, cabbages and turnips. The Army of the Rhine has now been without bread for eleven days."[49]

Hunger seemed all the more insidious because the individual could do so little to combat it. If his rations were reduced, he could, in theory, make up the difference by buying food locally with his own money, but in practice that was seldom a realistic alternative. The very presence of the army in the local community resulted in shortages and price rises, and the troops were quick to claim that local traders were hoarding and concealing their stocks. Besides, army pay remained lamentably low, was generally paid some months in arrears, and was seriously eroded by inflation. The troops' assignats were, understandably, often refused in local shops, especially when the unit was on foreign soil. And only too often the French themselves had requisitioned or stolen everything of value in the community, reducing everyone—local people and soldiers alike—to new depths of suffering. "Since the armies have been in the area the villages are all completely ruined," admitted one soldier from Sarrelibre, "it is impossible to find anything whatsoever."[50] Further east, in the Palatinate, Rémy Thirion wrote with a compassion that verged on the poetic that the countryside had been systematically stripped of everything of value. "They will remember us for a long time," he said, "since we left them with nothing but the eyes to cry with."[51] Hence the misery suffered by the men was real, and the debts they ran up often sizable. Many of the letters they sent to brothers or parents were little more than thinly concealed pleas for money to help tide them over a period of crisis or to buy urgent necessities they could not afford otherwise. When men faced the sort of grinding poverty experienced in the armies, only gifts of money could serve any useful purpose. Parents had to be told of the depths to which their sons had sunk, and they had to be discouraged from irrelevant acts of indulgence. Jean-Baptiste Daoust, for instance, was less than

pleased to receive a parcel from home containing stockings, hand-
kerchiefs, and cake; only cash could repay the debt he had incurred
in keeping himself alive.[52]

Yet it should not be supposed that army life was one long and
bitter catalog of deprivations, even in the eyes of those forced to
experience it. Day-to-day existence was hard, and the soldiers
were often impecunious, but they were young men in the prime of
life, who could all cite moments of enjoyment and relaxation, of
pleasure and discovery, which had helped brighten their dull
routine. There were the simple pleasures of the table and the local
inn, when they could afford them, which so contributed to the
reputation of garrison towns for being noisy and boisterous. There
were the consoling pleasures provided by the local girls in the
communities through which they passed, to whom, if the men's
writings are any guide, French soldiers were wont to show great
courtesy, even a certain chivalry.[53] There were the unaccustomed
comforts of being billeted on local families, of sleeping in a warm
bed under a solid roof, of sharing a family meal, of being surrounded once again by women and children. Some men became so
well established that they stayed, or married one of the daughters
of the house and became part of a Belgian or a German family.[54]
Even in the darkest moments of the war, the determination to
enjoy life seemed very natural to men in daily contact with injury
and death and often took the form of a taste for revelry and hard
drinking, the most traditional outlet for the men of the regiments. Joliclerc, for example, presents himself as the very epitome
of a carefree and hard-bitten hedonist, refusing to see in his
penchant for wine any hint of irresponsibility and mercilessly
mocking the concern of his peasant mother to save and to provide
for the future. "When I have money," he boasts, "I spend it on
food and drink," the generous and open-hearted response of a man
who has no immediate worries and no desire to accumulate property. But then, he was a committed Republican soldier who saw
his future in the military and had no thoughts or expectation of

returning to the family holding. Property had little appeal for him. He lived for the present, and lived intensely, for the simple reason that in the army there was no promise of tomorrow.[55]

The activities of the soldiers brought them into frequent conflict with the local civilian population. It could hardly be otherwise. The code of values which pertained in the regiments was very different from the traditional values of French rural life. Cautious and suspicious villagers, anxious to protect their lands and their property, found themselves the victims of requisitions, theft, and simple maurauding by hungry and high-spirited soldiers. Men and women concerned for their personal safety found that the army brought dramatic increases in crime, in violence, and in physical assaults. Village morals were outraged by the easy virtue of many of the troops, by the attacks on village girls and the many allegations of rape and indecency, and by the often undignified conduct of the crowds of women who accompanied the regiments, whether as army wives or as camp followers and common prostitutes.[56] Village custom and religious beliefs were assaulted when soldiers, in the name of the French Republic, stripped churches and carried off statues of saints, pillage sanctified with the title of dechristianization. In garrison towns especially, so many circumstances could give rise to raised voices and lost tempers; many of the soldiers were youthful and ill-disciplined, noisy and belligerent, especially when they ran into local youths in bars and country inns. If the brawls which ensued were little different from those which broke out between gangs of town youths or between boys from rival villages after Saturday night balls, the fact that soldiers were pitted against part of the local community did irreparable harm to the reputation of the military. Besides, the army did not always show great tact in its handling of community problems. Where villagers proved recalcitrant, it was always too easy to pull a saber or to threaten instant reprisals in order to get one's own way. The result, in many instances, was mutual incomprehension, with the soldier despising his civilian counterpart for being cowardly and treacherous, while the civilian responded by seeing in every soldier a potential bully who might be expected to put the safety of the community at risk.[57]

With the passage of time this gulf would become more difficult to bridge, as the soldiers grew more professionalized and the ideal of a citizen-army faded into folklore. By the end of the decade the army had become a powerful and largely independent estate which brooked little interference or criticism from civilian sources, a fact that could only have had an important effect on the mentality of the individual soldier. If many among them still dreamed of their *congé* and of a safe return to the farm or the workshop, an increasing number had spent their lives in the service of the French Republic and knew no other culture than that of the regiments. They accepted quite willingly the authority and discipline of the army, and they enjoyed the company of their peers. They gave little thought to the traditional concerns of the young, to marriage and children and a plot of land to farm. They dreamed not of their future demobilization or even of peace, but of recognition and promotion through the ranks. For the ordinary soldier, it was a source of pride to be chosen as a corporal by his fellows, a token of their esteem which he valued and appreciated. For the officer, despite the expense involved, promotion could become an end in itself, and for some a matter of obsessive concern.[58] This in turn had serious implications for relations between military and civilian society. For such deeply engrained military values, a life-style and culture divorced from the rest of the community, guaranteed that men who knew no other trade than soldiering and no other milieu than the army should feel confused and even alienated by the daily concerns of civilian life. They were intolerant of what they saw as the greed of the civilian population and angered by their failure to share the dangers to which soldiers were exposed. They failed to understand the nagging worries of ordinary people about the loss of income through requisitions or of their sons to the recruiting officer. But such incomprehension was not a one-sided affair. Civilians, too, became critical of the abuses and

exaggerated demands of the military, and, especially in the countryside, they came to view the soldiers as outsiders, even enemies,
who represented the interests of Paris and the revolutionary state
and who threatened rather than protected their communities'
traditions.

7

THE SOLDIERS AND THE STATE

I F THE LOGIC OF THE REVOLUTION PUSHED FRANCE
into a European war, so the fact of being at war had important repercussions on the domestic character of the Revolution. Not only were the soldiers at war, but the entire country was
increasingly mobilized in their support. In particular, the process
of militarization which France underwent during the 1790s
changed the nature and ambition of the revolutionary state. With
an army of half a million men at its command, central government
could aspire to greater influence and could enforce its will more
effectively. The state could seek to intervene in areas where ancien
régime governments had held back—in the workings of the local
economy, for example, or in the largely autarchic world of village
politics. This development was quite involuntary: it resulted from
the demands of the soldiers and the economic requirements of war.
A country geared to fighting a long and exhausting war could not
behave in the same way as it had done during periods of peace. It
did not enjoy the same liberty of action, the same freedom of
choice. The declaration of hostilities pushed France ineluctably in
the direction of greater centralization, effectively ending the Revolution's liberal and decentralizing phase of 1789 to 1791 and
changing the whole character of the regime. As Theda Skocpol
puts it, "this act set in motion the processes of government
centralisation and popular political mobilisation that were to
culminate first in the Montagnard Terror of 1793–94, and then in

the Napoleonic dictatorship."[1] And as government power increased, so the powers of the center encroached upon the liberties
that individual citizens enjoyed.

The extent of government intervention was itself largely determined by the needs of its soldiers. It was not simply a question of
ideology, for centralist aspirations remained evident during the
Directory, just as they had been during the Jacobin Republic.
With the extension of war fronts into Italy, Germany, and Spain,
the needs of the army greatly increased, and central involvement
would take many different forms. As troops were marched to and
from the battle fronts, they had to be provided with hospitality
and accommodation, and individual towns found themselves specially designated by the government as overnight stops for the
armies. Where garrisons were imposed for reasons of defense or
policing, they, too, had to be supported by the local community.
Taxes and contributions were required to help pay the army's
spiraling costs, which meant that taxpayers had to be cajoled into
parting with their hard-earned income. Recruitment, likewise,
was too important to be left to local patriotism or local enthusiasms: where communities showed a reluctance to provide men for
the regiments, they had to be persuaded, bullied, and finally
compelled to obey the law. And where that reluctance extended to
matters of supply—to grain and bread, meat and wine, fodder
and straw, mules and horses—again the government found itself
forced to adopt a harshly interventionist line, overruling the
interests of local people and imposing the priorities of the center.
All this may seem very natural, even self-evident, to a modern
reader accustomed to the level of sacrifice demanded by the total
warfare of the twentieth century. But in the France of the eighteenth century it represented an intrusion by the state into the
affairs of local communities that extended far beyond what was
accepted by custom and practice.

Local communities, especially in rural areas, had traditionally
retained a large measure of control over their own affairs, unchecked by either central or provincial government. They had

been expected to pay their taxes to the state and supply their quota of men for the militia, but beyond that there had been little need to refer local decisions to central authority. Parish and community had been the main decision-making agencies in village affairs.[2] With the coming of the Revolution in 1789 there had been a rapid flurry of administrative reform which resulted in the creation of elected municipal councils in each of approximately forty thousand towns and villages; and the insistence—one might almost say obsession—of the early revolutionaries with the principle of answerability ensured an endless succession of electoral consultations at the very lowest level of civil administration. Devolution of responsibility was deemed by many to be the Revolution's most important legacy to local government, the liberation of the people from the stultifying deference of the eighteenth century. And while the insistence on election might be shown to have worked extremely badly—many of those who became mayors in small agricultural and pastoral communities were barely literate and understood little of the complex legislation with which they were inundated—the fundamental message of the early Revolution was clear. Far from wishing to concentrate power in its ministries, it wanted to spread decision taking as widely as possible throughout the community and to involve the people, even at village level, in the running of their day-to-day affairs. Both in the sphere of local administration—through the mayor and his *conseil-général*—and in the administration of justice—in the form of the justice of the peace and the canton—devolution and decentralization were to be assured.

Although the failure of this ideal was not due solely to the war or to the demands of the military, they played a significant part. Tax collection when there was a war to be won could not reasonably be left to illiterate or innumerate countrymen who showed themselves to be incapable of interpreting tax laws. Where army requisitions were at stake, the government had to have men it could rely upon as mayors and *adjoints,* men who could be trusted to deal with official correspondence and to maintain the accurate registers of births and marriages which formed the basis of the military levies. Again, when the moment came for the village *tirage,* it was critical that the mayor should be a man of sufficient caliber to impress his fellow villagers, a man who understood his obligation to the state and did not allow himself to be swayed by considerations of sympathy or friendship. In practice, of course, many fell scandalously short of this expectation. Some were prosecuted for derilection of duty, for forging municipal records or burning incriminating evidence, or for showing favor to friends and relatives. Others, less spectacularly, discovered that the post they had accepted as a largely honorific position in the community had become too arduous and time-consuming; their business interests were suffering; or they were condemned to make enemies among their family and neighbors. By the Year VII, few mayors or municipal officials seemed to have much appetite for the role the government expected them to play. They had become highly unpopular and were even slightly despised for seeming to take the side of the government against their fellow villagers, especially over the vexed question of recruitment. The result was perfectly predictable. After a number of years it became almost impossible to find men of adequate standing in their community who were willing to assume an office no longer seen as desirable or entirely honorable.[3] The viability of the whole democratic structure that had been so carefully created in 1790 was put at risk.

Yet neither the Jacobins nor those who replaced them seemed greatly concerned. In the context of the war, local government had diminished in status and importance. Increasingly, indeed, it had come to be seen as an arm of the central executive, with the mayor and his municipal council as simple cogs in the administrative machine. Generals and ministers now saw efficiency, not democratic answerability, as the principal quality of good administration. They looked to mayors and town councils to carry out the letter of the law rather than to quibble about its effect on the local economy. And since the cause of victory was too important to be put at risk by local scruples or sectional interests, the role which local people were expected to play underwent a dramatic transformation. They were expected to impose and implement central directives. They were given endless bureaucratic chores like taking censuses and drawing up lists of commodities that might be useful to the armies. They were expected to report to the Ministry of the Interior about the state of public opinion in their commune, to warn Paris of possible kernels of opposition or revolt. Thus the contribution of local government became more clearcut and more repressive. Mayors were to police public opinion in their communes and to denounce those who shielded draft-dodgers or connived at tax evasion, who refused to billet troops or cheated on their requisitions. Failure to do so implied incompetence or ill will. In the Basses-Alpes, for instance, the generals commanding the Armée d'Italie repeatedly criticized the local district and communal authorities for not doing enough to help reduce the high desertion levels in the area.[4] Were they not there to help the cause of the nation? Kellermann expressed the view that in mountainous departments like the Basses-Alpes, criss-crossed by soldiers on their way to and from the front, the most essential task for local government should be the maintenance of roads and the building of bridges across the many rivers and torrents.[5] It should, in other words, concentrate on matters which served to ease the movement of the military, matters which served national interests but which were perceived by the local community as being at best rather marginal to their daily lives.

If local concerns came to be treated rather lightly in France itself, they mattered even less in those territories which were either occupied or annexed. Here public opinion could be safely sublimated to serve the immediate military interest, and although the forms of political institutions imposed on France's neighbors varied widely—from direct annexation and subdivision into French-style departments, as happened in Belgium and Piedmont, to the creation of sister states like the Batavian Republic or the Cisalpine Republic—the decisions taken never conflicted with the needs of the army. When military strategy demanded that the newly formed Italian republics should be relegated to the role of international bargaining chips, for example, the diplomats obligingly complied.[6] Either local people were cowed into submission, or power was handed over to the small groups of patriots and Republicans within each country who were already ideologically committed to the French cause. As for the costs of the invasion, they were, as far as possible, to be borne by the grateful populations of the new republics. In September 1793, the Committee of Public Safety admitted as much when it ordered commanders in occupied territory to procure as much as possible of their food and supplies from local sources; and in the following year four *agences de commerce* were set up to accompany the armies, their main task being to take everything that might have a strategic importance and ensure that it was sent immediately to France.[7] Besides these seizures, French agents were to impose taxes and war contributions and to force local communities to contribute toward French military levies. They were to show no scruples or favors; they were, after all, at war, and, as Hoche reminded his divisional commanders on the Moselle, there was only one thing that they should never forget—the fact that they were in a rich country, a country that could afford to pay.[8] For those who tried to refuse, the French reserved a wide armory of punitive devices from billeting soldiers to taking hostages. In the last resort they could simply let their troops loose on the hapless citizenry.

Requisitions, added tax burdens, and forced loans did nothing, either in France or in the lands the French annexed, to improve the public image of the army or to increase respect for the uniform of the Republic. Nor, of course, did the acts of violence and vandalism with which the troops became associated; the distinction between legal requisitions and simple pillage was not always easy to maintain. If civilians were quick to complain about the wrongs they suffered at the hands of a licentious soldiery, their complaints were seldom wholly unfounded. Young men who found themselves miles from home, without responsibilities in the towns where they were stationed, bored and footloose or desperate for instant pleasure before facing another campaign, and generally without the money they needed to buy themselves a few hours of oblivion—there was ample scope for conflict with the local people. Drinks went unpaid in village bars, disputes flared up over money or girls, and the armies left trails of drunken destruction behind them. Soldiers were held responsible for acts of sacrilege against Church property at the height of the Terror; they were blamed for stealing crops and for burning communal woods to keep themselves warm. They could also be astonishingly lacking in sensitivity toward the people among whom they were stationed. In the Roussillon, for instance, the French showed an ill-concealed contempt for Catalan culture and threatened to impose the French language on the Catalans, thus "removing those impure local idioms which debase mankind and alienate their intellectual faculties."[9]

There were, indeed, almost as many causes of conflict as there were disputes or brawls. Nor was it always misconduct by the troops which sparked off animosity: the performance of their military duties could itself antagonize local people. This was especially true where the state used the army for internal policing—work carried out under the Directory by troops assigned to the domestic *divisions militaires*.[10] The units which carried out these policing functions were indistinguishable from those who fought in the armies of the frontier; indeed, in the South they were often units which had just completed a turn of duty in Italy or the Pyrenees. Their mandate was to work alongside the gendarmerie, supporting and supplementing the gendarmes where law and order were threatened with breakdown. They were placed at the disposal of civil authorities to enforce government policy, and were used extensively to track down army deserters and refractory conscripts, to prevent outbreaks of rioting, and to disperse illegal gatherings. From the Directory's point of view, the advantage of military policing was obvious. It removed control from local communities whose loyalty was often uncertain, replacing it with that of an army that had proved itself in putting down popular insurgency in Paris during the Year III. But local people often saw things very differently. And the fact that the army was increasingly used in a policing role against brigands and counterrevolutionaries, many of whom enjoyed tacit local support, led to charges of malpractice and brutality by the forces of order. Such was the level of popular antagonism, indeed, that even some of the generals became alarmed, reminding their men that they should reserve their efforts for the Republic's enemies, and that "the soldiers of liberty should always remember that the nation had provided them with arms in order to protect its citizens, not to oppress them."[11] But the government's aim was that the law should be enforced, not that the soldiers should be loved for enforcing it. Increasingly, that aim could be said to have been achieved. Public opinion could safely be disregarded as the fickle force it was.

The one area which continued to cause embarrassment was recruitment. At no point during the 1790s did the government succeed in persuading the population at large that military service was a duty incumbent upon every citizen. With the introduction of annual conscription in the Year VII, it might be argued that the basis had been laid for a smooth system of recruitment for the future, one that would be recognized as workable and as essentially fair. But that was for the future. The levels of draft evasion and desertion in the Year VII were among the highest of the entire war, with the young continuing to respond by fleeing to the woods, feigning sickness, or offering violence. The problem of disobedience and the connivance of parents, officials, and entire communities remained a serious rebuke to a state which claimed to control the persons of its citizens. Unchecked desertion, sometimes by groups of twenty, sixty, or even a hundred soldiers in a single night, had serious implications for the morale of those left behind. Just as important, the fact that so many young men continued to live at liberty in their communities was a damaging daily reminder that the government's pretensions far exceeded its capabilities. Despite all the innovation of the revolutionary years, large parts of France remained traditional and largely autarchic, impervious to the propagandist appeal of the nation-state. And although it is true that the state now had resources at its command with which to cajole and coerce opinion, it was unable to force on a reluctant peasantry sacrifices which they continued to regard as burdensome and unnatural. With time, many of these attitudes would, of course, change, and the experience of war during the Revolution and Empire would be one of the most important single motors of that change. But attitudes would not be transformed overnight: in the most refractory areas, like the Lozère, popular distaste for personal service survived long into the Third Republic and would be overcome only in the great recruitment campaigns of World War I.[12] The legislation of the 1790s must be seen as a first step in a protracted process of political socialization.

CONCLUSION

PIERRE PERDIGUIER, A CARPENTER FROM THE LITtle village of Morières in the Vaucluse, was one of many young men who volunteered for service in the armies of the Revolution. He served bravely in the Armée d'Italie and was elected by his fellows to the rank of captain. He saw himself as a patriotic citizen whose duty was to defend France and its Revolution against foreign aggression, and when he returned from the wars to resume his trade and bring up his family of seven children, he enjoyed a certain standing, a certain prominence, in his local community. Yet in 1815, at the time of the Second Restoration, Perdiguier was no longer a local hero. His service rendered him politically suspect to the royalists of the Southeast; the fact that he had volunteered was taken as proof that he was a political zealot devoted to the Republican cause, while his promotion only served to convince them that he was a notorious *rouge,* a man of extreme radical views who posed a threat to public order. He and several members of his family were arrested. Even his ten-year-old son, Agricol, was set upon by royalist revelers in the street and attacked and beaten by other children at school. The whole family became reviled and ostracized, treated as social outcasts from a society in which any whiff of Republicanism now caused outrage.[1] Yet the Perdiguiers would seem to have been honest folk, farmworkers and tradesmen who played a valuable part in the life of the community. Their reputation stemmed from one single decision—that of the young Pierre to join the volunteers of Avignon in the revolutionary cause. That single fact was sufficient to label him as a radical extremist, because only radicals of the most extreme persuasion would have dreamed of volunteering in the revolutionary cause.

This was the stereotype of the revolutionary soldier passed down to the nineteenth century, a stereotype which enjoyed wide credence both in France and elsewhere. Twenty-five years of European warfare did much to reinforce it. Besides, the Revolution had, through its relentless propaganda, gone far to create this picture in the first place—that of the volunteer as a committed Republican, a man of principle who opposed tyranny and privilege with the same passion that he reserved for the armies of Austria and Prussia. The volunteer of 1791 marching out of his village with gaiety in his heart and the cheers of his fellow villagers ringing in his ears; the passionate recruit of 1793 scornfully refusing to let his name be entered in the ballot; the soldier of the Year II with the *Père Duchesne* in his knapsack and a continent at his feet—all are integral parts of the image of the revolutionary soldier which the revolutionaries themselves promoted. Theirs was in every sense a revolutionary army, different from every other army that Europe had known.

Others saw that army in a very different light, just as they defined the purpose of the war very differently from the revolutionary leaders. Whether from complacency or from military judgment, the generals of the other European armies of the day were not immediately impressed by the claims of the French for their poorly trained mass armies, unschooled in eighteenth-century battlefield techniques. The Austrian and Prussian commanders remained unconvinced of the military virtues of the pike or the tactical supremacy of the bayonet in close combat. And if in the long term the lessons learned from fighting the French were to bring reforms to every land army in Europe, these lessons were not immediately apparent. Even Prussia, where Stein and Hardenberg

were impelled to introduce root-and-branch military reform following upon defeat at the hands of Napoleon, remained uncon-
cerned by the sight of the French armies of the 1790s. As Gordon
Craig has shown, the Prussian authorities continued to trust in
their own institutions and to distrust, even to patronize, the new
French state. Only in 1806, after rout at Jena and the entry of
Bonaparte's armies into Berlin, did the Prussians come to realize
that there were real military benefits to be derived from a system
in which the individual soldier could feel that his contribution
was appreciated and rewarded. The reforms which followed were
to become a model for all Europe.[2]

In our own century, the Republican and Marxist traditions so
dominant in French revolutionary historiography have felt no
reason to question the nineteenth-century's heroic view of the
revolutionary soldier. Because he emerged from the ranks of the
people, he had every interest in fighting for the cause of the people
in what was essentially a political war. In Albert Soboul's phrase,
"it was not the corporal's baton that got the soldiers of the Year II
to march into battle: they were fighting for their own cause; why
would they have been tempted to desert?" In the same vein Soboul
describes the unique role idealism played in the ranks of the
Republican army: "In the Year II the army of the Republic was a
truly revolutionary army, intimately tied to the popular classes of
society and an instrument of defence for the social and political
conquests of these classes. Its inflexible morale, supported by an
enthusiasm emanating from the very depths of the people, its
exceptional ability to create and reconstitute its officer ranks, to
reform itself and to recover after defeats, allowed it to face up to
the enemy in the most difficult conditions, and then to achieve
victory."[3]

The soldiers of the Republic, in short, were different from the
soldiers who manned the other armies of Europe. They were free
men who could think for themselves, free men who realized the
justice of their cause and who fought for that cause with a new and

burning sense of involvement. And that political element, in fighting a revolutionary war and pursuing a revolutionary goal, was what made them invincible.[4]

How far can this highly idealized picture be sustained? Or must it be dismissed, not without regret, as a colorful and persistent strand of the mythology of revolutionary France? One of the principal aims of the present book—albeit an aim that has sometimes been subsumed rather than explicit—has been to reassess the character of the revolutionary armies, and in particular to examine them through the prism of the individual soldier's feelings and aspirations. To what extent did the Revolution achieve what it promised, the creation of a new kind of army where the rights of man would be respected and traditional authority revised, an army where the private soldier, the volunteer of 1791, the infantryman at Valmy, the fresh recruit of the Year II rapidly trained in arms and thrown into battle, would enjoy the same civil rights and privileges as the officer to whom he was answerable? In what measure can the battalions who served in Belgium or in Italy be seen as truly "revolutionary?"

To be excessively revisionist, to attempt to deny the importance of revolutionary innovation in the military sphere, would clearly be absurd. A great deal was achieved in these years which revolutionized the soldier's lot. The structure of the revolutionary armies was more democratic than any in Europe at the time, with noble privilege ended and military careers thrown open to talent. The infantryman enjoyed the same rights at law as his officers: indeed, for much of the Revolution it was the officer who risked being shunned and regarded as suspect by his political masters. The infantryman had the right to be judged by his peers, and could no longer be beaten and humiliated in the name of an authoritarian and hierarchical military discipline. Recruitment was radically reformed to eliminate unfair discrimination and to compel men from all social classes to make sacrifices in the name of the nation. New tactics were evolved to make better use of the young mass armies which France now had at her disposal. And the government laid new emphasis on questions of pay and supply in an attempt to ensure that the recruit would be given the logistical support he required—support in the form of provisioning, of billeting, of efficient weapons and sufficient ammunition, of care when he was wounded, of pensions for his dependents if he were to be killed. The Revolution, in short, sought to treat the soldier as a citizen who was performing an honorable task in the service of the nation, a task which the rest of the nation had a duty to respect and reward. Even if it often failed badly in this aim—whether through communications breakdowns or administrative inefficiency or, most commonly of all, through financial crises which left the army denuded of funds—the very fact that the soldier was addressed and treated as a privileged member of French society gave him a status and a self-respect which had been denied to the armies of the ancien régime.

The most critical change sought by the Revolution, however, concerned the political status of the soldier. If he were to be a citizen first and a soldier second, he must enjoy the same civil rights as his fellows. And these must include political rights, rights which were universally denied to serving soldiers elsewhere in Europe. Under the Jacobin Republic, in particular, the soldier was encouraged to exercise these rights: he was entitled to vote in elections, to militate in political causes, and to join political clubs and popular sections. He was invited to take part in colorful festivals with a clear political message; to attend ideologically explicit plays in the theaters of local towns; and to read a selection of political newspapers, including some of the most radical papers then circulating among the civilian population. Through speeches and exhortations, songs and military symbols, the government attempted to educate the soldier not just in citizenship but in republican political ideas. And although the political propaganda in the armies might be less explicit after the Jacobins fell from power, it did not disappear. All the governments of the 1790s continued to proselytize among the troops. All sought to use ideology to create close bonds between the army and the state. All

194 The Soldiers of the French Revolution

seemed to believe that their cause would be best served by a politically conscious and educated soldiery.

Yet this picture of a politically conscious army, believing deeply in the revolutionary ideals for which they were fighting, must be treated with a certain caution. Despite the insistence of the revolutionaries that this was what they sought to create, despite the political credos expressed by individual soldiers in their journals and correspondence, there are reasons for examining the concept critically. Did the government really have any interest in encouraging free political thought among the men on whose force it was dependent for its continued existence? Or was not the political message a consistently narrow one, a reflection of the prevailing ideology which would help to cement military discipline in the ranks? Throughout the period there was potential tension between the conflicting aims of ideological activism and political control, between the army as a revolutionary force and the army as an instrument of state. Under the Jacobins, the pendulum seemed to swing in the direction of activism, with soldiers encouraged to denounce their officers for political crimes, even if they did so at the expense of traditional army discipline. Under the Thermidorians and during the Directory it swung back in the direction of authority, as courts showed greater severity over disciplinary offenses and the position enjoyed by the officers was again strengthened. But in neither period was the political arm willing to contemplate any loosening of the ties that bound the army to the state. Control was always more important than ideology; ideology, indeed, must be seen as an important means of exercising control. Inasfar as a revolutionary army must also be an army of the politically aware, it would always be bedeviled by conflicts and contradictions. The least that can be said is that throughout the Revolution the political leadership remained profoundly aware of them.

If the revolutionaries chose to educate the army, it was very largely because they saw politically conscious troops as more dependable in the immediate context of the Revolution. Unlike a purely professional force, they would feel some loyalty to the idea of revolution and would therefore be less likely to be subverted by counterrevolutionaries, royalists, or enemy agents. They would not be so liable to be led astray by their officers or to become subservient to an aristocratic high command. Given the character of the ancien régime army and the Revolution's early experience of treason among the old officers of the line, this suspicion of traditional military authority is easy to understand. At certain moments, indeed—particularly when the émigrés were plotting to invade from Turin and Coblentz and in the months which followed Dumouriez's defection—the suspicion which the political leaders harbored of their military counterparts seemed almost boundless. They feared the ambitions of the generals almost as much as they feared their military strength. They wanted to avoid the dangers of Caesarism, the dangers of a military coup that could allow the generals to assume political control of the state. Against those who argued that military efficiency demanded a more disciplined and professional army, the revolutionaries would point to the political risks involved, preferring to put their trust in generals with a proven political record and recruits drawn from a wide spectrum of French society. Of course these fears had more than a little basis in fact. French officers did harbor political ambitions, as was demonstrated both by the damaging spate of defections in 1792–93 and by Bonaparte's final seizure of power on 18 *brumaire*. But the continued strength of such fears does once again suggest that the purpose of political education in the revolutionary armies was a very limited one, that of containing the ambitions of the soldiery and imposing the authority of the state.

The level of political consciousness had therefore to be carefully controlled. The Jacobins were no more prepared to tolerate the growth of *hébertiste* cells in the Armée du Nord in the Year II than was the Directory to accept the spread of neo-Jacobin ideas in the ranks of the Armée d'Italie three years later. Political expression was firmly circumscribed, and ideology could easily blend into indoctrination. But this in turn leads to further questions. Was the process of political education successfully carried out? Did the soldiers of the Revolution believe what they were told? Did they become truly converted to the ideas they heard repeated all around them? And would they continue to hold these views once they were demobilized into civilian life? In short, did the Revolution succeed in creating a truly revolutionary army, or was it simply an army of enthusiastic young soldiers for whom political indoctrination formed a part of the overall process of motivation and military training?

The answers to these questions must, I think, be less unequivocal and more nuanced than the answers given by Albert Soboul. If it is true that the first volunteers were deeply committed to the Revolution in whose name they served, the men of subsequent levies had seldom chosen to serve and were much less political in outlook. Of course the whole spirit of the revolutionary battalions helped to provide them with motivation and a sense of identity, inculcating a feeling of national solidarity and shared experience, a sense of belonging to the French nation, which had had no counterpart during the ancien régime. The more democratic army structure, the forced camaraderie of long campaigns, the portrayal of the enemy as tyrants and slaves—all played their part in forging that identity. In the Year II in particular, a heady cocktail of military success and political propaganda helped to convince many among them, disoriented and highly impressionable as they were, that their cause was the cause of liberty and revolution. But there is little evidence that many emerged from that experience as committed Jacobins; still less that they were prepared to disobey the orders of their superiors in the cause of the Jacobin Republic. The impact of those long hours of political education by officers and deputies-on-mission would seem to have been severely limited.

If some soldiers talked effusively of the liberties they were bringing to the benighted peoples of Europe and boasted of their republican ideals, they were relatively few in number. Most restricted themselves to discussing the everyday concerns of military life, the taste of victory and the bitterness of defeat, the shortfalls in supply, the weariness and discomfort, and the almost permanent penury which they suffered. From their diaries and correspondence they emerge less as revolutionary activists than as a cross-section of the youth of France, passively accepting the duties prescribed for them. Their reactions extended across the entire gamut of human response, from keenness to apathy, from commitment to revulsion. Many still sought escape through desertion. And if small neo-Jacobin cells persisted in the armies under the Directory, there had been little hint of rebellion when the Jacobin government in Paris was brusquely overthrown. The soldiers accepted the Thermidorian regime with hardly a murmur. As campaign followed campaign, they saw themselves more and more as career soldiers who belonged in the armies and knew no other world. Some gave up all thought of a return to civilian life, dreaming instead of promotion through the ranks, with all the honors and rewards that that might bring and prepared to follow anyone who would guarantee their self-respect. Many, indeed, showed scant regard for the Directors as political leaders of the Revolution, but by then they had arguably ceased to be a revolutionary army, committed to a revolutionary ideal. When Napoleon Bonaparte launched his bid for power, promising an end to chaos and corruption and an honored place for the army in the affairs of the nation, the soldiers rallied willingly to his cause. Brumaire was their *journée,* too.

NOTES

ABBREVIATIONS

A.D.: Archives Départementales, A.G.: Archives de la Guerre (Vincennes), A.N.: Archives Nationales

1. THE REVOLUTION AND ITS SOLDIERS

1. An extreme example is R. Phipps, *The Armies of the First Republic,* 5 vols (London, 1926–39).
2. S. F. Scott, *The Response of the Royal Army to the French Revolution* (Oxford, 1978), pp. 171–74.
3. D. M. G. Sutherland, *France, 1789–1815: Revolution and Counterrevolution* (London, 1985), pp. 270–71.
4. G. Lefebvre, *The French Revolution,* vol. 2 (London, 1962), p. 167.
5. J. Solé, *La Révolution en Questions* (Paris, 1988), p. 237.
6. The work of Albert Sorel is typical of this very Republican approach.
7. G. Lefebvre, *The Great Fear of 1789: Rural Panic in Revolutionary France* (London, 1973).
8. Sutherland, *France, 1789–1815,* pp. 135, 149.
9. N. Hampson, *The Terror in the French Revolution* (London, 1981), p. 5.
10. H. Morse Stephens, *The Principal Speeches of the Statesmen and Orators of the French Revolution,* 2 vols. (Oxford, 1892), 1:276–78.
11. Billaud-Varenne, *Rapport fait à la Convention Nationale au nom du Comité de Salut Public,* 1 floréal II.
12. Stephens, *Statesmen and Orators,* 2:304–32.
13. T. C. W. Blanning, *The Origins of the French Revolutionary Wars* (London, 1986), pp. 205ff.
14. J. Servan, *Le Soldat-citoyen, ou vues patriotiques sur la manière la plus avantageuse de pourvoir à la défense du royaume* (Neufchâtel, 1780).
15. Dubois-Crancé, *Observations sur la constitution militaire proposée au Comité Militaire* (Paris, 1789), a point of view he restated in his *Lettre à l'armée* in February 1793.

16. A. Soboul, *Les Soldats de l'an II* (Paris, 1959), p. 25.
17. P. Goubert and M. Denis, eds., *1789: Les Français ont la parole* (Paris, 1964), pp. 209ff.
18. Soboul, *Soldats,* pp. 25–27.
19. Ibid., pp. 24–25.
20. Scott, *Response,* esp. chapter 2, pp. 46–80.
21. M. Reinhard, "Observations sur le rôle révolutionnaire de l'armée dans la Révolution Française," *Annales historiques de la Révolution Française* (1962), pp. 170–73.
22. Reinhard, "Observations," p. 170.
23. For a fuller discussion, see Scott, *Response,* pp. 67ff.
24. A.N., D§1–16, "Pétitions de militaires et dénonciations d'officiers inciviques."
25. P. Dufay, *Les Sociétés populaires et l'armée: 1791–1794* (Paris, 1913), pp. 24–25.
26. J.-P. Bertaud, *La Révolution armée: les Soldats-citoyens et la Révolution Française* (Paris, 1979), pp. 47–48; Scott, *Response,* pp. 93–95.
27. J. Leverrier, *La Naissance de l'armée nationale, 1789–94* (Paris, 1939), p. 64.
28. G. Bodinier, *Les Officiers de l'armée royale combattants de la Guerre d'Indépendance des Etats-Unis* (Vincennes, 1983), pp. 403–33.
29. Scott, *Response,* p. 109.
30. D. Greer, *The Incidence of the Emigration during the French Revolution* (Cambridge, Mass., 1951), p. 25.
31. For a full discussion of the build-up of legislation against émigrés, see J. Vidalenc, *Les Emigrés français* (Caen, 1963), chapters 1 and 2.

2. RESTRUCTURING THE ARMIES

1. J.-P. Bertaud, *La Révolution armée: les Soldats-citoyens et la Révolution Française* (Paris, 1979), pp. 35–36.
2. A. Corvisier, *L'Armée française de la fin du dix-septième siècle au ministère de Choiseul: Le Soldat,* 2 vols. (Paris, 1964), p. 109.
3. S. F. Scott, *The Response of the Royal Army to the French Revolution* (Oxford, 1978), appendix 2, pp. 217–24.
4. Bertaud, *La Révolution armée,* p. 36.
5. M. Reinhard, "Observations sur le rôle révolutionnaire de l'armée dans la Révolution Française," *Annales historiques de la Révolution Française,* 1962, p. 172.
6. E. G. Léonard, *L'Armée et ses problèmes au dix-huitième siècle* (Paris, 1958), pp. 47–53.
7. Léonard, *L'Armée,* p. 225.
8. Corvisier, *L'Armée française,* esp. pp. 91–100.
9. J. Chagniot, "Quelques aspects originaux du recrutement parisien au

milieu du dix-huitième siècle," in *Recrutement, mentalités, sociétés: Colloque international d'histoire militaire* (Montpellier, 1974), pp. 112–13.

10. For a discussion of army tactics in the eighteenth century, see E. Hublot, *Valmy, ou la défense de la nation par les armes* (Paris, 1987), pp. 48ff.
11. Bertaud, *La Révolution armée*, p. 36.
12. Corvisier, *L'Armée française*, p. 174.
13. A. Soboul, *Les Soldats de l'an II* (Paris, 1959), p. 20.
14. Corvisier, *L'Armée française*, p. 711.
15. Bertaud, *La Révolution armée*, pp. 36–38.
16. I. Cameron, *Crime and Repression in the Auvergne and the Guyenne, 1720–1790* (Cambridge, 1981), esp. p. 73.
17. D. Bien, "La réaction aristocratique avant 1789: l'exemple de l'armée," *Annales: E.S.C.*, 29 (1974), p. 29.
18. Bien, "La réaction," pp. 519–22.
19. C. Achard, "Le recrutement de la milice royale à Pézenas de 1689 à 1788," in *Recrutement, mentalités, sociétés*, p. 45.
20. P. Laporte, "La milice d'Auvergne, 1688–1791," *Revue d'Auvergne* 71 (1957), p. 24.
21. A. Corvisier, *Armies and societies in Europe, 1494–1789* (Bloomington, 1979), pp. 32–36.
22. Achard, "Recrutement de la milice," p. 48.
23. A. Soboul, *L'Armée nationale sous la Révolution, 1789–94* (Paris, 1945), p. 81.
24. Corvisier, *L'Armée française*, pp. 123–25.
25. Soboul, *L'Armée nationale*, pp. 27–31.
26. J. Servan, *Le Soldat citoyen* (Neufchâtel, 1780), esp. pp. 451–58.
27. Hublot, *Valmy*, pp. 66–67.
28. Ibid., p. 57.
29. J. Leverrier, *La Naissance de l'armée nationale, 1789–94* (Paris, 1939), p. 57.
30. Scott, *Response*, pp. 24–25, 191–92.
31. D. Berlemont, "Le militaire est-il un modèle de citoyen? (septembre 1792 à juillet 1794)," mémoire de maîtrise, Université de Paris-I, 1987, p. 6.
32. For a full discussion of the work of the Constituent Assembly in this field, see Bertaud, *La Révolution armée*, pp. 56–71.
33. Scott, *Response*, p. 73.
34. The texts of the laws that are referred to here can be found in A.N., AD[VI] 48, "Droits civils des militaires."
35. Hublot, *Valmy*, pp. 68–70.
36. G. Michon, "La justice militaire sous la Révolution," *Annales révolutionnaires* 14 (1922), pp. 1–25.
37. Bertaud, *La Révolution armée*, p. 158.
38. G. Noel, *Au Temps des volontaires, 1792: Lettres d'un volontaire de 1792* (Paris, 1912), p. 3.

39. Bertaud, *La Révolution armée*, p. 159.
40. Scott, *Response*, p. 179.
41. V. Fanet, "Dugommier d'après sa correspondance," *Carnet de la Sabretache* (1902), pp. 537ff.
42. Dubois-Crancé, *Lettre à l'armée*, February 21, 1793, and *Rapport sur l'embrigadement*, 13 *frimaire* II.
43. Soboul, *L'Armée nationale*, pp. 93–96; Leverrier, *La Naissance*, pp. 70–71.
44. For a full discussion of the respective images of the soldier and the officer presented in the speeches and reports of the Year II, see the *mémoire* by Dominique Berlemont cited in note 31.
45. A.N., AD^VI 48, decree of the Convention dated 18 *prairial* II.
46. A. Meynier, "L'armée en France sous la Révolution et le Premier Empire," *Revue d'études militaires* (1932), pp. 17–23; also Michon, "La justice militaire," pp. 127ff.

3. RECRUITING THE SOLDIERS

1. Chevalier des Pommelles, *Observations sur le recrutement et l'emplacement de l'armée active par cantons et par départements* (Paris, 1789), pp. 4–7.
2. A. Corvisier, *L'Armée française de la fin du dix-septième siècle au ministère de Choiseul: Le Soldat*, 2 vols. (Paris, 1964, pp. 415–18.
3. E. Déprez, *Les volontaires nationaux, 1791–1793* (Paris, 1908), p. 10.
4. L. de Cardénal, *Recrutement de l'armée en Périgord pendant la période révolutionnaire, 1789–1800* (Perigueux, 1911), pp. 49–50.
5. J.-P. Bertaud, *Valmy: la Démocratie en armes* (Paris, 1970), pp. 189–90.
6. For a local example, see J. Delmas, *La Patrie en danger: les Volontaires du Cantal* (Paris, 1902); also Bertaud, *Valmy*, p. 193.
7. A. Soboul, *Les Soldats de l'an II* (Paris, 1959), pp. 69–71.
8. See chapter 6; also J.-P. Bertaud, *La Révolution armée: les Soldats-citoyens et la Révolution Française* (Paris, 1979), pp. 218–24.
9. X. de Pétigny, *Un Bataillon de volontaires: le Troisième bataillon de Maine-et-Loire, 1792–96* (Angers, 1908), pp. 65–67.
10. Bertaud, *La Révolution armée*, pp. 66–68.
11. A.G., Vincennes, X^w 16, list of volunteers for the canton of Aurillac, 1791.
12. A. Crépin, "Armée de révolution, armée nouvelle: l'exemple de la Seine-et-Marne," thèse de troisième cycle, Université de Paris-I, 1979, pp. 66–74.
13. J.-P. Bertaud, *Valmy*, p. 219.
14. A.G., Vincennes, X^w 95, list of enrollments for the District of Versailles, 1792.
15. A.D. Cantal, L202, letter from Mayor of Montsalvy to District of Aurillac, July 8, 1792.
16. Delmas, *La Patrie*, p. 192.

17. A.N., F⁹ 160, minutes of department of Aude, February 18, 1792.
18. Bertaud, *Valmy*, pp. 219–48.
19. *Le Moniteur*, vol. 14, p. 248.
20. Soboul, *Les Soldats*, p. 106.
21. Bertaud, *La Révolution armée*, pp. 85–88.
22. D. Berlemont, "Le militaire est-il un modèle de citoyen?," mémoire de maîtrise, Université de Paris-I, 1987, p. 42.
23. A. Forrest, *Déserteurs et insoumis sous la Révolution et l'Empire* (Paris, 1988), p. 40.
24. M. Giraud, *Levées d'hommes et acheteurs de biens nationaux dans la Sarthe en 1793*, (Le Mans, 1920), pp. 98–99.
25. G. Sangnier, *La Désertion dans le Pas-de-Calais de 1792 à 1802* (Blangermont, 1972), p. 47.
26. A. Forrest, *The French Revolution and the Poor* (London, 1981), pp. 147–48.
27. Forrest, *Déserteurs*, p. 44.
28. Soboul, *Les Soldats*, p. 119.
29. Bertaud, *La Révolution armée*, p. 166.
30. Forrest, *Déserteurs*, p. 47.
31. Crépin, "Armée de révolution," p. 267.
32. Letter of Carnot, Delbrel, and de Sacy, quoted in Soboul, *Les Soldats*, pp. 111–12. See also on the subject of replacement B. Schnapper, *Le Remplacement militaire en France* (Paris, 1968), p. 17.
33. Bertaud, *La Révolution armée*, pp. 138–39.
34. A.D., Seine-et-Oise, series R (unclassified), list of men abandoning their regiments in 1814 (District of Rambouillet).
35. A.G., Vincennes, Xʷ 6, report from District of Saint-Girons, 12 *thermidor* III.
36. G. Vallée, *La Conscription dans le département de la Charente, 1798–1807* (Paris, 1936), p. 15.
37. Vallée, *La Conscription*, pp. 10–11.
38. J.-A. Castel, "L'application de la Loi Jourdan dans l'Hérault," mémoire de maîtrise, Université de Montpellier, 1970, p. 7.
39. Forrest, *Déserteurs*, p. 51.
40. For a fuller discussion of forms of evasion, both semilegal and completely illegal, see Forrest, *Déserteurs*, chapter 3.
41. M. Brunet, *Le Roussillon: une Société contre l'Etat, 1780–1820*, (Toulouse, 1987), pp. 321–32.

4. REVOLUTIONIZING THE SOLDIERS

1. M. Ozouf, "La Révolution française et l'idée de l'homme nouveau," in *The Political Culture of the Revolution*, ed. C. Lucas (Oxford, 1988), pp. 213–32.
2. R. C. Cobb, *The People's Armies* (London, 1987), pp. 22–23 and 159ff.
3. R. C. Cobb, *Terreur et subsistances* (Paris, 1965), p. 98.

4. M. Henriot, *La Révolution en Côte-d'or: le Club des Jacobins de Sémur, 1790–95* (Dijon, 1933), pp. 307–8.

5. P. Leuilliot, *Les Jacobins de Colmar* (Strasbourg, 1923), p. xxx.

6. E. Leleu, *La Société populaire de Lille* (Lille, 1919), pp. 77–78.

7. P. Dufay, *Les Sociétés populaires et l'armée, 1791–94* (Paris, 1913), p. 152.

8. General Herlaut, *Le Colonel Bouchotte, ministre de la Guerre en l'an II*, 2 vols. (Paris, 1946), p. 242.

9. J.-P. Bertaud, *La Révolution armée: les Soldats-citoyens et la Révolution Française* (Paris, 1979), p. 145.

10. E. Maury, ed., *Lettres de volontaires républicains, 1791–94* (Troyes, 1901), p. 11.

11. L.-G. Pélissier, *Lettres de soldats, 1792–93* (Paris, 1891), p. 5.

12. Dufay, *Les Sociétés populaires*, p. 66.

13. M. Kennedy, *The Jacobin Clubs in the French Revolution*, vol. 2, *The Middle Years* (Princeton, 1988), p. 112.

14. A. Chuquet, *Wissembourg* (Paris, 1893), p. 44; P. Leuilliot, *Colmar*, p. 37n.; M. Delarue, "L'Education politique à l'armée du Rhin, 1793–94," mémoire de maîtrise, Université de Paris-Nanterre, 1968, pp. 102–9.

15. J. A. Lynn, *The Bayonets of the Republic* (Urbana, 1984), p. 156.

16. R. C. Cobb, "La campagne pour l'envoi de l'armée révolutionnaire dans la Seine-inférieure," *Terreur et subsistances*, pp. 95–120.

17. Leleu, *Lille*, p. 12.

18. The discussion which follows is largely drawn from the papers of the société populaire held in the Archives Municipales in Lille. See, in particular, the minutes of the society for 1793 and the Year II (A.M., Lille, 18,326 and 18,330), the register of members of the society (A.M., Lille, 18,336), and correspondence with the Armée du Nord (A.M., Lille, 17,954).

19. General Herlaut, "Le général baron Dufresse," *Revue du Nord* 14 (1927), p. 170.

20. Leleu, *Lille*, p. 82.

21. A.M., Lille, 18,229, "Etat nominatif des citoyens composant les différens bureaux de la Société Populaire de la ville de Lille," an II.

22. Cobb, *The People's Armies*, p. 173.

23. A.M., Lille, 17,955, minutes of Société Populaire of Lille, October 7, 1793.

24. Leleu, *Lille*, p. 94.

25. G. Aubert, "La Révolution à Douai: la Société Populaire de Douai," *Annales historiques de la Révolution Française* 14 (1937), pp. 426–27; O. Bled, *Les Sociétés populaires à Saint-Omer pendant la Révolution* (Saint-Omer, 1907), pp. 71–90.

26. General Herlaut, "La républicanisation des états-majors et des cadres de l'armée pendant la Révolution," *Annales historiques de la Révolution Française* 14 (1937), p. 387.

27. Lynn, *The Bayonets*, pp. 162ff.
28. Bertaud, *La Révolution armée*, p. 214.
29. Lynn, *The Bayonets*, p. 279.
30. For a full discussion of political propaganda to the armies, Delarue's thesis is again a most informative source, especially pp. 186–224.
31. J.-M. Levy, "La vertu aux armées pendant la Révolution Française," *Cahiers d'histoire* 12 (1967), p. 359.
32. Lynn, *The Bayonets*, pp. 83, 158.
33. J.-P. Bertaud, *La Vie quotidienne des soldats de la Révolution: 1789–99* (Paris, 1985), pp. 134–37; *La Révolution armée*, pp. 147–52.
34. Lynn, *The Bayonets*, p. 147.
35. A.M., Lille, 18,326, minutes of Société Populaire of Lille, 16 *frimaire* II.
36. P. Courteault, *La Révolution et les théâtres à Bordeaux* (Paris, 1926), pp. 120–50; Delarue, "Education politique," pp. 130–32; J. J. Barbé, "Le théâtre à Metz pendant la Révolution," *Annales historiques de la Révolution Française* 4 (1927), p. 380; Bonnal de Ganges, *Les Représentants du peuple en mission près les armées, 1791–97*, 4 vols. (Paris, 1898–99), p. 307.
37. A. Soboul, "Sur la mission de Saint-Just à l'armée du Rhin," *Annales historiques de la Révolution Française* 26 (1954), pp. 195ff.
38. S. Bianchi, *La Révolution culturelle de l'an II* (Paris, 1982), p. 76.
39. Ozouf, *La Fête révolutionnaire*, pp. 14–40.
40. Delarue, "L'Education politique," pp. 124–25.
41. R. Legrand, "Les fêtes civiques à Abbéville," *Bulletin de la Société d'émulation historique et littéraire d'Abbéville* 24 (1978), pp. 373–426.
42. *La Soirée du camp* 11 (12 *thermidor* II).
43. J. Barada, "Lettres de Joseph Ladrix, soldat de la Révolution," *Carnet de la Sabretache* 8 (1925), p. 108.
44. H. Gough, *The Newspaper Press in the French Revolution* (London, 1988), p. 104.
45. For a detailed discussion of the military press during the Revolution, see M. Martin, "Journaux d'armées au temps de la Convention," *Annales historiques de la Révolution Française* 44 (1972), pp. 567–605.
46. A. Mathiez, "La presse subventionnée de l'an II," *Annales révolutionnaires* (1918), pp. 112–13; Lynn, *The Bayonets*, pp. 126–29.
47. *Bulletin de l'Armée des Côtes de Brest*, esp. issues 26, 37, and 39.
48. *Bulletin de l'Armée du Midi*, issues of September 11 and September 27, 1792.
49. *Argus du Département du Nord: L'Ami Jacques*, issue 6 (April 7, 1792).
50. Martin, "Journaux d'armées," pp. 587–88.
51. *L'Avant-garde de l'Armée des Pyrénées-orientales* (Perpignan, an II); the examples cited are from issues 29 (25 *messidor*) and 32 (9 *thermidor*).
52. *La Soirée du camp*, issue 1 (2 *thermidor* II).
53. Ibid., issue 13 (14 *thermidor* II).
54. Bertaud, *La Révolution armé*, p. 217.

55. D. Berlemont, "Le militaire est-il un modèle de citoyen? (septembre 1792 à juillet 1794)," mémoire de maîtrise, Université de Paris-I, 1987, pp. 123–34.
56. Delarue examines the role of these agents in considerable detail ("L'Education politique," pp. 168–78).
57. J. Godechot, *Les Commissaires aux armées sous le Directoire* (Paris, 1937), pp. 11–32.
58. J.-P. Gross, *Saint-Just: sa politique et ses missions* (Paris, 1976), esp. p. 85.
59. Gross, *Saint-Just*, pp. 191–92.
60. Levy, "La vertu," pp. 360–65.
61. G. Michon, "La justice militaire sous la Convention à l'armée des Pyrénées-orientales," *Annales historiques de la Révolution Française* 3 (1926), p. 39.
62. Delarue, "L'Education politique," p. 55.
63. Lynn, *The Bayonets*, pp. 13–14.
64. Godechot, *Les Commissaires*, p. 34.
65. A good example is the *Journal des défenseurs de la patrie*, published between April 1796 and March 1802.
66. I. Woloch, *Jacobin Legacy: The Democratic Movement under the Directory* (Princeton, 1970), pp. 134–35, 165–69.

5. PROVIDING FOR THE SOLDIERS

1. A. Soboul, *Les Soldats de l'au II* (Paris, 1959), p. 127.
2. R. Devleeshouwer, *L'Arrondissement du Brabant sous l'occupation française, 1794–95* (Brussels, 1964), pp. 119–20.
3. P. Wetzler, *War and Subsistence: The Sambre and Meuse Army in 1794* (New York, 1985), p. xvii.
4. A.N., AD^VI 45, instruction on the functions of commissaires des guerres, *ventôse* of the Year III.
5. R. Werner, *L'Approvisionnement en pain de la population du Bas-Rhin et l'Armée du Rhin pendant la Révolution (1789–97)* (Strasbourg, 1951), p. 597.
6. J.-P. Bertaud, *La Révolution armée: Les Soldats-citoyens et la Révolution Française* (Paris, 1979), pp. 239–40.
7. Werner, *Approvisionnement*, p. 596.
8. A.D., Rhône, 1L843, instruction of commissaire-ordonnateur des guerres of 21st Division Militaire, 15.ii.II.
9. M. Brunet, "Les armées de la Révolution et la population roussillonnaise, 1791–94," *Anneles du Midi* 83 (1971), p. 226.
10. Devleeshouwer, *Brabant*, p. 126.
11. A.N., AD^VI 45, mémoire on commissaires des guerres, 10 *brumaire* II.
12. A.N., AD^VI 45, decree on commissaires des guerres, 16 April 1793.
13. Wetzler, *War and Subsistence*, pp. 269–93, provides an analysis of personal dossiers of commissaires with the Army of the Sambre-et-Meuse.

14. A.D., Vaucluse, 1L344, letter from commissaire des guerres in Avignon to Department of Vaucluse, 5 *thermidor* VII.
15. A.D., Vaucluse, 1L344, letter from commissaire Sartelon in Avignon to Department of Vaucluse, 18 *floréal* IV.
16. A.D., Rhône, 1L843, letters of commissaire-ordonnateur des guerres of 21st Division Militaire, 24.i.II and 1er *nivôse* II.
17. Devleeshouwer, *Brabant,* pp. 143–44.
18. A.G., Vincennes, X^w 30, letter from Niderbaum of 5e Bataillon de la Drôme, 29 *frimaire* II.
19. A.G., Vincennes, X^w 5, letter from municipal council of Foix (Ariège), 16 *thermidor* III; A.D., Vosges, L539, letter from Clément, chef du 37e escadron de gendarmes, 14 *fructidor* VII.
20. A.D., Rhône, 1L844, ministerial instruction dated 4 September 1792.
21. A.D., Basses-Alpes, L224, correspondence on the forest at Tournoux, n.d.
22. A.D., Vaucluse, 1L344, letter from Sartelon to administration of Vaucluse, 14 *brumaire* V.
23. Soboul, *Les Soldats,* pp. 127–43; Bertaud, *La Révolution armée,* pp. 239–41.
24. A.D., Hautes-Alpes, L843, correspondence dated 6 *germinal* II, 11 and 16 *frimaire* IV.
25. Soboul, *Les Soldats,* pp. 144–53.
26. A.D., Hautes-Alpes, L844, minutes of minister of finance on supply of saltpeter, 2 *prairial* VII.
27. J.-P. Bertaud, *La Vie quotidienne des soldats de la Révolution, 1789–99* (Paris, 1985), p. 62.
28. General Herlaut, *Le Colonel Bouchotte, ministre de la guerre en l'an II,* 2 vols. (Paris, 1946), 1:142–67.
29. Ibid., p. 177.
30. Soboul, *Les Soldats,* p. 157.
31. Ibid., p. 159.
32. A.G., Vincennes, X^w 41, requisition order by District of Saint-Gaudens, 24 June 1793.
33. A.D., Rhône, 1L769, decree of Convention of 14 March 1793.
34. A.D., Hautes-Alpes, L915, census of pack animals, cantonal returns for 1792.
35. J.-P. Bertaud, "Contribution à l'étude des transports militaires dans les Pyrénées, 1794–95," *Actes du 94e Congrès National des Sociétés Savantes* (1969), pp. 209–11.
36. A.N., AD^VI 63, projet de décret presented jointly by Comité de Guerre and Comité des Secours Publics, 1791.
37. A.N., AD^VI 63, report from Armée des Ardennes, an II.
38. A.D., Bouches-du-Rhône, L785, decree of 6 *messidor* II.
39. A.D., Rhône, 1L221, report on conditions in military hospital at Mâcon, 1 *pluviôse* II.

40. V. Fanet, "Dugommier, d'après sa correspondance," *Carnet de la Sabretache* (1902), p. 537.
41. A.D., Haute-Vienne, L375, report on military hospital at Limoges, 9 *vendémiaire* V.
42. A.N., AD^VI 63, staff list of military hospital at Verdun.
43. General Herlaut, *Bouchotte*, 1:226.
44. A.D., Rhône, 1L902, letter from adjoint of minister of war to commissaire-général of Armée des Alpes, 24.ii.II.
45. A.D., Hautes-Alpes, L931, letters of 14, 22, and 29 *prairial* VII.
46. A.N., AD^VI 63, report of Boy, chirurgien-aide-major of Armée du Rhin, to Société Populaire in Strasbourg, 4 *pluviôse* II.
47. A.D., Rhône, 1L903, report of comité militaire in Lyon, 2 June 1793.
48. M. Reinhard, "Nostalgie et service militaire pendant la Révolution," *Annales historiques de la Révolution Française* 30, (1958), esp. pp. 1–9.
49. J. Lynn, *The Bayonets of the Republic* (Urbana, 1984), p. 109.
50. A.D., Basses-Alpes, L224, report from maréchal-du-camp in Basses-Alpes, 28 August 1792.
51. A.N., AD^VI 74, law of 8 February 1793.
52. I. Woloch, *The French Veteran from the Revolution to the Restoration* (Chapel Hill, 1979), pp. 83–84; A. Forrest, *The French Revolution and the Poor* (London, 1981), pp. 148–50.
53. A.N., AD^VI 74, decree of 27 *nivôse* II.
54. Woloch, *The French Veteran*, pp. 78–89.
55. A.D., Rhône, 1L921, correspondence on issue of passes to the Invalides in Paris, 1792–an III.

6. THE SOLDIERS AND THEIR WORLD

1. For a discussion of the value of these journals and letters, see J.-P. Bertaud, *La Révolution armée: les Soldats-citoyens et la Révolution Française* (Paris, 1979), pp. 218–24 and 352. Excellent use is also made of soldiers' letters in the same author's subsequent work, *La Vie quotidienne des soldats de la Révolution, 1789–99* (Paris, 1985).
2. E. Picard, *Au Service de la nation: Lettres de volontaires, 1792–98* (Paris, 1914), pp. i–xx.
3. F.-X. Joliclerc, *Ses lettres, 1793–96* (Paris, 1905), pp. 20–21.
4. A.G., Vincennes, X^w 49 (Indre), letter of 26 *messidor* II; Bertaud, *La Révolution armée*, p. 219.
5. A.G., Vincennes, X^w 29 (Deux-Sèvres), letter of 5 *thermidor* II.
6. A.D., Loir-et-Cher, F 2196, correspondence of Louis Godeau, letter of 27 *messidor* II.
7. J. Barada, "Lettres d'Alexandre Ladrix, volontaire de l'an II," *Carnet de la Sabretache* 9 (1926), p. 13.
8. A.D., Indre, L 778, letter of 11 *messidor* II.

9. A.D., Loir-et-Cher, F 2196, letter of 8 *pluviôse* III.
10. Barada, "Lettres d'Alexandre Ladrix," p. 84.
11. A. Pioger, "Lettres de Pierre Cohin, volontaire à l'Armée du Nord, à des membres de sa famille, 1777–1794," *Annales historiques de la Révolution Française* 27 (1955), p. 131.
12. L. Duchet, *Deux volontaires de 1791: les Frères Favier de Montluçon* (Montluçon, 1909), p. 65.
13. A.G., Vincennes, X^w 29 (Deux-Sèvres), letter of 10 *fructidor* II.
14. Joliclerc, *Lettres*, p. 155.
15. G. Pages, "Lettres de requis et volontaires de Coutras en Vendée et en Bretagne," *Revue historique et archéologique du Libournais* 190 (1983), p. 158.
16. Pages, "Lettres de requis," p. 159.
17. F. Vermale, "Lettres à un soldat de l'an II," *Annales historiques de la Révolution Française* 8 (1931), p. 137.
18. Bertaud, *La Révolution armée*, p. 220.
19. M. Demay, "Les volontaires auxerrois de 1792 aux armées de la République," *Bulletin de la Société des sciences historiques et naturelles de l'Yonne* 28 (1874), pp. 577–78.
20. A.G., Vincennes, X^w 49 (Indre), letter of 23 *prairial* II.
21. Duchet, *Deux volontaires*, pp. 93–94.
22. A.G., Vincennes, X^w 7 (Ariège), letter of 1 *germinal* II.
23. L.-G. Pélissier, *Lettres de soldats, 1792–93* (Paris, 1891), p. 5; Pioger, "Lettres de Pierre Cohin," p. 129.
24. Picard, *Au Service de la nation*, p. 48.
25. G. Noël, *Au Temps des volontaires, 1792: Lettres d'un volontaire de 1792* (Paris, 1912), p. 13.
26. E. Maury, *Lettres de volontaires républicains* (Troyes, 1901), pp. 20–21.
27. "Lettres de campagne du sergent-major Dumey de la 8e Demi-brigade," *Carnet de la Sabretache*, 3e série, 1 (1913), p. 612.
28. A.G., Vincennes, X^w 57 (Loiret), letter of 16 October 1792; A.G., Vincennes, X^w 61 (Maine-et-Loire), letter of 14 *frimaire* II; Maury, *Lettres*, p. 16.
29. A.G., Vincennes, X^w 66 (Meuse), letter of 2 *floréal* II.
30. A.D., Mayenne, L 1028, letter of 2 *pluviôse* III.
31. Capitaine de Bontin and Lieutenant Cornille, "Les volontaires nationaux et le recrutement de l'armée pendant la Révolution dans l'Yonne," *Bulletin de la Société des sciences historiques et naturelles de l'Yonne* 66 (1912), pp. 592–93. 93.
32. A.G., Vincennes, X^w 7 (Ariège), letter of Jean Dascin (undated).
33. A.D., Loir-et-Cher, F 2196, letter of 10 *messidor* IX.
34. A.D., Indre, L 778, letter of 16 *messidor* II.
35. A.D., Loir-et-Cher, L 615, letter of 23 *fructidor* II.
36. Joliclerc, *Lettres*, p. 98.
37. A.G., Vincennes, X^w 66 (Meuse), letter of 12 *germinal* II.

38. A.D., Loir-et-Cher, F 2196, letter of 27 *vendémiaire* VIII.
39. Noël, *Au Temps des volontaires*, p. 42.
40. J. Bernet, "Document inédit: Lettres de soldats compiégnois à leurs familles sous la Révolution," *Annales historiques compiégnoises modernes et contemporaines* 2 (1978), p. 47.
41. A.G., Vincennes, X^w 7 (Ariège), letter of 9 *ventôse* II.
42. Noël, *Au Temps des volontaires*, p. 36.
43. F. Vermale, "Lettres inédites d'un sous-lieutenant de l'Armée des Alpes," *Annales historiques de la Révolution Française* 6 (1929), p. 70.
44. Bontin and Cornille, "Volontaires nationaux," p. 590.
45. Joliclerc, *Lettres*, p. 19.
46. Duchet, *Deux volontaires*, p. 58.
47. A.G., Vincennes, X^w 61 (Maine-et-Loire), letter of 26 *prairial* III.
48. Picard, *Au Service de la nation*, p. 22.
49. Demay, "Les volontaires auxerrois," p. 546.
50. A.G., Vincennes, X^w 49 (Indre), letter of 1 *ventôse* II.
51. A.G., Vincennes, X^w 66 (Meuse), letter of 21 *pluviôse* II.
52. Demay, "Les volontaires auxerrois," pp. 585–86.
53. Picard, *Au Service de la nation*, pp. xiii–xiv.
54. Vermale, "Lettres inédites d'un sous-lieutenant de l'Armée des Alpes," p. 58.
55. Joliclerc, *Lettres*, pp. 35–36, 166.
56. Bertaud, *La Vie quotidienne*, pp. 157–63.
57. A. Forrest, *Déserteurs et insoumis sous la Révolution et l'Empire* (Paris, 1988), pp. 197–203.
58. Vermale, "Lettres inédites d'un sous-lieutenant de l'Armée des Alpes," p. 56.

7. THE SOLDIERS AND THE STATE

1. T. Skocpol, *States and Social Revolutions* (Cambridge, 1979), pp. 185–86.
2. P. M. Jones, "Parish, Seigneurie, and the Community of Inhabitants in Southern Central France during the Eighteenth and Nineteenth Centuries," *Past and Present* 91 (1981), passim.
3. A. Forrest, *Déserteurs et insoumis sous la Révolution et l'Empire* (Paris, 1988), pp. 246–52.
4. A.D., Basses-Alpes, L 224, letter from General Moulin to Department of Basses-Alpes, 17 *prairial* III.
5. A.D., Basses-Alpes, L 224, letter from General Kellermann to Department of Basses-Alpes, 12 May 1793.
6. S. Woolf, *A History of Italy, 1700–1860: The Social Constraints of Political Change* (London, 1979), pp. 157, 165.
7. R. Devleeshouwer, *L'Arrondissement du Brabaut sous l'occupation française, 1794–95* (Brussels, 1964), p. 133.

8. T. C. W. Blanning, *The French Revolution in Germany: Occupation and Resistance in the Rhineland, 1792–1802* (Oxford, 1983), p. 73.

9. M. Brunet, "Les armées de la Révolution et la population roussillonnaise, 1791–94," *Annales du Midi* 83 (1971), p. 232.

10. The activity of one of these *divisions militaires* is discussed by J. Devlin, "The Army, Politics, and Public Order in Directorial Provence," D.Phil. diss., Oxford University, 1987.

11. A.D., Basses-Alpes, L 224, order to all troops in the Basses-Alpes, 5 *prairial* IV.

12. Y. Pourcher, *Les Maîtres de granit: les Notables de Lozère du dix-huitième siècle à nos jours* (Paris, 1987), p. 36.

CONCLUSION

1. A. Perdiguier, *Mémoires d'un compagnon* (Paris, 1964), pp. 53–62.

2. G. Craig, *The Politics of the Prussian Army, 1640–1945* (London, 1968), pp. 20–21.

3. A. Soboul, *Les Soldats de l'an II* (Paris, 1959), p. 6.

4. Soboul, *Les Soldats,* p. 281.

NOTE ON SOURCES

This essay is intended to provide a general conspectus, not to give an exhaustive list of everything that has been published on the armies during the revolutionary period. It is necessarily selective without, I hope, being too idiosyncratic. In particular, I have not given a detailed listing of primary sources, although in individual chapters—most notably that on supply—they form a substantial part of the source material. Primary documents used are to be found in the Archives Nationales in Paris, the Bibliothèque Nationale, also in Paris, the Archives de Guerre at Vincennes and in various departmental and municipal archives in French provincial cities. The reader wishing detailed scholarly references should turn to the notes section.

SECONDARY SOURCES

Those who wish to place the revolutionary wars within the general political context of the French Revolution, can begin with a wide range of possible textbooks. Georges Lefebvre, *The French Revolution,* 2 vols. (London, 1962) gives considerable prominence to the war, within a Marxist interpretation of the Revolution. Michel Vovelle, *The Fall of the French Monarchy, 1787–92* (Cambridge, 1984), discusses the circumstances in which war came to be declared. François Furet and Denis Richet, *The French Revolution* (London, 1970) offer an alternative reading of the period, as does D. M. G. Sutherland, *France, 1789–1815: Revolution and Counterrevolution* (London, 1985), for whom the war, emigration, and royalism assume a central role. For a discussion of the nature of the war itself, see T. C. W. Blanning, *The Origins of the French Revolutionary Wars* (London, 1986).

On the armies themselves, surprisingly little is published in English, and so I make no apology for concentrating on books in French. Most valuable are the works of Jean-Paul Bertaud, whose *La Révolution armée: Les Soldats-citoyens et la Révolution Française* (Paris, 1979) is the most authoritative recent study of the subject. Also of interest are the same author's collection of documents on the revolutionary armies, *Valmy: La Démocratie en armes* (Paris, 1970), and his study of army life, *La Vie quotidienne des soldats de la Révolution, 1789–99* (Paris,

1985). Older and more consciously Jacobin works on the military abound. The most useful among them include Jules Leverrier, *La naissance de l'armée nationale, 1789–94* (Paris, 1939), and the works of Albert Soboul, most notably *L'Armée nationale sous la Révolution, 1789–94* (Paris, 1945) and *Les Soldats de l'an II* (Paris, 1959). All concentrate heavily on the experience of 1793–94 and are Republican in tone. Far less is available for the Directorial period; perhaps the best introduction is provided by Albert Meynier's long article, "L'Armée en France sous la Révolution et le Premier Empire," *Revue d'études militaires* (1932). A good conspectus is offered by Marcel Reinhard, "Observations sur le rôle révolutionnaire de l'armée dans la Révolution Française," *Annales historiques de la Révolution Française* (1962).

A masterly study of the French army at the end of the ancien régime is provided by André Corvisier, *L'Armée française de la fin du dix-septième siècle au ministère de Choiseul: Le Soldat,* 2 vols. (Paris, 1964); see also Corvisier's general study, *Armies and Societies in Europe, 1491–1789* (Bloomington, 1979). Lee Kennett, *The French Armies in the Seven Years' War* (Durham, 1967) is also useful for an understanding of what the Revolution had to build on. The full extent of the difficulties facing the military at the end of the ancien régime is exposed in E.-G. Léonard, *L'armée et ses problèmes au dix-huitième siècle* (Paris, 1958), while the legacy of the American War among the French officer class is examined in G. Bodinier, *Les Officiers de l'armée royale combattants de la Guerre d'Indépendance des Etats-Unis* (Vincennes, 1983). The question of whether there was an aristocratic reaction among the military is treated by David Bien, "La réaction aristocratique avant 1789: l'exemple de l'armée," *Annales: E.S.C.* 29 (1974).

The transformation of this Royal Army into the army of the Revolution is the subject of an excellent work by S. F. Scott, *The Response of the Royal Army to the French Revolution* (Oxford, 1978). See also two articles by the same author: "The Regeneration of the Line Army during the French Revolution" in *Journal of Modern History* (1970), and "The French Revolution and the Professionalisation of the French Officer Corps, 1789–93," in *On Military Ideology,* ed. M. Janowitz and J. van Doorn (Rotterdam, 1971). The legislation affecting the armies is very well presented in Jacques Godechot's *Les Institutions de la France sous la Révolution et l'Empire* (Paris, 1968), and, somewhat less digestibly, in A. Picq, *La Législation militaire de l'époque révolutionnaire* (Paris, 1932). For a discussion of tactics and military motivation, see John A. Lynn, *The Bayonets of the Republic* (Illinois, 1984), a highly readable monograph on the Armée du Nord between 1791 and 1794, and E. Hublot, *Valmy, ou la défense de la nation par les armes* (Paris, 1987).

On recruitment, besides general works like Bertaud and Soboul, much must be drawn from local and regional studies. Among the best of these are L. de Cardénal, *Recrutement de l'armée en Périgord pendant la période révolutionnaire, 1789–1800* (Périgueux, 1911); X. de Pétigny, *Un Bataillon de volontaires: le Troisième Bataillon de Maine-et-Loire* (Angers, 1908); and the classic work of Gustave Vallée, *La Conscription dans le département de la Charente, 1798–1807*

(Paris, 1936). A more general discussion is in E. Déprez, *Les Volontaires nationaux, 1791–93* (Paris, 1908). For an analysis of the cognate problems of desertion and draft-dodging, see A. Forrest, *Déserteurs et insoumis sous la Révolution et l'Empire* (Paris, 1988), and its English translation, *Conscripts and Deserters: The Army and French Society during the Revolution and Empire* (New York, 1989); for links between recruitment and poverty, see the same author's *The French Revolution and the Poor* (London, 1981). Replacement and substitution are discussed by I. Woloch, "Napoleonic Conscription: State Power and Civil Society," *Past and Present* 111 (1986), and by Bernard Schnapper, *Le Remplacement militaire en France* (Paris, 1968). An excellent collection of papers on the problems of recruitment can be found in *Recrutement, mentalités, société: Colloque international d'histoire militaire,* published by the Centre d'Histoire Militaire at the University of Montpellier (Montpellier, 1974).

The role of revolutionary politics in the armies has been subjected to much historical discussion, not all of it objective. Among the most committed is the work of General Herlaut, a convinced supporter of the Jacobin Republic, who wrote biographies of *Le Colonel Bouchotte, ministre de la Guerre en l'an II,* 2 vols. (Paris, 1946), and of *Le Général rouge Ronsin* (Paris, 1956). Note also his article on "La républicanisation des états-majors et des cadres de l'armée pendant la Révolution," in the *Annales historiques de la Révolution Française* for 1937. More dependable is Marcel Reinhard's two-volume biography of *Le Grand Carnot* (Paris, 1950–52). Georges Michon, author of *La Justice militaire sous la Révolution* (Paris, 1922) and of several articles on the operation of military justice, puts the Jacobin case with some skill. On a similar theme, see J.-M. Lévy, "La vertu aux armées pendant la Révolution Française," *Cahiers d'histoire* 12 (1967), p. 359. For the *armées révolutionnaires* of the Paris sections, nothing has remotely equalled Richard Cobb's study, now published in English as *The People's Armies* (London, 1987), as well as Cobb's essays in *Terreur et subsistances* (Paris, 1965). And for the longevity of Jacobinism in the military, there is Isser Woloch's authoritative *Jacobin Legacy: The Democratic Movement under the Directory* (Princeton, 1970).

The political education of the soldiers is discussed by both Bertaud and Lynn, and also in two excellent although unpublished dissertations: D. Berlemont, "Le Militaire est-il un modéle de citoyen?" (maîtrise, Université de Paris-I, 1987), and M. Delarue, "L'Education politique à l'Armée du Rhin" (maîtrise, Université de Paris-Nanterre, 1968). The military press, besides the papers themselves, can be studied through Marc Martin, "Journaux d'armées au temps de la Convention," *Annales historiques de la Révolution Française* 44 (1972), pp. 567–605; the financing of newspapers sent to the armies is examined by Albert Mathiez, "La presse subventionnée en l'an II," in *Annales révolutionnaires* (1918). A discussion of the military press is also to be found in H. Gough, *The Newspaper Press in the French Revolution* (London, 1988). On revolutionary fêtes, Mona Ozouf's *La Fête révolutionnaire* (Paris, 1976) is the standard work. On the theater and propaganda, see J.-J. Barbé, "Le théâtre à Metz pendant la Révolution," *Annales historiques de la Révolution Française* 4 (1927), 380, and P. Courteault, *La Révolution et les théâtres à Bordeaux* (Paris, 1926).

On the role of provincial Jacobin clubs, the most exhaustive work is that of Michael Kennedy, *The Jacobin Clubs in the French Revolution,* vol. 1, *The First Years,* and especially vol. 2, *The Middle Years* (Princeton, 1982 and 1988). Among the many works on individual Jacobin clubs which throw light on their connection with the military are those local histories dealing with societies in the north and east of France, notably P. Leuilliot, *Les Jacobins de Colmar* (Strasbourg, 1923); E. Leleu, *La Société Populaire de Lille* (Lille, 1919); O. Bled, *Les Sociétés populaires à Saint-Omer pendant la Révolution* (Saint-Omer, 1907); and G. Aubert, "La Révolution à Douai—la Société Populaire de Douai," *Annales historiques de la Révolution Française* 14 (1937), pp. 426–27. Also worth consulting are M. Henriot, *La Révolution en Côte d'Or: le Club des Jacobins de Sémur* (Dijon, 1933), and the rather tendentious general book by Pierre Dufay, *Les Sociétés populaires et l'armée: 1791–1794* (Paris, 1913).

Much of the political education in the armies was imposed by the government and its deputies-on-mission. Studies of their influence can be found in Bonnal de Ganges, *Les Représentants du peuple en mission près les armées, 1791–97,* 4 vols. (Paris, 1898–99), and J. Godechot, *Les Commissaires aux armées sous le Directoire* (Paris, 1937). Saint-Just was the best known of these deputies; see J.-P. Gross, *Saint-Just: sa politique et ses missions* (Paris, 1976); B. Vinot, *Saint-Just* (Paris, 1986); and A. Soboul, "Sur la mission de Saint-Just à l'Armée du Rhin," *Annales historiques de la Révolution Française* 26 (1954), p. 195.

Supply and provision are comparatively neglected topics in the historiography of the armies, and the reader is forced to turn to local studies and monographs. In English, Peter Wetzler has written on *War and Subsistence: The Sambre and Meuse Army in 1794* (New York, 1985); in French, there are several good regional histories, most notably R. Devleeshouwer, *L'Arrondissement du Brabant sous l'occupation française, 1794–95* (Brussels, 1964) and R. Werner, *L'Approvisionnement en pain de la population du Bas-Rhin et de l'Armée du Rhin pendant la Révolution, 1789–97* (Strasbourg, 1951). The health of the troops, likewise, has attracted far less interest than the armies as fighting units. On homesickness, there is an excellent article by Marcel Reinhard, "Nostalgie et service militaire pendant la Révolution," in *Annales historiques de la Révolution Française* 30 (1958). On pensions and the care of veterans, see Isser Woloch, *The French Veteran from the Revolution to the Restoration* (Chapel Hill, 1979).

Of the soldiers' own writings, there is, happily, something of a plethora, much of it published during the more militaristically patriotic years of the Third Republic between 1871 and 1914. The journals can be deceptively enthusiastic and even jauntily Republican in tone. Among the more famous are L. Larchey, *Journal de marche du sergent Fricasse, 1792–1802* (Paris, 1882), and A. and J. Bricard, *Journal du canonnier Bricard, 1792–1802* (Paris, 1891). More recent published memoirs include P.-R. Girault, *Mes campagnes sous la Révolution et l'Empire* (Paris, 1983). Collections of soldiers' letters have also been published. Among the most useful of these are E. Picard, *Au Service de la Nation: Lettres de volontaires, 1792–98* (Paris, 1914); E. Maury, *Lettres de volontaires Républicains, 1791–94* (Troyes, 1901); F.-X. Joliclerc, *Ses lettres, 1793–96* (Paris, 1905); L. Duchet, *Deux volontaires de 1791: Les Frères Favier de Montluçon* (Montluçon, 1909); and G. Noël, *Au Temps des volontaires, 1792: Lettres d'un volontaire de 1792* (Paris, 1912).

Finally, there is some valuable literature on the army in its wider social and political context. For a general introduction to the role played by armies in Europe at the time, see Geoffrey Best, *War and Society in Revolutionary Europe, 1770–1870* (London, 1982). The relationship between the military and the growth of the state is discussed by Theda Skocpol, *States and Social Revolutions* (Cambridge, 1979). More specifically, Clive Emsley deals with "The Impact of War and Military Participation on Britain and France, 1792–1815," in *Artisans, Peasants and Proletarians, 1760–1860* (London, 1985). The relations between French armies and the civilian population is discussed by Michel Brunet, both in his thesis, *Le Roussillon: une société contre l'Etat, 1780–1820* (Toulouse, 1987), and in an article, "Les armées de la Révolution et la population roussillonnaise, 1791–94," *Annales du Midi* 83 (1971), p. 226. The same problems are well illustrated in several studies of French occupation elsewhere in Europe, most notably in T. C. W. Blanning, *The French Revolution in Germany: Occupation and Resistance in the Rhineland, 1792–1802* (Oxford, 1983); in Jacques Godechot, *La Grande Nation: L'Expansion révolutionnaire de la France dans le monde de 1789 à 1799* (Paris, 1983); and in Stuart Woolf, *A History of Italy, 1700–1860: The Social Constraints of Political Change* (London, 1979). Also invaluable is the collection of papers given at the Brussels Colloquium on the French Military Occupation, held in January 1968 and published under the title of *Occupants, occupés, 1792–1815* (Brussels, 1969).

INDEX

Library of Congress Cataloging-in-Publication Data
Forrest, Alan I.
The soldiers of the French Revolution / Alan Forrest.
Includes bibliographical references.
ISBN 0-8223–0909-2. — ISBN 0-8223-0935-1 (pbk.)
1. France—History, Military—1789–1815. 2. France.
Armée—History—Revolution, 1789–1799. 3. Soldiers—
France—History—18th century. I. Title.
DC151.F68 1989
944.04—dc20   89-35875 CIP